W9-AMY-402

The Words Upon the Window Pane

Manuscript Materials

THE CORNELL YEATS

PLAYS

The Countess Cathleen, edited by Michael J. Sidnell and Wayne K. Chapman
The Words Upon the Window Pane, edited by Mary FitzGerald
The Hour-Glass, edited by Catherine Phillips
The Herne's Egg, edited by Alison Armstrong
Purgatory, edited by Sandra F. Siegel
The Death of Cuchulain, edited by Phillip L. Marcus

POEMS

The Early Poetry, Volume I: "Mosada" and "The Island of Statues," edited by George Bornstein
The Early Poetry, Volume II: "The Wanderings of Oisin" and Other Early Poems to 1895, edited by George Bornstein
The Wind Among the Reeds, edited by Carolyn Holdsworth
"In the Seven Woods" and "The Green Helmet and Other Poems," edited by David Holdeman
The Wild Swans at Coole, edited by Stephen Parrish
Michael Robartes and the Dancer, edited by Thomas Parkinson, with Anne Brannen
The Winding Stair (1929), edited by David R. Clark
Words for Music, Perhaps, edited by David R. Clark
New Poems, edited by J. C. C. Mays and Stephen Parrish
Last Poems, edited by James Pethica

The Words Upon the Window Pane
Manuscript Materials

BY W. B. YEATS

EDITED BY

MARY FITZGERALD

Cornell University Press

ITHACA AND LONDON

The preparation of this volume was made possible in part by grants
from the National Endowment for the Humanities, an independent federal agency.

First published 2002 by Cornell University Press
Printed in the United States of America

Library of Congress Cataloging-in-Publication Data

Yeats, W. B. (William Butler), 1865–1939.
The words upon the window pane : manuscript materials / by W. B. Yeats ; edited by Mary FitzGerald.
p. cm. — (The Cornell Yeats)
Includes bibliographical references.
ISBN 0-8014-4047-5 (cloth)
1. Yeats, W. B. (William Butler), 1865–1939. Words upon the window pane—Criticism, Textual. 2. Yeats, W. B. (William Butler), 1865–1939—Manuscripts. 3. Swift, Jonathan, 1667–1745—Drama. 4. Spiritualists—Drama. 5. Seances—Drama. I. FitzGerald, Mary, 1946–2000 II. Title.

PR5904 .W7 2002
822'.8—dc21 2002023729

Cornell University strives to utilize environmentally responsible suppliers and materials to the fullest extent possible in the publishing of its books. Such materials include vegetable-based, low-VOC inks and acid-free papers that are recycled, totally chlorine-free, or partly composed of nonwood fibers. For further information, visit our website at www.cornellpress.cornell.edu

1 3 5 7 9 cloth printing 10 8 6 4 2

THE CORNELL YEATS

The volumes in this series present all available manuscripts, revised typescripts, proof-sheets, and other materials that record the growth of Yeats's poems and plays from the earliest draftings through to the lifetime published texts. Most of the materials are from the archives of Senator Michael Yeats, now in the care of the National Library of Ireland, supplemented by materials held in the collection of the late Anne Yeats; the remainder are preserved in public collections and private hands in Ireland and around the world. The volumes of poems, with a few exceptions, follow the titles of Yeats's own collections; several volumes of plays in the series contain more than one play.

In all the volumes, manuscripts are reproduced in photographs accompanied by transcriptions, in order to illuminate Yeats's creative process—to show the poet at work. The remaining materials—such as clean typescripts and printed versions—are generally recorded in collated form in an apparatus hung below a finished text. Each volume contains an Introduction describing the significance of the materials it includes, tracing the relation of the various texts to one another. There is also a census of manuscripts, with full descriptive detail, and appendixes are frequently used to present related materials, some of them unpublished.

As the editions seek to present, comprehensively and accurately, the various versions behind Yeats's published poems and plays, including versions he left unpublished, they will be of use to readers who seek to understand how great writing can be made, and to scholars and editors who seek to establish and verify authoritative final texts.

THE YEATS EDITORIAL BOARD

Contents

Acknowledgments

Mary FitzGerald's tragic death in August 2000, following a long battle against cancer, left her edition just short of completion. We have assembled the parts, slightly modifying some of them, built an *apparatus criticus* of variants in secondary typescripts and proof-sheets, and composed an Introduction based on her article titled "'Out of a medium's mouth': The Writing of *The Words Upon the Window-pane*," published in the *Colby Library Quarterly* 17, no. 2 (June 1981):61–73.

We know that she would have wished to acknowledge the assistance given her in the libraries where she worked in close partnership with her husband, Richard Finneran, especially the National Library of Ireland, in Dublin, and the Houghton Library at Harvard University; both libraries generously provided photocopies of some of their holdings. We have also to thank on her behalf the staff of the British Library Manuscript Room, where play scripts submitted to the Lord Chamberlain for licensing are now stored, along with a card index. The staff of the Special Collections at the Frank E. Melville Junior Library, State University of New York at Stony Brook, courteously provided us with microfilms of Yeats manuscripts at the National Library of Ireland in their possession, from which most of the photographs in this volume were made. Unpublished materials are used with the kind permission of the following: Colin Smythe, Ltd., on behalf of Anne Gregory de Winton and the estate of Catherine Kennedy; the Henry W. and Albert A. Berg Collection of the New York Public Library Astor, Lenox and Tilden Foundations; and Michael and Anne Yeats for the unpublished letter by George Yeats. The illustration of the frontispiece of the 1934 Cuala Press edition of the play appears courtesy of the Division of Rare and Manuscript Collections, Cornell University Library.

During her work, Mary FitzGerald was supported by sabbatical grants from the University of New Orleans and the Louisiana State University system, and by a research grant from the National Endowment for the Humanities. Our work and the publication of her edition have been supported by generous grants awarded to the Department of English at Cornell University from the Atlantic Philanthropies. Behind all these, of course, lies the cooperation of Michael Yeats of Dublin and the late Anne Yeats; they have made all the volumes in this series possible, and all students of the poet owe them an enormous debt of gratitude.

STEPHEN M. PARRISH

Cornell University

ANN SADDLEMYER

University of Toronto

Census of Manuscripts

BL(2) See **BL Add. MS 55879**, below.

BL Add. MS 55878 In the British Library. Page proofs of *Wheels and Butterflies* containing "Press" copy of *The Words Upon the Window Pane*, stamped "R. & R. Clark Ltd. / 6 Aug 1934 / Edinburgh." and FIRST PAGE PROOF. Revisions are limited to corrections of punctation and printer's errors, but queries are answered by WBY in ink. On the title page the printer asks, "Two of the plays have been *produced* and two *performed.* Do you wish to make this distinction, or which should be used throughout?" The response, signed WBY, is "performed throughout." This is followed by a fresh suggestion, "—it might be better—First performed at the Abbey Theatre on 17th November 1930," to which Yeats responded "Yes."

BL Add. MS 55879 Abbreviated as BL(2) in the *apparatus criticus*. Author's marked proofs of *The Words Upon the Window Pane* for *Collected Plays* (1934) in the British Library.

BL Add. MS 55885 Page proofs of *The Words Upon the Window Pane* in *Wheels and Butterflies*, volume 4, stamped "Feb 1939." A few revisions in blue pencil are copied from earlier texts.

BL Add. MS 55892 Second and third page proofs of *Plays*, volume 5, stamped "12 July 1935" and showing a few corrections by Mrs. Yeats, probably made in 1939.

H(1) Nineteen leaves of buff paper, approximately 33 by 25.5 cm, tipped into a binder; all leaves are in WBY's holograph, with his page numbers in upper-right corners. There are six different papers, three ruled with blue lines, three unruled, bearing various watermarks: (1) crown emblem and GOVERNMENT / 207; (2) emblem of Britannia seated; (3) BALLYCLARE / CO ANTRIM; (4) PIRIE; (5) SWAGGART; one leaf is unmarked. Most contain fair copy, lightly revised. Seventeen rectos are filled; 15^r has only nine lines of text; 19^r is three-fourths full; 2^v has only a single word, "ASTRAY." The versos of leaves 3 and 4 contain drafts relating to facing rectos; 6^v has a draft substituting for a passage on 6^r. Leaf 19 is signed at end of the text: "Oct 1930 / WBYeats. / Coole Park." Cataloged as f Ms Eng 338.9 in the Houghton Library, Harvard.

H(2) Typescript of twenty-three leaves of unwatermarked typing paper approximately 27.9 by 21.6 cm, ribbon copy with typed date: "March 1931." On the title page is a cast list. The text appears to be typed from the revised Harvard MS, H(1), but there are a few scattered variations.

Page 3 has two pencil insertions of words or letters left out by the typist, not in WBY's hand; page 14 has one, page 18 has one, and page 21 has one. There are pencil marks opposite names in the cast list. Cataloged as b MS Am 1787 (604) in the Houghton Library, Harvard.

LCP Play scripts, proofs, printed copies, with some manuscripts, submitted to the office of the Lord Chancellor for licensing. In the card file at the Manuscript Room of the British Library, *Words Upon the Window Pane*, indexed as 1937/3, and licensed on 13/1/37 for production at the Arts Theatre, Cambridge, is a twenty-six-page carbon typescript in a blue paper binder inscribed "Abbey Theatre / Dublin" and stamped "National Theatre Society LTD." There are occasional revisions or corrections, none in WBY's hand. Classified as Add. MS 53544 in the British Library.

NLI(2) Twenty-six-page ribbon typescript of "The Words Upon the Window Pane" with leaves numbered 1–27 (but with no page 21), bearing revisions in WBY's hand. All pages measure 8 by 10 inches, and all are watermarked SWIFT BROOK BOND and / or EXTRA SUPERFINE. This typescript serves as the base text from which is hung the apparatus of variants found in other typescripts and proof-sheets. Classified as 8768(2) in the National Library of Ireland.

NLI(3) Twenty-seven-page carbon typescript, not the same typing as NLI(2), but on the same paper with the same watermarks. Bears scattered revisions and insertions; at top of the first page is "Corrected. W. B. Y. / Oct 27." Classified as 8768(3) in the National Library of Ireland.

NLI(4) Another twenty-seven-page carbon typescript, identical with NLI(3), bearing a typed cast list and occasional stage directions in pencil in the hand of Lennox Robinson. Written on a cover page in pencil are what appear to be two alternate titles: "Perfect Harmony" and "White Dice," both deleted; "Prompt Copy" is written on the title page. For these phrases in the text, see the Cuala edition, below, original page 38, l. 6, and original page 50, l. 21. Inscribed on the first page is "—W.K. 25/11/30." Classified as 8768(4) in the National Library of Ireland.

NLI(5) Printer's proof of the play with title page and a Cuala Press emblem: THE CUALA PRESS DUBLIN IRELAND MCMXXXIV. On the title page is written "Press" in ink. A dedication page reads "In Memory of Lady Gregory in whose house it was written." Preceding the text is a page headed "PERSONS OF THE PLAY," listing seven characters, without the "Two or three other people" of NLI(4). At end is the Cuala imprint: "Finished in the last week of January nineteen hundred and thirty four." Pages 9–33 of the Introduction follow, through Part XII; text of the play runs through pages 34–58. Scattered revisions in ink and pencil are limited to corrections of printer's errors, such as supplying an accent for "séance." Classified as 30,211 in the National Library of Ireland.

NLI 13,582 Rapallo Notebook E containing entries from about May 9, 1928, to about January 1929; among these are drafts of "The Resurrection" and portions of "A Vision." The notebook measures 30 by 22 cm and is bound in yellow boards decorated with vertical stripes. On leaves 17^v–28^r is a manuscript scenario of "Words Upon the Window Pane," followed on leaves 28^v–30^r by drafts of "For Anne Gregory." The draft of the play is completed on leaves 33^v–40^v.

NLI 15,598 Corrected galley proofs of the "Introduction"—revised to "A Commentary"—to *The Words Upon the Window Pane* for *The Dublin Magazine*. Printed date "November, 1930."

NLI 30,185 Revised page proofs of *The Words Upon the Window Pane* in the Coole edition of *Plays*, volume 4 (pp. 349–369) dated "7 Oct 1932" in printer's stamp. Revisions are limited to punctuation, spelling, and spacing save for three earlier readings restored by Yeats, in ink. A slip attached to the proofs in the NLI identifies this text as page proof of the "Coole Edition": "WBY used these in preparing copy for 'Wheels and Butterflies,' 1934."

NLI 30,324 Corrected pages from *The Dublin Magazine* issues of October through December 1931 and January through March 1932, containing an introductory essay to *The Words Upon the Window Pane*, version of the Cuala Press edition of 1934.

NLI 30,325 A twenty-two-page typescript of the Introduction to "Words Upon the Window Pane," dated November 1930.

NLI 30,545 The "White Vellum Notebook," in private hands, contains drafts toward Part II of the Introduction, or "Commentary," published with the play, dated "Nov. 1, 1931." The notebook is abbreviated as MBY 545 in other volumes in this series.

NLI 30,874 Eight-page typescript dated "Nov. 1, 1931," of "Commentary," Part II, to "Words Upon the Window Pane," with a few revisions which appear to be made by the typist.

READING One-page unrevised typescript of a portion of Part II of the Introduction to *The Words Upon the Window Pane*, classified as Acc MS 842 in the Reading University Library.

Introduction

Inscribing James A. Healy's copy of the Cuala Press edition of *The Words Upon the Window Pane* (1934), W. B. Yeats noted: "I wrote this play as a help to bring back a part of the Irish mind which we have been thrusting out as [if] it were foreign. Now that our period of violent protest is over we claim the Anglo-Irish eighteenth century as our own."[1] Although this affirmation of the Anglo-Irish Protestant Ascendancy was a new theme for Yeats's plays, it was already familiar to readers of his poetry and prose. He had given it defiant and memorable formulation on June 11, 1925, in an address to the Irish Senate:

> I am proud to consider myself a typical man of that [Anglo-Irish] minority. We . . . are no petty people. We are one of the great stocks of Europe. We are the people of Burke; we are the people of Grattan; we are the people of Swift, the people of Emmet, the people of Parnell. We have created the most of the modern literature of this country. We have created the best of its political intelligence.[2]

In poetry, Yeats further expanded this exalted idea of Anglo-Irishness, claiming a glorious past for his ancestors and a continuing legacy of generous civility for his descendants:

> . . . I declare
> They shall inherit my pride,
> The pride of people that were
> Bound neither to Cause nor to State,
> Neither to slaves that were spat on,
> Nor to the tyrants that spat,
> The people of Burke and of Grattan
> That gave, though free to refuse—[3]

The fusion of past and future in these lines suggests that the Anglo-Irish heritage fully inhabits the present, much as the Georgian architecture of certain Dublin streets assures that the

---

[1]Quoted in Michael B. Yeats, *'Something to Perfection Brought': The Cuala Press* (Stanford, Calif.: Associates of the Stanford University Library and the Department of Special Collections, 1976), n.p. Later published editions of *Words Upon the Window Pane* read "Window-pane."

[2]*The Senate Speeches of W. B. Yeats*, ed. Donald R. Pearce (Bloomington: Indiana University Press, 1960), p. 99.

[3]*The Tower*, ll. 126–133, in *The Variorum Edition of the Poems of W. B. Yeats*, ed. Peter Allt and Russell K. Alspach (New York: Macmillan, 1957; revised third printing, 1966), p. 414.

eighteenth century fully inhabits the twentieth. This continuing presence of the past, hinted in the poetry and prose, is actually accomplished onstage in Yeats's *The Words Upon the Window Pane*, when the passionate words of Jonathan Swift come tumbling out of a medium's mouth. In that dramatic moment, Yeats quite literally "bring[s] back a part of the Irish mind" into his own Irish present and extends it into his children's children's future.

As Daniel Harris has shown in *Yeats: Coole Park and Ballylee*,[4] Yeats associated Anglo-Irish greatness particularly closely with Lady Gregory and her family, and so it is not surprising that his first specifically Anglo-Irish play should have been written, like *The Tower*, at her Coole Park estate, a setting that had more to do with the shaping of the play than has previously been suspected. More surprising, perhaps, is Yeats's choice of Jonathan Swift as the hero of his Ascendancy play. Given a choice among Berkeley, Burke, Emmet, Grattan, Parnell, and Swift, Yeats settled upon Swift with apparent ease. Possibly he saw Swift's life as the most intrinsically interesting, because of its romantic triangle. A drama about Berkeley, Burke, or Grattan might have demonstrated passionate thought, but it would have made less effective theater than one about the passionate emotion of Swift. A play about Emmet or Parnell might have provoked nationalist feelings that would have confused the issue and obscured his point. But a play about Swift could allow Yeats to subsume politics under personal character, and besides, like Yeats, Swift was both politician and poet. In fact, Jonathan Swift as the subject of a play had been in Yeats's mind for some time, as had the idea of incorporating a séance: as early as August 2, 1929, he had written to Lady Gregory, "When I have finished my present task 'Stories of Michael Robartes' . . . I shall begin my spiritualistic play about Swift"; while convalescing in Italy the following April he was reading not only Swift's diary to Stella but his correspondence with Pope and Bolingbroke and in June told Olivia Shakespear that he was still "read[ing] Swift constantly"; by late August 1930 he was preparing to write, and by September 5, three days before his arrival at Coole, he informed his hostess that he had finished the first draft.[5]

As can be seen from the manuscripts, although the writing of the play ought to have given Yeats at least as much trouble as others of his plays and poems, it did not. He immediately selected an especially felicitous episode from Swift's life for his central action, the incident concerning a letter Vanessa wrote to Stella asking whether she and Swift were man and wife. This incident allowed Yeats to dramatize the confrontation within the romantic triangle at the peak of its frustrated intensity and to focus attention on Swift's reasons for not marrying—as Yeats saw them—his overriding fear of flaccidity of thought in the coming generations and his personal dread of passing a hereditary madness to his children,[6] reasons that Yeats validates dramatically in his play by presenting twentieth-century Dubliners as the silly if likeable group around the medium's table, obviously no match for Swift's contemporaries. Yeats's use of a séance as a frame device thus permits him to compare the present with the past and to bring the past into the present. Everything fits. Not a word is wasted. *The Words Upon the Window*

---

[4]Daniel Harris, *Coole Park and Ballylee* (Baltimore: Johns Hopkins University Press, 1974).

[5]Yeats to Lady Gregory, NLI 30,179; Yeats to Olivia Shakespear, June 1, 1930, *The Letters of W. B. Yeats*, ed. Allan Wade (London: Rupert Hart-Davis, 1954), p. 776.

[6]Modern Swift scholarship discounts this view, but Yeats held the older belief that Swift lapsed into mental illness in his later years. The newspaper accounts of the Abbey Theatre production of a Swift play in January 1913 by G. Sidney Paternoster suggest that it presented madness as Swift's reasons for not marrying Stella; Paternoster, *The Abbey Theatre: The Rise of the Realists 1910–1915*, ed. Robert Hogan with Richard Burnham and David P. Poteet (Dublin: Dolmen Press, 1979), pp. 244–245. For a modern diagnosis, see Irvin Ehrenpreis, *The Personality of Jonathan Swift* (Cambridge: Harvard University Press, 1958).

Pane is a tightly constructed masterpiece of Yeats's later period, and it has merited excellent critical analysis.[7] Two aspects of the play, however, have remained mysterious to scholars: the uncharacteristic ease with which he assembled his characters and developed his plot, and the uncharacteristic speed with which he wrote the play.

Unlike most of Yeats's plays, *The Words Upon the Window Pane* seems to have sprung virtually full grown from the mind of its creator. In Rapallo Notebook E,[8] the first draft shows the central dramatic confrontation between Swift and Vanessa almost exactly as it eventually appears in the published versions of the play. The séance is somewhat more sketchily presented at first, but the text as a whole rapidly achieves its final form—so rapidly, in fact, that Curtis Bradford assumed that intermediate drafts must have existed between the initial scenario, "one of the longest Yeats wrote and one of the most detailed,"[9] and the final draft. As Bradford noted, Yeats works out the central conflict on the very first attempt. Moreover, close examination of the Rapallo Notebook reveals that his handwriting shows no hesitation in the writing of the central action involving Swift and Vanessa. It is clearly a first draft, but it is a draft obviously informed by a fairly complete idea of the play.

There is a plausible explanation for all this: Yeats was probably working from his recollection of an earlier play. Among Lady Gregory's papers in the Berg Collection of the New York Public Library are copies of a deservedly unknown one-act play called *Swift and Stella*, authored by Charles Edward Lawrence (1870–1940), Lady Gregory's editor at John Murray's, Ltd.[10] The Berg copies are acting texts sent by Lawrence to Lady Gregory in 1930, but the play itself is of earlier date. It had first appeared in 1926 as one of several one-act dramas based on historical figures, which Lawrence published in *The Cornhill Magazine*, the house journal of Murray's.[11]

Swift and Stella is a terrible play. Although it was not Lawrence's first attempt in the genre, it is easily his worst, sharing and indeed perfecting his general failings as a dramatist. It is virtually

[7]See, for example, Douglas N. Archibald, "*The Words Upon the Window-Pane* and Yeats's Encounter with Jonathan Swift," in *Yeats and the Theatre*, ed. Robert O'Driscoll and Lorna Reynolds (Toronto: Macmillan of Canada, 1975), pp. 176–214; Curtis B. Bradford, *Yeats at Work* (Carbondale: Southern Illinois University Press, 1965), pp. 217–236; David R. Clark, *W. B. Yeats and the Theatre of Desolate Reality* (Dublin: Dolmen Press, 1965), pp. 60–84; Thomas Flanagan, "A Discourse by Swift, A Play by Yeats," *University Review* (Dublin) 5 (spring 1968): 9–22; John Rees Moore, *Masks of Love and Death* (Ithaca: Cornell University Press, 1971), pp. 249–267; Ann Saddlemyer, "Yeats's Voices in the Theatre," in *Literature and the Art of Creation*, ed. Robert Welch and S. B. Bushrui (Gerrards Cross: Colin Smythe, 1988), pp. 153–173; and Peter Ure, *Yeats the Playwright* (New York: Barnes and Noble, 1963), pp. 84–112. See also the Yeats chapter in *Anglo-Irish Literature: A Review of Research*, ed. Richard J. Finneran (New York: Modern Language Association of America, 1976), pp. 216–314.

[8]See the entry for NLI 13,582 in the Census of Manuscripts.

[9]Bradford, *Yeats at Work*, p. 218.

[10]C. E. Lawrence, *Swift and Stella: A Play in One Act*, Repertory Plays no. 65 (Boston: Gowans and Gray, 1927). Lawrence and Lady Gregory were professional friends. In 1903, he sent her a copy of his *The Trial of Man*, and in an unpublished letter on April 22, 1903, he wrote appreciatively of her perceptive comments about it. She preserved letters of his from the front, letters about Irish writers, and letters about her business affairs. From these and from references to him in her journals, it is clear that Lawrence knew Yeats as well. On several occasions he sent her copies of his books, although their friendship apparently cooled in 1924, when he read the manuscript of her memoirs and detected anti-English feeling, as noted in *Lady Gregory's Journals*, vol. 1, ed. Daniel J. Murphy (Gerrards Cross: Colin Smythe, 1978), pp. 580–581. In later journal entries, she noted that amicability had been restored and that he attended the Abbey Theatre on May 15, 1930 (*Journals,* vol. 2, ed. Daniel J. Murphy [Gerrards Cross: Colin Smythe, 1987], pp. 71 and 517).

[11]C. E. Lawrence, "Swift and Stella," *Cornhill Magazine*, n.s. 60, no. 360 (June 1926): 672–681. All subsequent references are to this text.

devoid of dramatic action. It consists entirely of Swift's reporting to Stella a conversation he has just had with Vanessa, prompting Stella to ask why Swift has never proposed marriage, and Swift to reveal immediately the secret he has kept from her all his life, the fact that they are illegitimate brother and sister. As if this were not bad enough, the characters are poorly drawn and oversentimentalized—Lawrence manages to reduce both Swift and Stella to the level of stock figures—and the dialogue is impossibly melodramatic, as in the following exchange:

> SWIFT. Stella, a tragedy has happened since we met. (*Stella remains silent.*) Stella, you do not speak; but I tell you that a tragedy has happened, or will happen. Death is flying on his speediest wings to bring the only comfort to a wounded—a broken—heart—the wounded heart of—a fool.
>
> STELLA. Nay! Jonathan!
>
> SWIFT. Vanessa!
>
> STELLA. Oh, must we speak of it?

Or this, which shows almost no regard for the rhythms of ordinary speech:

> STELLA . . . Why do you further torture that always tortured soul?
>
> SWIFT. It is the result of life, Stella. Life without stress and agony would be impossible to me. Always I have suffered—nay, always I have fought against anguish of heart and body, enduring the patronage and pity of lesser people. Ha! From the beginning, even from the beginning, men, whom with these present powers I could have crushed, ordered me here and there with their insolence, assisted me [*sic*], insulted me, made me eat the bitter ashes of a base dependence.
>
> STELLA. But that is past—and long past. It was a dream that is dead.
>
> SWIFT. Not dead and no dream; for its wounds—they bleed even in these hours. In my loneliness, as voices from the dead, as the voices of tempters whispering from a poisoned darkness, I hear again the old words.[12]

Obviously, *Swift and Stella* would not bear notice, were it not for the fact that it both predates Yeats's Swift play and anticipates it in subject, structure, treatment, and even dialogue.

It is highly probable that Yeats knew Lawrence's play. Circumstances argue that he certainly should have known it; indeed, it would have been very odd if he had not known it. When it first appeared in the June 1926 issue of *The Cornhill Magazine*—a year after his Senate speech—Yeats was saturating himself in the writings of eighteenth-century Irishmen. A few days before the publication of *Swift and Stella*, Lady Gregory noted in her journal that Yeats was "full of the 17th [*sic*] Century—Burke, Grattan, Berkeley, Swift—all the Protestant leaders did for Ireland's independence."[13] If she received *The Cornhill Magazine* at Coole, and as one of Murray's better-known authors she almost certainly did, Yeats might have read the play there, or she might have read it to him, as she often did because of his poor eyesight. Even if she did not regularly receive the magazine, Lawrence might well have sent her a copy, as he was not only her editor and friend but also an aspiring playwright who sought her advice. Then

---

[12]Ibid., 675–676.

[13]May 20, 1926, *Journals*, 2:99.

too, Yeats would almost certainly have seen the magazine at one or another of the clubs that he frequented,[14] and his abiding curiosity about Swift, particularly intense at this time, would have prompted him to read it, as would his awareness of Lawrence's link with Lady Gregory. At the very least, Lady Gregory could have read the play herself and then described its dramatic faults and failings to Yeats. The fact that Yeats's Swift play is a point-for-point improvement of Lawrence's mistakes suggests that he not only knew *Swift and Stella* but had also analyzed its weaknesses and knew how to remedy them. Both he and Lady Gregory had been "readers" for the Abbey Theatre since its inception; by 1926 dissecting the work of other playwrights was second nature for them both. It might well have been Lawrence's play that stimulated Yeats to consider writing one himself, and George Yeats for one urged him on.[15]

It would have been neither unprecedented nor unusual for Yeats to have borrowed an idea from another writer's work for his own use. He began his playwriting career that way with *The Countess Cathleen*, parts of which are a close translation from a French rendition of the folktale. His alleged raid on George Moore's idea for *Where There Is Nothing* was infamous in its day. He appropriated Lady Gregory's recollection of her nurse's account of the 1798 French landing for *Cathleen ni Houlihan*, and although Lady Gregory wrote most of the play, Yeats barely acknowledged her share.[16] He was perhaps genuinely unaware that Cathleen herself derived her dual nature as both old woman and symbolic figure from the character of Peg Inerny in Edward Martyn's *Maeve*, who is also a real woman and a symbolic incarnation of Ireland—a point Yeats noticed and praised in a rehearsal speech to the actors shortly before he "dreamed" his own Cathleen into existence.[17] For many years he collaborated with Lady Gregory in the writing of his own plays as well as hers, giving as well as taking plots, dialogue, and ideas at will, as he himself acknowledged and as another Yeats collaborator, Frank O'Connor, confirms.[18] Moreover, Patrick Diskin has demonstrated that even at the end of his life Yeats felt free to borrow and to improve a play he had read: his *Purgatory* is apparently based on James Clarence Mangan's translation of a German drama that Yeats would have read in *The Dublin Magazine*. As he did with *Swift and Stella*, Yeats took the characters, the central incident, and even some of the stage directions from his source and reshaped them for his own purposes.[19]

---

[14]As suggested by the late Dr. Oliver Edwards, whose kindness to other Yeatsians knew no bounds.

[15]*Explorations*, selected by Mrs. W. B. Yeats (London: Macmillan, 1962), p. 322: "My wife who urged me to do it added the detail about the medium refusing money and then looking to see what each gave." The failure of Arthur Power's short play *The Drapier Letters* during Horse Show week in August 1927 may have been an added stimulus. Yeats refers to Power's play in his Introduction to Percy Arland Ussher's translation of *The Midnight Court and The Adventures of a Luckless Fellow* (London: Jonathan Cape, 1926), p. 6n. When *The Drapier Letters* was produced, Yeats and the author discussed Swift at length; see Arthur Power, "A Contact with Yeats," in *W. B. Yeats: Interviews and Recollections*, ed. E. H. Mikhail (London: Macmillan, 1977), 1:191.

[16]*Seventy Years: Being the Autobiography of Lady Gregory*, ed. Colin Smythe (Gerrards Cross: Colin Smythe, 1974), pp. 2–3; W. B. Yeats, "Modern Ireland: An Address to American Audiences, 1932–33," ed. Curtis Bradford, in *Irish Renaissance*, ed. Robin Skelton and David R. Clark (Dublin: Dolmen Press, 1965), p. 18; James Pethica, "'Our Kathleen': Yeats's Collaboration with Lady Gregory in the Writing of *Cathleen ni Houlihan*," *Yeats Annual No. 6*, ed. Warwick Gould (London: Macmillan, 1988), pp. 3–31.

[17]Lady Gregory, *Our Irish Theatre* (Gerrards Cross: Colin Smythe, 1972), p. 28; and *The Variorum Edition of the Plays of W. B. Yeats*, ed. Russell K. Alspach (New York: Macmillan, 1966), p. 232.

[18]Frank O'Connor, *A Short History of Irish Literature: A Backward Look* (New York: Capricorn Books, 1967), pp. 168–169.

[19]Patrick Diskin, "Yeats's Purgatory and Werner's *Der vierundzwanzigste Februar*," *Notes & Queries*, n.s. 26, no. 4 (August 1979): 340–342.

The external evidence, then, strongly suggests that Yeats knew and did not hesitate to rework Lawrence's *Swift and Stella*, and that it is the chief source for *The Words Upon the Window Pane*; but the most convincing argument is the internal evidence offered by the plays themselves. Both begin with Swift's rage over the letter that Vanessa writes to Stella. Both center on Swift's explanation of why he has not married. Both contain the line, "I am a woman, Jonathan." Both end with Swift's quoting the same scriptural passage. But there, happily, the resemblance largely ends. Yeats's sense of conversation and of construction had little in common with Lawrence's. Typically, where Lawrence is rhetorical and content to report the action in his play, Yeats is succinct and presents his action directly. For example, Lawrence's major scene, the confrontation between Swift and Vanessa, is already over by the time the curtain rises. His Swift merely describes to Stella his furious (and apparently wordless) reaction to Vanessa's letter:

> I carried her letter back to her at Marlay Abbey. In my anger—now I can see it—I rode those miles through the dark and the mire with never the lamp of a single star to brighten my wrath and misery, and saw nothing of the way. I sprang up the stairs, passed [*sic*] her woman, and into the room. She was there, standing; I can see her face yellow with fear—her eyes—waiting. I flung the letter on to the table. . . . She shrank at the sight of it as though struck in the heart. I thought she would fall. I saw death in her eyes. I went.[20]

Though there is more passion in the telling of this offstage event than in anything that happens onstage in *Swift and Stella*, the episode is robbed of greater dramatic impact because the audience overhears it instead of seeing it directly, and it is robbed of suspense because the audience has already learned what the letter was about. In *The Words Upon the Window Pane*, by contrast, Yeats does not have his characters describe their conflict; he presents Swift and Vanessa directly onstage—without warning—in the midst of their angry confrontation and enhances the dramatic potential of the scene by making the audience figure out for themselves what is happening between the two—and even who they are! Moreover, he works a subtle transformation on Lawrence's "overhearing" scene. His audience "overhears" the encounter between Swift and Vanessa in a more sophisticated sense than Lawrence could have foreseen, and in the process he elaborates his theme: by having Swift and his ladies speak through the mouth of a medium, Yeats brings the past to life in the present. His audience experiences the event not only as it once occurred, but also as it occurs in front of them—and as it recurs endlessly. Their initiation in this principle is forceful and direct. In Rapallo Notebook E, Yeats writes: "Suddenly Swift's voice, speaking through medium: 'You have written to her. What if she and I are married? What right have you to ask questions?'"[21] In the final version, this becomes: "How dare you write to her? How dare you ask if we were married? How dare you question her? . . . You sit crouching there. Did you not hear what I said? How dared you question her?"[22]—a series of questions that heightens the dramatic impact of Swift's introduction to the audience, establishing him immediately as a formidable and angry figure. It is interesting, too, that in "crouching" in reaction to Swift's onslaught, Yeats's Vanessa more closely resembles

[20]Lawrence, *Swift and Stella*, p. 678.
[21]Bradford, *Yeats at Work*, p. 222.
[22]*Variorum Plays*, p. 948.

Lawrence's Vanessa, "shrinking" from the sight of the letter. Other bits of dialogue show similarities in theme and content, if not in style.

Stage business, too, is often similar, and here again, Yeats improves on Lawrence. In Lawrence's play, Swift is denied a dramatic entrance, as he is already in the room, waiting for Stella, when the curtain rises. In Yeats's play, Swift's entrance is unexpected and dramatic because he has been in the room all along—indeed, Yeats's point is that Swift is always in the room. In both plays, all action takes place in a single sitting room; but whereas in *Swift and Stella* this leads to an unintentional stasis, in *The Words Upon the Window Pane*, the stasis is deliberately chosen. Yeats seats his characters around a table, and their arrested motion focuses all attention on the spoken word and makes the simple act of rising from the table (as the medium does when Swift possesses her) tremendously significant. In Lawrence's play, when Stella learns why Swift has never married her, she exits through the door, distraught, leaving him to pace aimlessly in the room. In Yeats's play, when the guests have departed, the medium/Swift goes through similar motions. The most striking similarity, however, is that both plays end with Swift alone onstage, uttering the same final cry. As Lawrence has it, Stella leaves, and Swift quotes Job:

> *(For a moment as the door closes behind her Swift hides his face in his hands. Then he walks to and fro, slowly, and gradually breaks into speech.)*
> SWIFT. Darkness! Darkness! Darkness! . . . *(then with an anger of passion)* Let the day perish wherein I was born, and the night in which it was said, there is a man child conceived. Let that day be darkness; let not God regard it from above, neither let the light shine upon it. Let darkness and the shadow of death stain it; let a cloud dwell upon it, let the blackness of the day terrify. As for that night let darkness seize . . . *(Curtain.)*[23]

Obviously, the length of this quotation diminishes the dramatic potential of the ending. An actor would have to reduce it to rant or to muttering, either one of which leaves Swift a pathetic character rather than a passionate or powerful one. Yeats's ending is more forceful and more effective. The audience has been raised to a pitch of tension at the climax of the medium's monologue by Swift's complete possession of her body as well as of her voice. He has pounded violently on the door in a futile attempt to escape his purgatory in the room and has since been quieted by the end of the séance. The fact that the other characters in the play regard the séance as a failure has a further calming effect as well as a dramatically ironic one, and Yeats deliberately has the characters take their leave one by one to emphasize a gradual return to normalcy. Lulled into thinking that Swift is now "gone," the audience also learns that he has really been present, as Corbet's questioning of the medium makes it clear that she does not know who Swift is and cannot therefore have been "acting." Corbet leaves, and the room is apparently restored to its former order, so much so that the medium, Mrs. Henderson, can now begin that most ordinary of rituals, the making of a pot of tea. The audience is completely unprepared—and in a better sense perfectly prepared—for the reappearance of Swift, who establishes himself by slowly counting on his fingers the "five great Ministers" and "ten great Ministers" who were his friends, riveting the audience's attention on the hands of the medium. The audience is once again caught up in the reality of his presence, and Yeats allows the resulting tension to lapse only slightly, as Mrs. Henderson subsides into her own voice long

---

[23]Lawrence, *Swift and Stella*, p. 681.

enough to verify that she does not recognize what is happening to her (she still thinks that she is hunting for the tea things). It also allows her to pick up the saucer that once again focuses the audience on her hands, which have become the dramatic symbol of her repossession by Swift only seconds before. As she is overtaken by Swift's presence for the last time, her grasp fails, the crockery slips and shatters, and Swift's voice cries out of her: "Perish the day on which I was born!"[24] That single, desolate sentence distills the full impact of the play into a powerful final image for the audience to carry away from the theater, fixing Yeats's portrait of Swift indelibly in the mind as a passionate—even terrifying—tragic figure. It also elicits fear and pity as efficiently as they have ever been elicited on the modern stage.

Every difference between the two plays—and there are many—is a Yeatsian improvement on a Lawrentian mistake. Where Lawrence uses past tense, Yeats uses present. Lawrence's poor dialogue and tangled syntax give way to short, vivid sentences. Where Yeats retains the use of monologue, as he does for Vanessa's long speech, he organizes it around a vivid image, the "ivory dice" she compares herself to.[25] Similarly, in Swift's long speech to Stella there is an anchoring image in Yeats—the words cut into the window pane, which finally emerged as the title. As for Swift's reasons for not marrying either woman, Yeats specifically repudiates in his Introduction the theory upon which Lawrence rests his play (though he does not name Lawrence), namely, that Swift and Stella were both the illegitimate offspring of Sir William Temple.[26] In its place, he offers the theory of Swift's supposed madness, the theory on which Sidney Paternoster based his four-act Swift play, which the Abbey produced in 1913 (though he does not cite Paternoster either). This theory, which is what Yeats believed that Swift would have believed, is more dramatically satisfying than the incest theory. Although the fear involved in both is the same—the risk of producing mentally damaged children—the "madness" theory locates the flaw in the protagonist, not in the marriage, and it accounts not only for why he will not marry Stella but also for why he will not marry Vanessa, a problem Lawrence's play leaves unresolved. Furthermore, it enables Yeats to use Swift's feared hereditary flaw as a symbol for his larger theme: the decline of contemporary society from its past greatness. Swift is elevated beyond merely personal failing and becomes instead a visionary who can foresee the dissolution that will eventually accompany democracy. This makes Yeats's play more universal in its appeal: its point is not the problem of a single man but rather of all mankind, not in past history but now.

Another major difference appears in the manner of exposition. Yeats heightens dramatic intensity by minimizing exposition, something he is more able to do than Lawrence, because his is a Dublin audience to whom Swift needs no introduction. Swift is still very much alive in his part of the old city: in the names of streets, in the various landmarks associated with his tenure as dean of St. Patrick's, in the mental hospital that he funded in his will, and in the living memory of the people. So Yeats is more free than Lawrence to present Swift as an "unknown" visitor, mysterious both to the onstage observers and to the audience. Instead of Lawrence's opening rant against conditions in Ireland and the comic foibles of the servant class, which establishes his Swift as a crotchety old complainer, Yeats's manner of exposition transfers the comic foibles to the bourgeoisie, as objectified in the séance-goers, and he avoids any direct commentary on the Dublin scene. Yeats places Swift in his historical context by subtly effective

[24]*Variorum Plays*, p. 956.

[25]See the discussion (pp. xxiii–xxiv) of his use of the phrase "White Dice," in NLI(4), as a possible heading or title.

[26]*Variorum Plays*, p. 966.

references to the fine old house in which the séance is held, a tactic that is dramatically superior not only because it is less obtrusive and more thematically coherent, but also because it draws attention early in the play to the room itself, which will become synonymous with Swift's contemporary presence and his continual reenactment of the past.

The most striking difference between the plays is, of course, Yeats's use of a frame plot, but even this can be seen as a modification of Lawrence's idea. It is, in fact, a complete transformation of the chief dramatic defect in *Swift and Stella*, the predominance of offstage action, into the major structural principle of *The Words Upon the Window Pane*. Yeats would easily have recognized that Lawrence's play fails because little or no action happens onstage, the most significant action has already occurred offstage, and the whole weight of the drama rests on the dialogue alone. The result is a one-act drawing-room tragedy that defies conventional dramatic wisdom, and loses. But although *The Words Upon the Window Pane* contains identical "faults," in Yeats's hands they become daring theatrical innovations in an experiment that works, and works beautifully. Like *Swift and Stella*, Yeats's play has little important "onstage" action: the séance is supposedly a failure. Similarly, it is dominated by an already completed action: Swift and the women have been dead for so long that they are only memories. Yeats also rests the entire weight of the drama on the dialogue: the medium's voice does the work of all three major figures (as well as her own and that of her controlling guide, Lulu). The visual perspective in the central confrontation is supplied through words alone: the audience creates for itself a pensive Stella, a "crouching" Vanessa, a broken and ugly Swift.

To trace the development of *The Words Upon the Window Pane* from its earliest draft "scenarios" through to its final form is relatively simple, as there are only two manuscripts, the Rapallo Notebook (NLI 13,582) and the Harvard Manuscript (H[1]), both of them incorporating drafts and fresh starts, but both moving through the entire play. (All other entries in the Census are typescripts or proof-sheets or printed versions, and their variant readings are supplied in apparatus entries beneath the first typescript, NLI[2]).

The two manuscripts reveal that from its beginning the play was made up of two scenes, or situations, that were given about equal space in all the texts. The first scene, which opens with a conversation between an old Dublin man and a young Cambridge man, offers a realistic portrayal of a group of people assembled in a Dublin house to take part in a séance. Dramatic tension arises from the mixed expectations and anxieties and demands of this group. Some in the group are "skeptics" (among them the young Cambridge man) who show uncertainty about what they are going to witness, but most are believers who are concerned about the "hostile force" that disrupted the last two séances. The old Dublin man, a wise and experienced séance-goer, tries to moderate and reconcile the conflicting and possibly disruptive opinions.

The second scene rises abruptly to a surrealistic level. It opens with startling power when the medium begins to speak in the voices of Jonathan Swift and the two women in his life, Vanessa and Stella. The medium's "control," first identified as "Silver Cloud," is Lulu, a little girl who died at the age of seven or eight; her thin voice contrasts startlingly with the powerful male voice of the aging Swift—both voices, of course, produced by the medium in her trance.

On the cover of the typescript of the play used as a prompt copy (NLI[4]) and bearing stage directions in the hand of Lennox Robinson, Yeats inscribed what appear to be two alternate titles but which could instead be keyed to the two scenes that make up the play. The first title is "Perfect Harmony," a phrase uttered in the realistic scene, quoting the medium and appealing for conditions that will allow the séance to take place: "Mrs Henderson says there must be perfect harmony." The second title is "White Dice," echoing the earliest version in the Rapallo Notebook (see p. 27, below), where she pleads with Swift to return her love and devotion.

> give your hand ~~again~~ I say – Give me your both your hands – I am woman put this hand upon my breast – O it is white, white as are the Gamblers dice, the little ivory dice.

At the close of the play the two scenes, one realistic and the other surrealistic, suddenly merge. After Mrs. Henderson sinks back in her chair, a quiet dialogue with the young Cambridge man is capped with a final despairing burst of Swift's voice: "Perish the day on which I was born."

The success of Yeats's experiment is rendered possible largely through the device of the medium, who summons the past into the present and allows it to unfold again with all the primal intensity of its first occurrence. The device may have suggested itself to Yeats because he associated mediumship with an act of dramatization, as he says in his Introduction to the play, or because he was familiar with séances and could therefore draw them from life.[27] For Yeats, of course, mediumship seemed as plausible as purgatorial atonement seemed to much of his audience. His familiarity with séances may be gauged from Lady Gregory's first reference to the play in her journal for September 18, 1930: "Yeats has been reading me his Swift play. . . . Very wild and terrible behind its flimsy setting, an *everyday* séance."[28] Even his use of the hymn by the nineteenth-century divine John Keble was standard practice. In addition, although his wife disapproved of spiritualism, he had for many years observed her entranced during their work on *A Vision*; as recently as January 1928, George Yeats had had an unfortunate experience while sleepwalking.[29] He might have arrived at the idea of the simple setting, then, through a convenient association of ideas. But he might also have been spurred on by *Swift and Stella*, which he would have recognized as a failed ghost play. The harmony of lovers in the drama is destroyed by the action of an absent figure, who is said to be recently dead or dying. Lawrence, of course, makes nothing of Vanessa's ghostly essence—she haunts the action only figuratively. But Yeats's interest in the traditional Japanese Noh play would have showed him richer possibilities, and besides, ghosts were very much on his mind when he wrote the play at Coole.

Yeats arrived at Coole Park for one of his many visits to Lady Gregory, who was by then terminally ill with cancer, on September 10, 1930. He arrived there from Oliver St. John Gogarty's house at Renvyle, not far away, where he and his wife had once encountered the ghost of a previous Renvyle owner, who appeared in their room while a séance was taking place downstairs.[30] Yeats had also seen a rhymed couplet that had been cut into the window pane of Gogarty's Dublin home, apparently in the Georgian era.[31] So, although Yeats's visit to Renvyle in 1930 had had nothing especially ghostly about it—he had gone there to sit for Augustus John's portrait of him—Gogarty's houses were rich with spirit associations for him and offered memories of a séance and of Georgian words upon a window pane.

---

[27]*Variorum Plays*, p. 967.

[28]September 18, 1930, *Journals*, 2:552 (emphasis added).

[29]W. B. Yeats, Introduction to "A Vision," in *A Vision* (London: Macmillan, 1962), pp. 20–21.

[30]Oliver St. John Gogarty, *As I Was Going Down Sackville Street* (London: Rich & Cowan, 1937), pp. 190–198; and *William Butler Yeats: A Memoir* (Dublin: Dolmen Press, 1963), pp. 21–22.

[31]Wade, *Letters*, p. 891.

Although Coole had no ghosts of its own, it held literary, historical, and Ascendancy associations for Yeats, and Lady Gregory had often said to him that she thought their spirits would haunt the library after their deaths, because they had written so many of their works together there. Moreover, in the autumn of 1930, Coole was being haunted by Vanessa herself—though from a distance. When Yeats arrived, he learned that Robert Gregory's widow and her husband, Guy Gough, were negotiating the purchase of Celbridge Abbey in County Kildare as their future permanent residence. This pained Lady Gregory, because it meant that her grandchildren would no longer live near her and that Coole would certainly be empty after her death.[32] The Goughs, however, were not troubled about this and were pleased with Celbridge Abbey, which had once been owned by the Vanhomrighs and later by Grattan. They told Yeats of the folk rumor that Vanessa had entertained Swift there and that she was said to haunt the bridge down to the present day.[33]

When not commiserating with Lady Gregory about the sad future of Coole, Yeats spent his time studying Berkeley, as she was reading Hone's recently completed manuscript of the life.[34] He also worked on revisions of his early stories for the projected Edition de Luxe of his works, stories he had first revised at Coole with her assistance.[35] In re-reading his *Rosa Alchemica*, he would have come across an echo of his own voice from 1897 in a passage that points to his long-held belief that presences linger in the places they have visited:

> . . . as I led the way up the wide staircase, where Swift had passed joking and railing, and Curran telling stories and quoting Greek, in simpler days, before men's minds, subtilized and complicated by the romantic movement in art and literature, began to tremble on the verge of some unimagined revelation. I felt that my hand shook, and saw that the light of the candle wavered more than it need have upon the gods and nymphs set upon the wall by some Italian plasterer of the eighteenth century, making them look like the first beings slowly shaping in the formless darkness.

Further along in this same passage, he sees a censer "with pieces of painted china" fallen from its place and hears a voice saying, "They have come to us . . . all that have ever been in your reverie, all that you have met with in books."[36]

The Words Upon the Window Pane appears to incorporate many of these Coole associations—Gogarty's houses, the haunted Celbridge Abbey, the echoes of his past words. In

---

[32]November 8, 1930, and March 30, 1931, *Journals*, 2:565–566, 601–602.

[33]July–October 1930, *Journals*, 2:538–557. See also Mackie Jarrell, "Jack and the Dane: Swift Traditions in Ireland," in *Fair Liberty Was All His Cry: A Tercentenary Tribute to Jonathan Swift*, ed. A. N. Jeffares (London: Macmillan, 1967), p. 335. Jarrell mentions that the estate was bought "by a Major Gough in the 1930s," notes that this is the only ghost story associated with Swift, and gives a description: "Vanessa's ghost (her name is 'Irished' as V'ennessa Vonbhombret) is said to have appeared to Jack Macan as he was crossing the rock bridge [near the rustic seat formerly called 'the Dean's Chair']. She told him not to go home by that way any more. He persisted, after still another warning, and on the third night she threw him into the river. It is said that if a person walks at twelve o'clock at night by the gate on the Temple Mill road he will see this noted Lady with a dog and fire coming from its mouth." It is not clear from Lady Gregory's journals how much of this legend the Goughs knew, but it is certain that they knew that Celbridge Abbey was thought to be haunted by Vanessa.

[34]September 29, 1930, *Journals*, 2:552.

[35]The Edition de Luxe, after Yeats's death renamed the Coole edition, never reached print, although much of it was set in proof.

[36]W. B. Yeats, *The Secret Rose* (London: Lawrence and Bullen, 1897), pp. 228–229.

transforming Lawrence's play Yeats uses Lawrence's Dublin setting, but he moves it from the deanery of St. Patrick's to Stella's house. He borrows the rhymed inscription from Gogarty's Dublin house and the séance from Renvyle, changing the lines to Stella's and the spirit to Swift's. He moves Vanessa's ghost from Celbridge Abbey to Stella's house in Dublin—where Vanessa in life would not have ventured—by extrapolating from Lawrence's off-stage confrontation as recounted to Stella by Swift. (This explains how Vanessa's ghost can be in the room with Swift and Stella; in Yeats's play, Swift mentally relives the encounter with her in telling it to Stella just as he relives the encounter with Stella herself immediately afterward.) Details from the passage in *Rosa Alchemica* lend themselves to the construction: Swift's former presence in an eighteenth-century room, "beings slowly shaping in the formless and void darkness," and even the falling china. So do phrases from *Swift and Stella*: "voices from the dead . . . whispering from a poisoned darkness," and "comings and goings in the moonless dark."

In his Introduction to the finished piece, Yeats says, "My little play *The Words upon the Window Pane* came to me . . . as a reward, as a moment of excitement."[37] It probably did. All the ingredients were present when he arrived at Coole, and the associations coalesced in the Ascendancy atmosphere of that great house, "Where passion and precision have been one, / Time out of mind" ("Upon a House Shaken by Land Agitation"). It happened very quickly. Lady Gregory records Yeats's presence at Coole on September 13, writing his poem about Anne Gregory's yellow hair; that poem appears alongside the draft of the play in Yeats's notebook. Lady Gregory's first record of what she always calls "Swift" or "his Swift play" is the reference on September 18 to the "everyday séance," by which time the play is "nearly ready now." It is "completed" by Sunday, September 28, and "finished" on October 1: "Yeats has finished his play. He had been waiting to get from Dublin a copy of Stella's poem for it. But I took down [Samuel] Johnson's sniffy essay on him in his Works from the Library Shelves—and there is the poem and he has used it." On October 4 she records that Yeats had "written the last words of his Swift play."[38]

Yeats left Coole on October 27 and two days later wrote to Lady Gregory from Dublin: "*Swift* is in rehearsal—I shall dedicate it to you."[39] It is the only one of his plays dedicated to her, although he had long ago given her his two volumes of *Plays for an Irish Theatre*, because they "are in part your own."[40] Not only did the play come quickly into existence, performance was just as immediate; *The Words Upon the Window Pane* opened at the Abbey Theatre on November 17, 1930. It is probably not mere coincidence that two days later, after the Irish papers containing notices of the performance had reached London, C. E. Lawrence inscribed a copy of his *Swift and Stella* for Lady Gregory—though it had been issued in paper covers fully three years earlier. If he wrote a letter in sending his play to her, the letter no longer survives.[41]

---

[37]*Variorum Plays*, p. 957.

[38]September 13–November 2, 1930, *Journals*, 2:552–561.

[39]Wade, *Letters*, p. 778.

[40]*Variorum Plays*, p. 232. Yeats dedicated the first American edition of *Where There Is Nothing* to Lady Gregory but subsumed that honor into the more general dedication of *Plays for an Irish Theatre* in 1911, by which time he had become dissatisfied with the play and rewritten it with her as *The Unicorn from the Stars*.

[41]The three copies of *Swift and Stella* which survive in the Berg Collection are uncut, including the one bearing the inscription "To Lady Gregory from C.E.L. 19 XI 30." Although it is possible that Lawrence had sent them at the time of the publication of the acting text in 1927 and later inscribed one for Lady Gregory, it seems more likely that he sent them in 1930, upon recognizing a similarity between Yeats's handling of Swift and Stella and his own. However it may

Yeats spent most of the 1931–1932 winter again at Coole, once more immersed in Swift as he worked on his introduction to the published play. From there he wrote to his wife, "I have just finished a beautiful & exciting second part to my commentary on the Swift play. I will bring it up & you can type it perhaps & O'Sullivan can have it if he likes. It is an interpretation of the séance in the light of Plotinus Ennead V.7—& is a thought that has been exciting me for weeks." His commentary, which George Yeats sent to James Starkey to be published in *The Dublin Magazine* (October–December 1931), initiated a debate between the Yeatses which returned to their discussions over the automatic script and *A Vision*, the second edition of which Yeats was still struggling over. George objected that his argument, "the dramatisation of the secondary and tertiary personalities of the medium," seemed "close to the old psychical research theory of the 'subconscious.'" Using examples from the characters in his play, she continued:

> If I had to interpret that 'commentary', I could not say that any 'spirit' were present at any séance, that spirits were present at a séance only as impersonations created by a medium out of material in a world record just as wireless photography or television are created; that all communicating spirits are mere dramatisations of that record; that all spirits in fact are not, so far as psychic communications are concerned, spirits at all, are only memory. I say 'memory' deliberately, because 'memory' is so large a part of all psychic phenomena. I dont remember any case in which a spirit (communicating through a medium) had during the latter part of his life or during any part of his life been cut off from that every day faculty of memory. Those people who were wounded in the head during war—they dont come—the insane dont come???—the spirits who tell us about their houses, their horse racing, their whiskeys and sodas, their children, their aunts and God knows whatnots, their suicides, were all mainly preoccupied during their lives with those things. Have we any record of a spirit communicating who had been at any period of his life been so physically or mentally incapacitated that memory, even 'subconscious' memory, had been obliterated?

Yeats replied immediately:

> I do not consider the fully separate spirit a passive mirror of timeless images but as a timeless act. This act appears to us through the antimony of past & future & loss of memory in the living man would be present in the act also. It may make communication difficult. If I think of John Smith who lost his memory from a blow on his head, I not only transfer that loss to the dramatization, in so far as that dramatization is from my suggestion, but think of him in just that part of his life, which is absent from his present state. If my 'subconscious' could think of him as he was when most alive, most completely himself, and do so with as great intensity as it now thinks of his tragedy he

---

have happened, the timing of Lawrence's inscription is extraordinary, and even more extraordinary is the uncut state of the books, which suggests that neither Yeats nor Lady Gregory tried to read the play—although Yeats's Swift play had just been produced, and although both of them later read Shane Leslie's Swift play and he pronounced it "rubbish" (January [21 or 22], 1931, *Journals*, 2:588). It is possible that one or both of them cut and read a fourth copy, which has now been lost, but it seems more likely that they did not read the play because they remembered it from its 1926 appearance in *The Cornhill Magazine* and therefore did not have to read it. Neither of them ever mentions it.

> would enter & direct the dramatization. It is because whatever is in time, is also in the timeless moment, that one is compelled in the pursuit of moral coherence to believe in re-birth. I admit the difficulty of timeless moments, but in some sense their selves [are] but parts of time; but what can we do with antinomies but symbolise their solution by some kind of Platonic myth.

Still not satisfied, he then sent "a different comment," which suggests not only the involvement of Yeats as author but of the audience as active spectators:

> Remember how many of what seems the laws of spirit life are but the pre-possessions of the living. A number of communicators have warned us against cremation on the ground that it is a shock to the departed spirit yet to think so would be to think that eastern races that have studied these things for centuries are more ignorant that we who have hardly studied at all. If I think of a man as having lost his memory from a blow on the head, my 'un-conscious' rejects him as possible testimony. I am more moved by my correspondents statement that I have turned a séance into a kind of wireless apparatus & denied that the spirits are there at all. If I drop that word 'unconscious' adopted out of mere politeness I may be better understood: the Daimon of a living man is a dramatist—what am I but my daimons most persistent drama—it dramatizes its fancies, characters out of fiction have written through the planchette—it dramatizes its knowledge, & when that is knowledge of other daimons it is as though it has lent them its dramatic power. The Spirit is thus present in a representation which is the child of the living & the dead. The separate daimon is not a passive timeless mirror but a timeless act which with your help enters time once more.[42]

When *The Words Upon the Window Pane* was finally published by the Cuala Press in 1934, Yeats's revisions to the original commentary as published in *The Dublin Magazine* reflected their debate and further enrich our understanding of the play. However, he did not forget his debt to Coole and his old friend, now dead. His simple dedication again paid tribute: "IN MEMORY OF LADY GREGORY IN WHOSE HOUSE IT WAS WRITTEN."[43]

[42]W. B. Yeats to George Yeats, November 1 and c. 25, 1931, and George Yeats to W. B. Yeats, November 24, 1931, both in the collection of Senator Michael Yeats; *Variorum Plays*, 975ff.

[43]W. B. Yeats, *The Words Upon the Window Pane* (Dublin: Cuala Press, 1934).

Transcription Principles and Procedures

Yeats's manuscripts are impossible to transcribe with absolute fidelity. Even the handwriting of his youth, with its occasionally erratic—and probably dyslexic—spelling, causes problems for the reader, and from the time of his early maturity onward, the speed with which he composed on paper gave rise to letter compression, shorthand versions of words and even whole phrases, and an almost indecipherable penmanship. In late life, when words obeyed his call, he wrote for eventual dictation to a typist with a swiftness and self-assurance born of a certainty that the scribblings would be remembered for what they signified in the white heat of creation, either by his own eye or by the eye of his wife George, whose handwriting bears an uncanny resemblance to his own, so much so that at times it is not possible to decide which of the two inserted a handwritten correction in a typed text. The manuscripts of *The Words Upon the Window Pane*, written by his own account in Lady Gregory's house during her final struggle against the cancer that would kill her, are entirely in his own hand and manifest all the idiosyncracies of his late-life manuscripts.

The photo-facsimiles of Yeats's notebook pages reproduced in this volume will allow students, magnifying glasses in hand, to puzzle out the extraordinary hieroglyphs and check the transcriptions for themselves. The manuscript pages are cleaner, of course, than the facsimiles, not only because they are larger but also because the clarity of the ink tends to be obscured by even the best photographic reproduction.

The principles according to which the transcriptions that follow were realized are listed below.

1. Where there is no reasonable doubt what word Yeats intended, even though the letters may be elided in the haste of writing, the word is generally transcribed in full, on the authority of his habit of so doing and his correct spelling of the word when it appears in other places. Where his spelling is indecipherable and in doubt—because the letters are indistinguishable from one another—the correct spelling is supplied. Where Yeats's writing is clear and letter compression is not in evidence, words are given exactly as he gives them, even when he misspells them, as he occasionally does with certain words and regularly with others.

2. Yeats frequently broke words at unusual points or broke words not normally divided. Such breaks are not usually represented in the transcriptions unless the width of the breaks approximates (or exceeds) the spacing he normally left between words, because such spacings tend to indicate that he considered the words in question to be two words (or ones needing a hyphen, though he rarely bothered to insert hyphens). Where he left a space for an apostrophe

but failed to insert it, the space is represented in the transcription. The photo-facsimiles, of course, allow the reader to judge of these distinctions.

3. The following typographical conventions have been adopted to represent the physical features of the text:

roman type	ink or pencil
boldface type	typescript or print
italic type	editorial comment

4. Illegible words and editorial conjectures are represented as follows:

[?]	an illegible word
[? ? ?]	several illegible words
[~~?~~]	a canceled illegible word
[?and]	a conjectural reading

5. Overwritings are indicated thus: ha{s ve = "have" revised to "has" by overwriting.

6. At various points in the drafts there are blots, or other obscure marks, that may have been made accidentally. In cases where their significance has not been determinded, they are silently omitted. On many drafts, foliation letters or numbers have been inserted by later scholars, typically in the upper corners of the leaf; these are omitted from the transcriptions.

7. Cancelation of single words or of words within a line is indicated by a horizontal cancelation line; these lines are straight even where Yeats's are wavy. Where he appeared to have intended to cancel an entire word but struck through only part of it, the cancelation in the transcription extends through the entire word. However, even when it seems likely that he meant to cancel an entire phrase or line, no word that he did not at least partially cancel is canceled in the transcriptions.

8. Cancelation of entire passages is indicated by a vertical line, or bracket, in the left-hand margin.

9. Yeats's "stet" marks are preserved, as are his underscorings to indicate italics.

10. Spacing and relative positions of words and lines attempt to approximate the originals as far as is possible, although the limitations of type in representing holograph material have resulted in various compromises.

11. In transcriptions of typescript material or printer's proofs, minor and obvious typing errors such as strikeovers, or obvious mistakes in typeset proofs, are generally not recorded, although revisions are shown when they seem significant. The *apparatus criticus* of variants, suspended from the earliest typescript, records only variants that can be attributed to Yeats; the record of variants in posthumous editions is carried forward in the indispensable *Variorum Edition of the Plays*, edited by Russell K. Alspach and Catharine C. Alspach.

The Words Upon the Window Pane

Manuscript Materials

The Rapallo Notebook

NLI 13,582

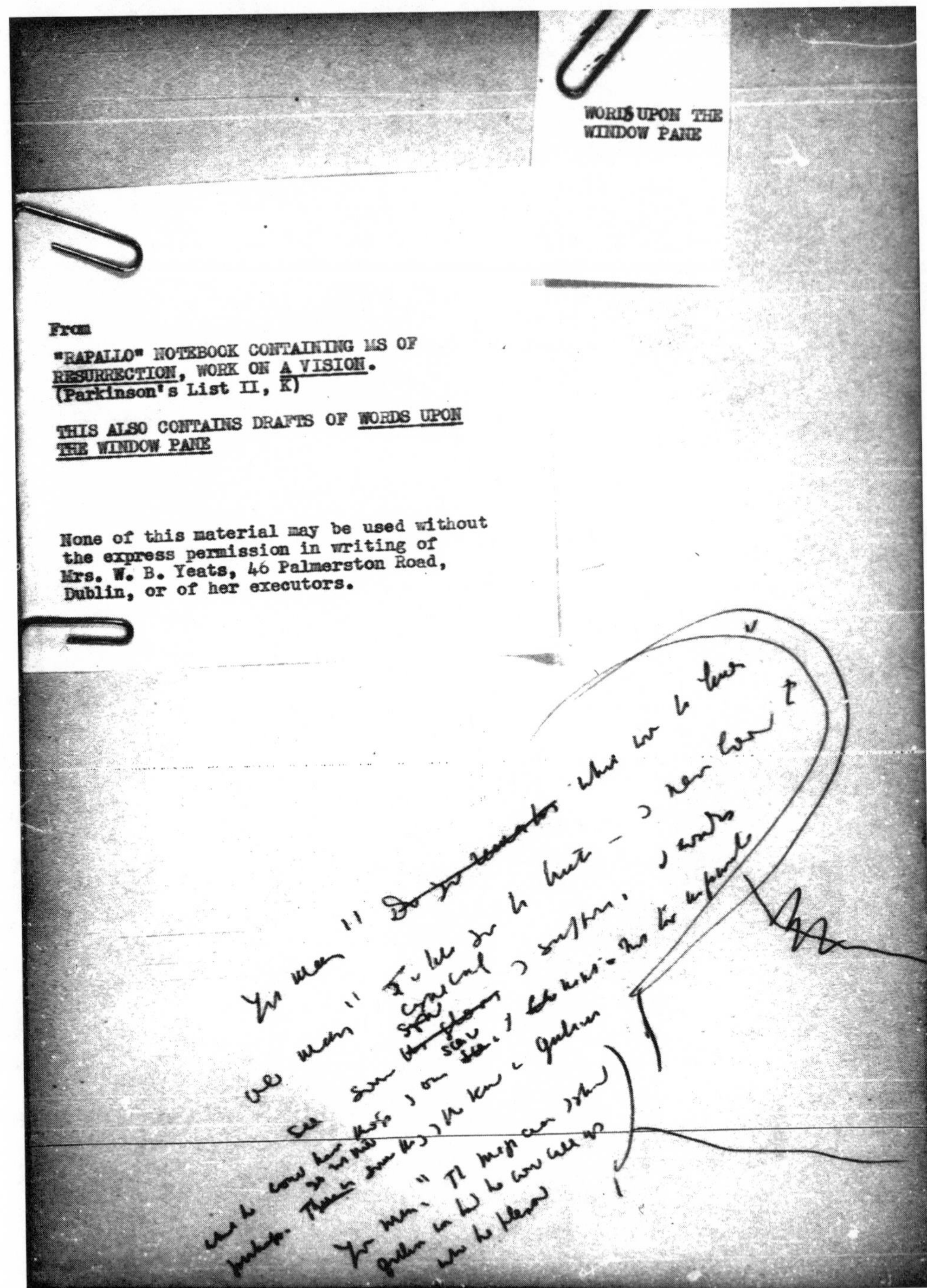
WORDS UPON THE
WINDOW PANE

From

"RAPALLO" NOTEBOOK CONTAINING MS OF
RESURRECTION, WORK ON A VISION.
(Parkinson's List II, K)

THIS ALSO CONTAINS DRAFTS OF WORDS UPON
THE WINDOW PANE

None of this material may be used without
the express permission in writing of
Mrs. W. B. Yeats, 46 Palmerston Road,
Dublin, or of her executors.

[NLI 13,582, 17v]

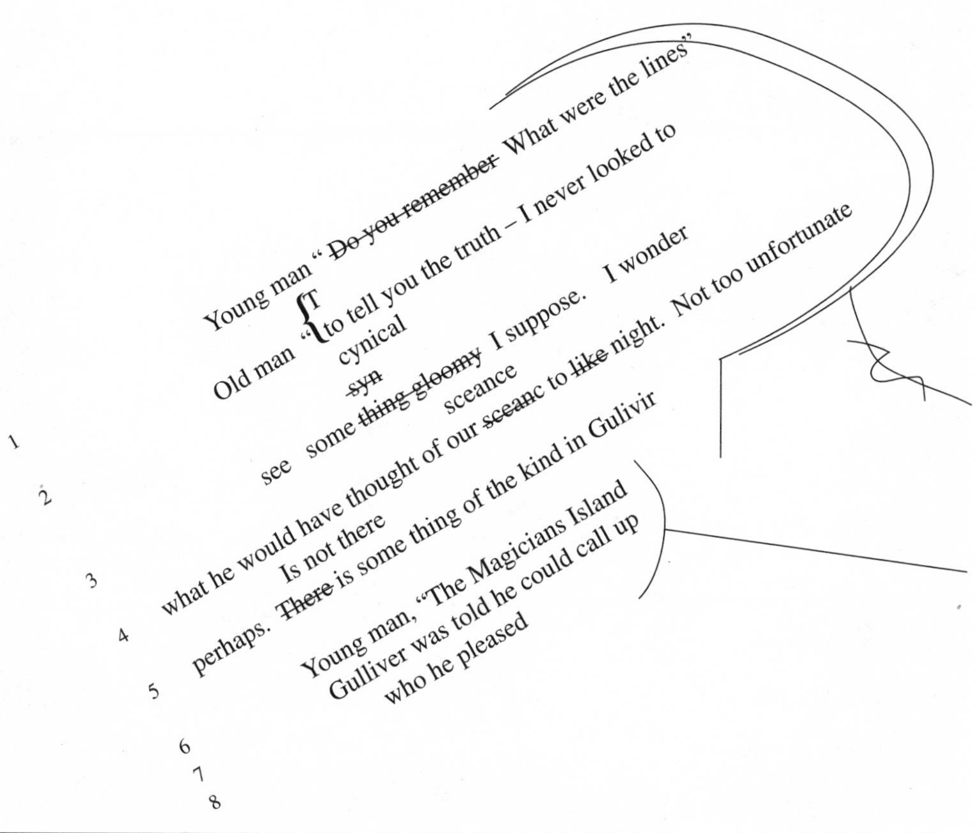

Young man " ~~Do you remember~~ What were the lines"

Old man " {T to tell you the truth – I never looked to

cynical

~~syn~~

see some ~~thing gloomy~~ I suppose. I wonder

sceance

what he would have thought of our ~~sceanc~~ to ~~like~~ night. Not too unfortunate

Is not there

perhaps. ~~There~~ is some thing of the kind in Gulivir

Young man, "The Magicians Island

Gulliver was told he could call up

who he pleased

1–5 Clued in following l. 18 on 18r, the facing recto.

6–9 Clued in to l. 22 on 18r.

[NLI 13,582, 18r]

[NLI 13,582, 18r]

Jonathan Swift
Scenario.

A large room in ~~house~~ Georgian house near
Dublin. – Two men enter one a young English man
the older man a Dublin man. ~~The old m~~an says
~~If you com~~ " ~~The inscription is on those windows~~ ~~We are~~
~~quite a new society~~ ~~The young man says~~ . The old man
says ~~"The Dub~~ ~~We have held our meeting here for~~
~~som t~~ ~~"Though we are quite an old society~~, we
~~have only met here some half a dozen tim~~es."
We held our first meeting in Molesworth St
~~We wanted a larger~~^ Mrs Patterson is so well ~~known~~ that
~~we found that we needed a larger room~~ known that we
had to get a larger ~~so~~ room." The Young Man
"A wonderful room for a lodging house". ~~O this~~
~~was not always a lodging house~~. This was somebodys town
house — not that it was exactly in the town – up to some
eighty years ago. Swift used to visit here, and if you will
come over here I will show you some lines he is
supposed to have [?scrawled] on the pane with a diymond," but you cant
read in this light.." ~~Young man~~ "I wonder what he would
have thought of the sceance to night – not much I imagine.
Young Man
~~Old Man~~ "O I dont know you remember
attended a kind of sceance,
the Magicians Island in Guliver. – Guliver ^ was told he could
raise from the dead any body he pleased. ~~Young Man~~ "Yes I

13 The upturned end of the downstroke on "y" in "somebodys" indicates an "s" to follow.
18 Lines 1–5 on the facing verso, 17v, were clued in here.
21–22 Lines 6–8 on 17v are clued in here.

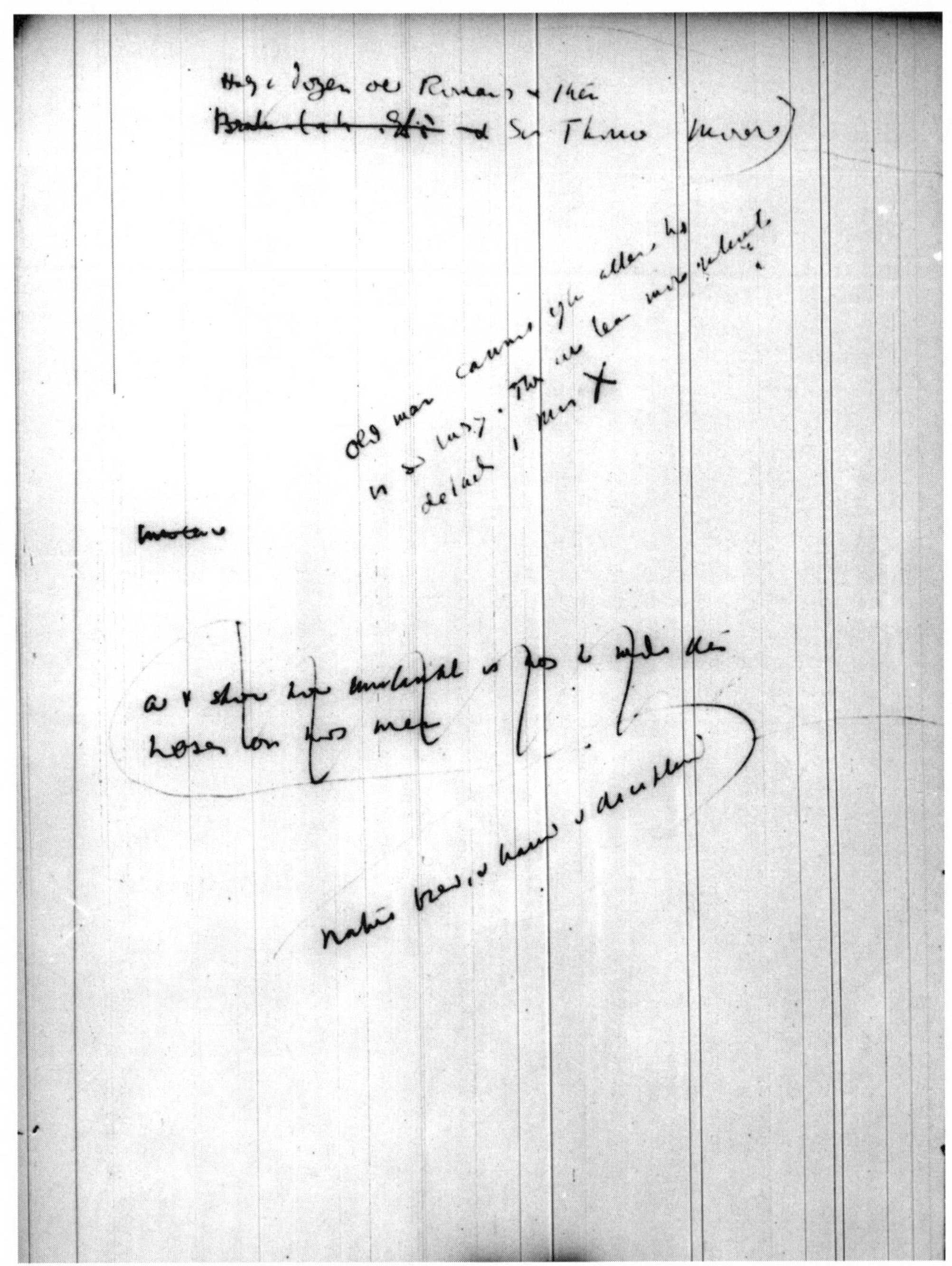

[NLI 13,582, 18v]

Half a dozen old Romans & then
~~Brutus, Cato, Etc &~~ Sir Thomas Moore

Old Man cannot often attend he
is so busy. Then we learn more relevant
details of Mrs. X

~~innocence~~

and to show how untamable it was he made them
horses or horse men

native bred, & learned & diciplined

1–2 clued in to l. 3 on the facing recto, 19r.
9 clued in to l. 15 on 19r.

[NLI 13,582, 19r]

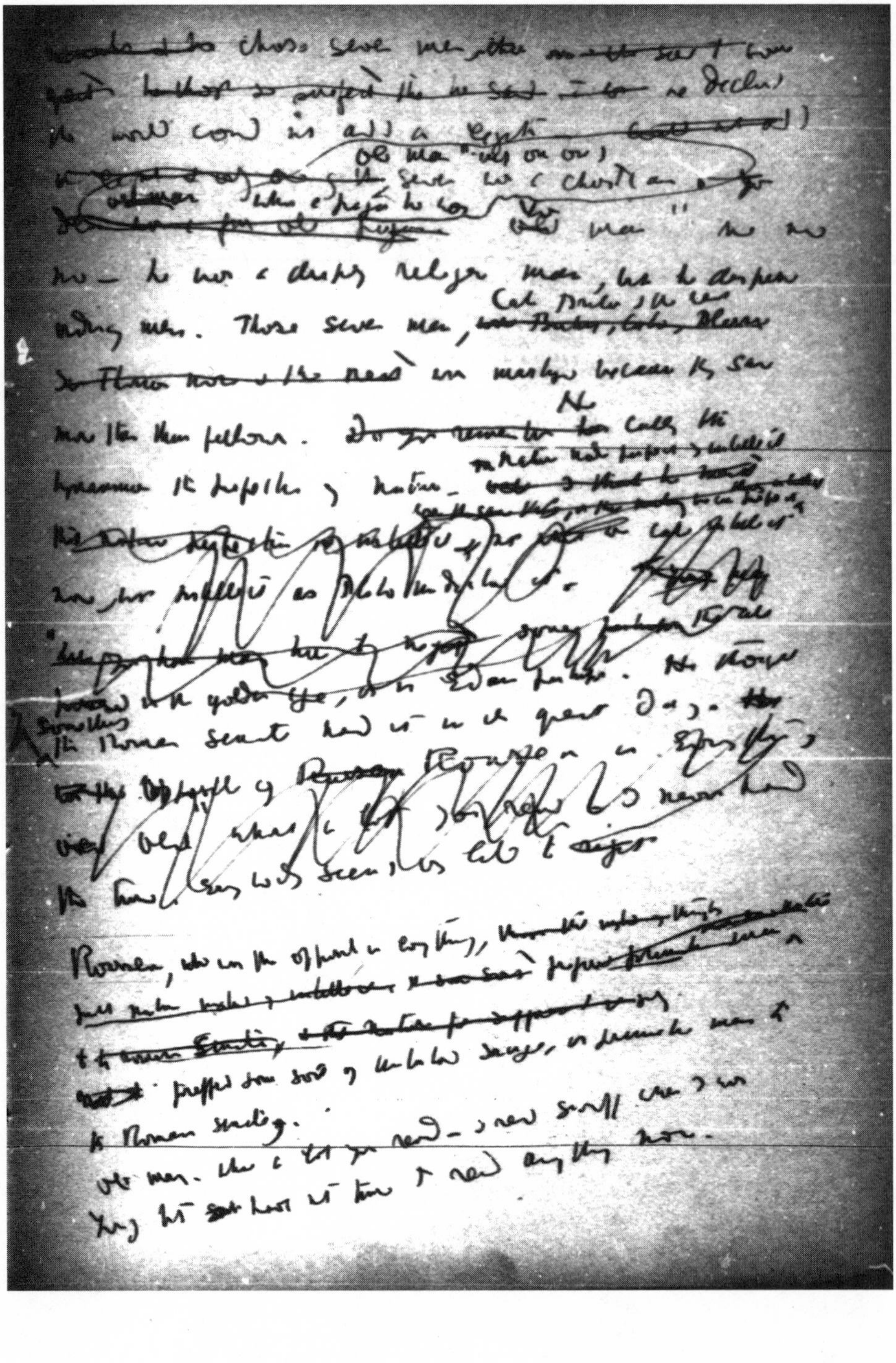

[NLI 13,582, 19r]

1 ~~remember & he~~ chose seven men, then ~~one who seemed to~~ some
2 ~~great~~ ~~he though so~~ [?~~perfect~~] ~~that he said the w~~ he declared
3 the world could not add an eighth – ~~could not add~~
Old Man "but one only
4 ~~an eight & only one of the~~ seven was a Christian. ~~You~~
old man What a pagan he was Young
5 ~~dean was a fierce old pagan~~ ~~Old~~ Man "No no
6 no — he was a deeply religious man, but he despised
Cato, Brutus & the rest
7 ordinary men. Those seven men, were ~~Brutus, Cato, Blessed~~
8 ~~Sir Thomas More & the rest~~ were martyred because they saw
He
9 more than their fellows. ~~Do you remember his~~ calling the
~~M~~ Nature made perfect by intellect
10 hynanmes the perfection of nature – ~~Well I think he meant~~
~~through intellect~~
~~were the same thing, or that nature became perfect~~ ^
11 that natural perfection of intellect & not what we call intellect
12 now, but intellect as Plato understood it. ~~"Young Man~~
13 ~~"Will you have many here to night~~ Some perhaps that all
14 possessed in the Golden Age, or in Edan perhaps. He thought
Something
15 ^the Roman Senate had it in its great day. ~~He~~
16 ~~was the opposite~~ of ~~Russeu~~ Rouseu in everything
17 ~~Old~~ Old "what a lot you read – I never had
18 the time. Every body seems very late to night

19 Rousseu, ~~who~~ was the opposite in everything, ~~though that~~ ~~might of~~ though
~~men~~ [?~~raw~~] ~~nature~~
20 [?~~just~~] ~~natural might of intellect~~, ~~& some sort~~ ~~preferred primitive men~~^
21 ~~to the Roman Senate,, & that nature was sufficient itself~~
22 ~~not to~~ preferred some sort of untutored savage, or primitive man to
23 the Roman Senate, –
24 Old Man. What a lot you read – I read Swift when I was
25 young but ~~since~~ have not time to read anything now.

---

2 "perfect" may be "purfect."
3 Lines 1–2 on the facing verso, 18v, are clued in here.
15 Line 8 on 18v is clued in here, at the caret.

[NLI 13,582, 19v]

[NLI 13,582, 19v]

Swift.

Scenario.

Conversation between old Dublin man, & young Cambridge man. ~~Swifts sig~~nature
on ~~window. Fine room for a lodging house~~ A sceance always here. Yes
Always. Fine room . . History of house . Swifts name on window pane.
What is it does not know. Cannot see in this light. Would he have thought
much of sceance or me to attend one. O I dont know the Magicians Island.
~~What a Pagan he was was. Seven men. One Christian~~. That was different
more modern. It was pure intellect, how he would have hated
all your [?prattering] about loved ones, & dear departed & all the
past . His love of intellect & what a pagan he was.

People have been coming in. Old man introduces Mrs L
Mr [?G]
Here is a young friend of mine ^ – from Oxford – think he was some kind of scepptic
but we all have to make a beginning. "O Mr [?G] I have had [?convincing] [?proofs]
My husband was killed in a flying accident two years ago – I nearly died of grief
told me to < even
& then some body ~~recommended~~ Mrs P – . Mrs P does not ^ know my
name & my husband came at once – at first it was very terrible
for all the death conditions came back. The breaking of something – knowledge that
he was falling, but is only at first. ~~He was very soon~~ O
~~almost~~ often
Old man. Yes that is ^ al~~ways th~~e way at first – they remember the death scene
Mrs L presently he called me by my Christian name, & then he told ~~all kinds~~ of
some things only both of us knew. Now I come to see him constantly &
ask his advice about every thing. Our son ~~who was~~ ~~he died~~ years
~~Young Man~~ ~~& years ago~~ is with him – he died when he was a little
boy but he has grown up there – he looks my husband tells
me as if he was thirty years ~~age~~ old – he will never grow

10–24 This whole block of lines is clued in to follow l. 5 on the facing recto, 20r.

[NLI 13,582, 20r]

[NLI 13,582, 20r]

Young Man ~~But~~ "But it does not need any great reading to see
how different they were. ~~Swift~~ Rous did not call up seven
to show the world could not add the eight, but an uneducated mob.
~~Old~~ All that is satirized in Gulliver & The Tale of a Tub.
Old Man

II.

(Old man says the people are late to night. As he is speaking
Young Miss Williams says ~~they are all here now they are~~ [?~~talking~~] ~~t~~ Mrs Patterson
they are before their time. It is early for every thing. Is introduced
to young man. It is his first sceance. He asks questions –
usual procedure
~~They~~ [~~?~~] She describes ~~usual procedure~~. ~~They give good descriptions~~. Listens
sceptical she says natural at first
He is ~~sceptical~~ but sh~~e says that is natural at first~~. Somehow they
describes sitters Lately horrid spirit has upset things
give good descriptions, Etc. ^ ~~Lately arrived a horrid spirit he~~ upsets
~~B~~ Mrs P ~~con~~ says connected with house perhaps
every thing. Mrs Patterson ~~thinks it is somebody connected with the house~~
~~such a ex~~ – discussions of similar cas
~~but nobody can think of any body~~, ~~& Young Man asks questions about some~~
gambler
~~cases~~. She tells of Abraham Williams & the [?Jambler]. But it is
not always the moment of death – ~~Sometimes an evil~~ S ~~There~~ are
~~even~~ [?~~some~~] There are spirits who go over & over guilty events of their past lives
and spirits they know ~~Young Man~~
~~a kind of penance she supposes~~: ~~He attends to House & description~~
{Old Man Why all good
~~of Achilles driving his hor~~ses. {old man ~~join~~ says it ~~does~~
[~~–?–~~] ~~that they are heard~~ – they have suffered so much, that they are
drawn back as it were must repeat some ~~p~~ past action, going a way
back into things that made [?us] suffer. ~~You rember that Oxford~~ Lady
~~who saw Marie Antoinete & wr & wrote about a book about it.~~ Young Man
gives example from Homer Achilles in a black chariot
this spirit is bad
Young woman is convinced this ~~spirit is~~ [?~~evil~~] ~~at any rate for he quite~~
spoilt two sceances
~~spoilt the last two~~ sceances. He would do nothing but pour out a lot
of abuse, always some woman – he said the most afful things –
Two
~~Some~~ of their members resigned. ~~And here is Mrs Patterson.~~

[NLI 13,582, 20v]

[NLI 13,582, 20v]

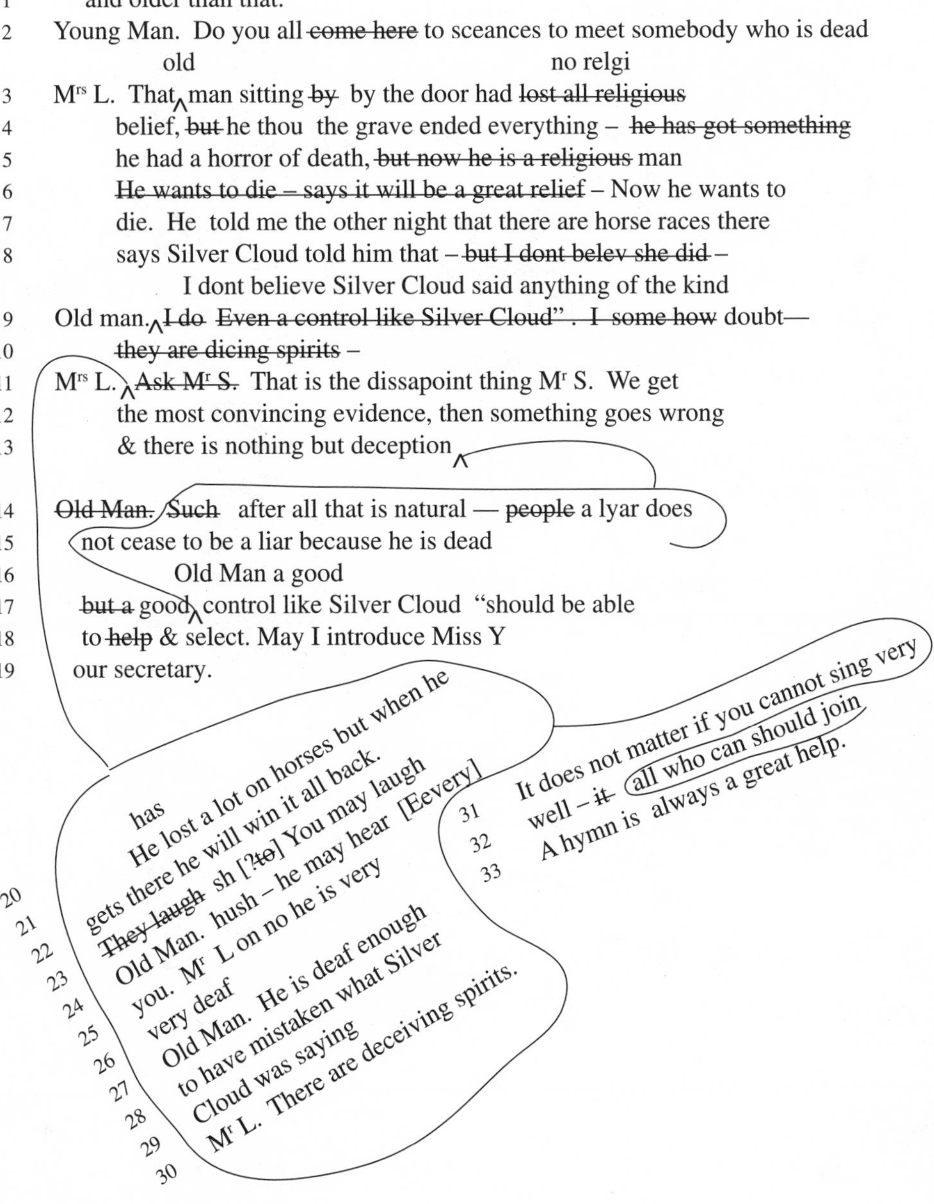

1 and older than that.

2 Young Man. Do you all ~~come here~~ to sceances to meet somebody who is dead

old no relgi

3 Mrs L. That^ man sitting ~~by~~ by the door had ~~lost all religious~~

4 belief, ~~but~~ he thou the grave ended everything – ~~he has got something~~

5 he had a horror of death, ~~but now he is a religious~~ man

6 ~~He wants to die – says it will be a great relief~~ – Now he wants to

7 die. He told me the other night that there are horse races there

8 says Silver Cloud told him that – ~~but I dont belev she did~~ –

I dont believe Silver Cloud said anything of the kind

9 Old man.^ ~~I do~~ ~~Even a control like Silver Cloud". I some how~~ doubt—

10 ~~they are dicing spirits~~ –

11 Mrs L.^ ~~Ask Mr S.~~ That is the dissapoint thing Mr S. We get

12 the most convincing evidence, then something goes wrong

13 & there is nothing but deception^

14 ~~Old Man.~~ ~~Such~~ after all that is natural — ~~people~~ a lyar does

15 not cease to be a liar because he is dead

16 Old Man a good

17 ~~but a~~ good^ control like Silver Cloud "should be able

18 to ~~help~~ & select. May I introduce Miss Y

19 our secretary.

has

20 He lost a lot on horses but when he

21 gets there he will win it all back.

22 ~~They laugh~~ sh [?~~to~~] You may laugh

23 Old Man. hush – he may hear [Eevery]

24 you. Mr L on no he is very

25 very deaf

26 Old Man. He is deaf enough

27 to have mistaken what Silver

28 Cloud was saying

29 Mr L. There are deceiving spirits.

30

31 It does not matter if you cannot sing very

32 well – ~~it~~ all who can should join

33 A hymn is always a great help.

[NLI 13,582, 21ʳ]

[NLI 13,582, 21r]

While they have been speaking various p persons half a dozen perhaps more,
have come & taken seats. The young woman says "A there is Mrs Patteson
medium
& goes over greet old ~~woman.~~ ~~Ol~~ Medium says now my dear
friends we will begin. ~~I say~~ [?~~pe~~] There some strangers among us
I want to explain that I do call up spirits – I make ~~a cond~~ the right
conditions that is all & they come. I do not know who is going to
come – they ~~mu~~ decide that – ~~but~~ the guides ~~all ways try to~~ do
but they cannot always succeed just at once
~~something~~ do they best, ~~& they do~~ ~~but cannot satisfy every body~~. ~~If you~~
~~want to speak to some dear departed one~~ [~~?~~] ~~they~~ ~~If they do~~ not find
~~your dear departed one this week~~ ~~you~~ I say to each one of [?us]
you, that ~~your~~ ~~dear departed one – &~~ If you want to speak to some
dear one who has passed on they will find for you but you have
patience. If they do not find to night, they may the next time we
or ~~it may they will that you will have to go to some other me~~
Now Miss X ~~A hymn p~~ A hymn please, the same verse we had
last time will do. (hymn) ~~for the sake of the new friends~~ who are
Now we will begin
here ~~to night) I say:~~ ~~No body should~~ You need not hold hands –
but nobody should move their leggs that interferes with the
magnetism. → ~~Miss X she is almost in trance~~ now –
~~She always makes that great~~ ~~snores like that when~~ she
Miss X always snores like that when she is going off
She will be in the trance in a moment. Child Spirit speaks
"Glad to see you friends. ~~"Silver Cloud~~ say good evening everybody"
says
X Miss X That is her child "Cilver Cloud –" ~~a little Indian gir~~
{T
{Child S There is somebody here for Lady ~~over there~~ by the door
Is recognised – ~~Another recognised –~~ Third spirit not recognized.
She says "drive that old man away – Who does he is an old

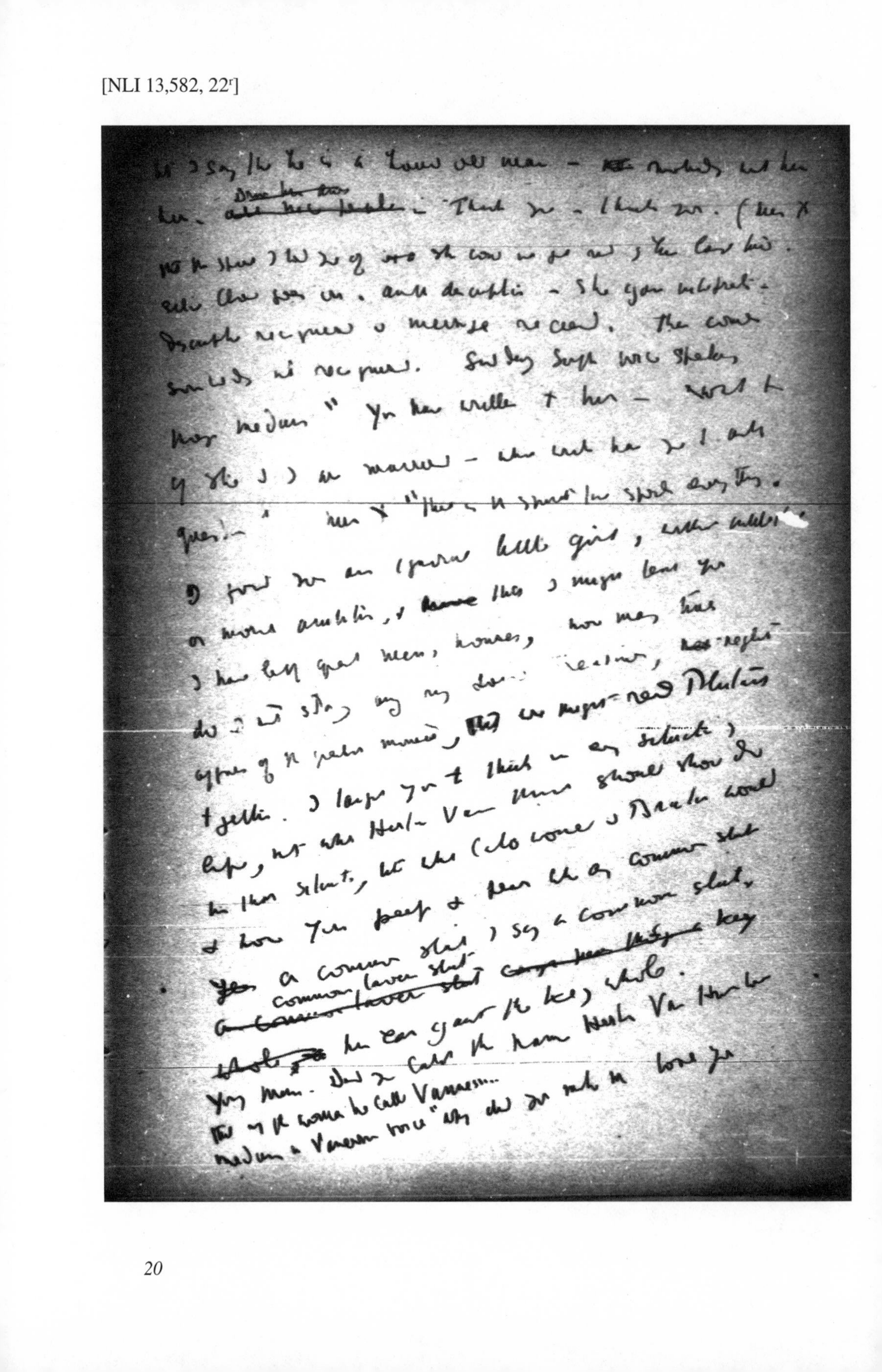

[NLI 13,582, 22r]

[NLI 13,582, 22^{r}]

but I say that he is a horrid old man – [?] Nobody want him
~~Drive him away~~
here. ~~All nice people~~ in Thank you – Thank you. (Mrs X
That the spirit I told you of ~~it e~~ She could not get rid of him last time.
Silver Cloud goes on. Another description – She again interprets –
description recognised & message received. Then comes
somebody not recognised. Suddenly Swifts voice speaking
through medium "You have written to her. [?Want to]
if she & I are married – wha write have you to ask
questions" Mrs X "That is the spirit that spoils everything.
I found you an ignorant little girl, without intellectual
or moral ambition, & ha~~ve~~ that I might teach you
I have left great mens houses, how many times
did I not stay [?] my Lord Treasurer, ~~neg~~ neglect
affairs of the greatest moment, that we might read Plutarch
together. I taught you to think in every situation of
life, not what Hester Van Homrigh should shoud do
in that situation, but what Cato would & Brutus would
& now you peep & peer like any common slut
~~Yes~~ a common slut I say a common slut,
common tavern slut
~~a common tavern slut caught pearing through a~~ key
~~whole, a~~ her ear against the key whole.
Young Man. Did you catch the name Hester Van Homrigh?
That was the woman he called Vanessa.
Medium in Vanessas voice "Why did you make me love you

[NLI 13,582, 22v]

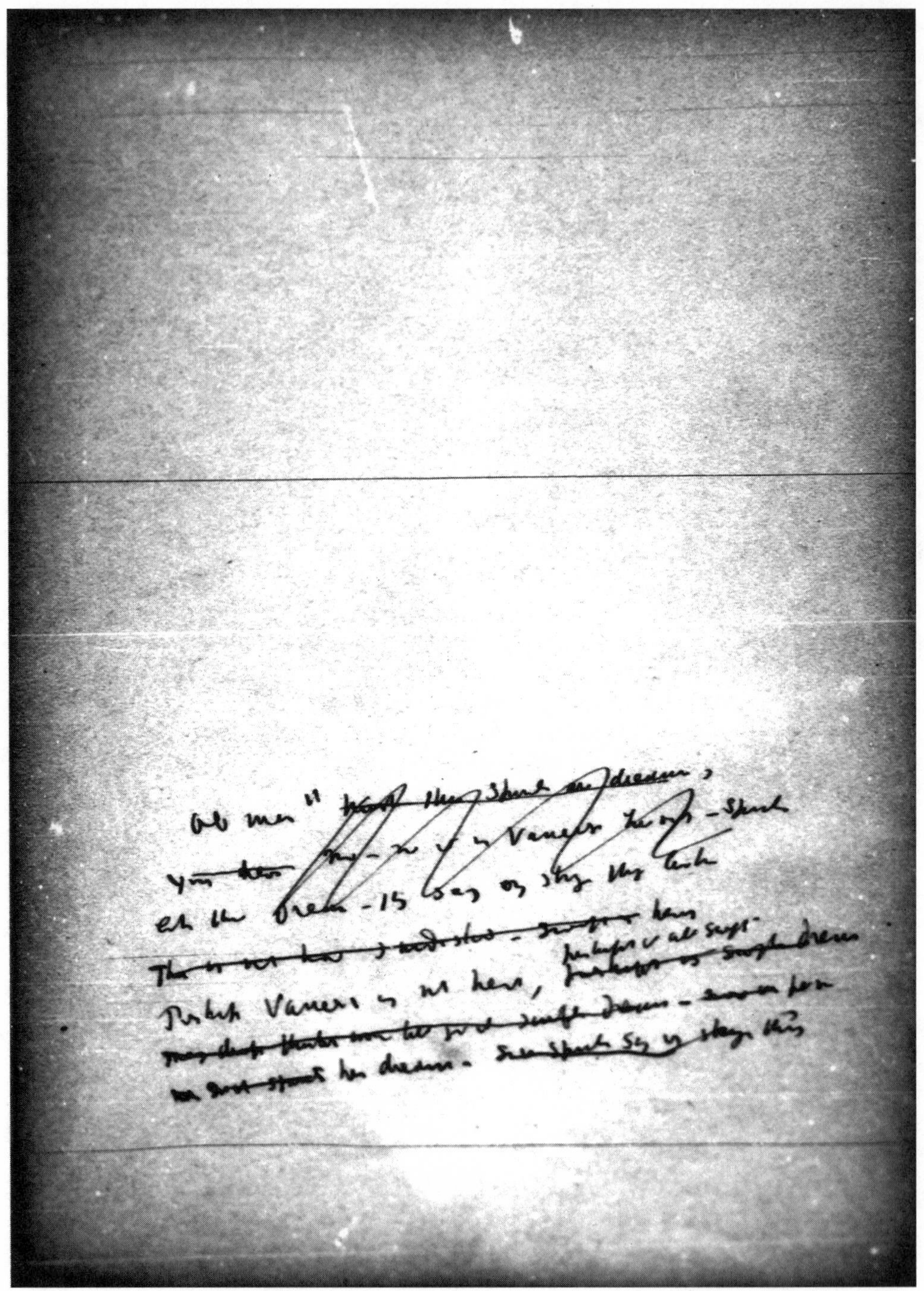

[NLI 13,582, 22ᵛ]

Old Man "~~Maybe these Spirits are dreaming~~
~~Young Man~~ No – No it is Vanessa herself – Spirits
like these dream – they say very strange things [?listen]
~~That is not how I understood. Swift was~~ hear
perhaps it all Swift
Perhaps Vanessa is not here, ~~perhaps its Swifts dreams~~
~~Maybe deep thinkers were all just Swifts dreams~~ – ~~Now one~~ person
~~no such spirits~~ his dreams. ~~Such spirits say very strange~~ thing

[NLI 13,582, 23r]

[NLI 13,582, 23^{r}]

Why did you let me spend hour after hour in your company
that old woman
Yo Man "~~My god she~~ wants us to believe that Vanessa is there too
talking through her mouth. ~~Other say~~ Silver Cd "There was only one spirit last
time & now there are two – is there no way of getting rid of them
and "how horrible it is like the horsse men in the Bible. Medium has
stood up Swifts voice 'I will stay one minute longer
– I will go where I am questioned" – How do you know what I have
to keep down what is in this flesh – ~~Am I to tell you when I~~ have
sworn never t to tell, to explain why I am not marry
Why I
I will go where I am not questioned, did I not tell ~~when we~~ first
~~read Pla~~ do whe we closed Plutarchs Alexander, I [?postponed]
that I wo could nev marry why I dreaded marriage?
Vaness Voice"

~~Do you think it is easy for me Vanessa~~
Y M
That old woman wants us to believe that Vanessa is there too
speaking through her Mouth
Swifts Voice "my god – do you think it is easy [?to]
me. I am a man in whom is strong, ~~& not~~
~~Vanessas Voice~~ I swore that I would never marry.
Vanessas Voice "If you are not married Cadenus
why should we not live like other men & women. ~~When I~~
~~followed you to Ireland, I left~~ It is ~~five years now since~~ you
came to my mothers house, & began to teach me. I loved you
from the first moment – I thought it would just enough to be near
you & speak to you – I followed to Ireland, five years ago & I
can bear no longer – It is not enough see you. It is not enough
to see enough, not enough to see & speak to you , not enough to see
& speak, & touch your hands when we meet

[NLI 13,582, 24[r]]

[NLI 13,582, 24r]

or part. Cadenus – Cadenus I am a woman, nor were th
Cato Brutus loved [?]
women Cato & Brutus loved any different. ~~"Swifts Voice~~ Old Women
stands up "Swifts Voice" I have that within me no child
must never inherit – Do you recall that day in London when
I got dizzie, I had to hold on to the book case
I almost fell. Dr Arbuthnot, you ~~nev~~ remember that wise
I told of ~~that afflic~~ of those attacks, & other things worse things
old man, ^ it was him who explained ~~it was then I resolved~~
{ knew }
Pope { [?new] } – You remember that line of his, that great wits
are allied, he wrote that because I told him
Vaness Voice "~~Yes~~ Great wits are ~~und~~ unto madness near
allied — ~~My blood is healthy, the Van Homrig has always~~ been
but Cadenus
~~healthy~~, ~~my~~ & if we had children my blood would made them healthy
~~the Van Homhir blood is healthy~~. ~~Swifts~~ Give me your hand
let may lay upon my heart, where the Van Homrig blood, the
(Old Woman stands up)
blood that has been healthy for generations. ^ ~~Swifts~~ "~~Gre~~at wit he said
"A great wit great intellect, – but if that is better,
than
~~than the heart,~~ [~~?~~] the foul blood clot, the foul heart
the [?serpents] fouled, ~~but it is not alone. Generation by generation~~ it is
~~growing It~~ I will "What if it be healthy, what if drown
~~many which many all in men is that is~~ [?~~men~~], ~~all~~
~~What if it drown all that is Jonathan Swift, that is~~ accursed to
[?to]
if my mind healthy. Do I add to all the common crowd,
cattle fill
~~those cattt~~ the ~~fie~~ the fields." Vanessa " Look at us Swift
it is your [?courage] that keeps you from me, give your hand ~~again~~
I say – Give me your both your hands – I am woman put this
hand upon my breast – O it is white, white as are the
Gamblers dice, the little ivory dice ~~that men throw~~.

[NLI 13,582, 24v]

[NLI 13,582, 24v]

~~So~~
Old woman rises & then sinks back again – Vanessas Voice
~~No No Cadenus – If you do not~~ ~~Do not think~~ it is
~~the strength of my arm that pulls you back Cade~~nus
~~it is my love~~ It is not my hands that pull you back
Cadenus. You love & I love – You are grown old
tho you want to grow old without children. Old
people are very solitary – their friends that remain are old too
& solitary – They ~~love~~ turn towards the young, but only their
children, or their childrens child – will endure an old man.
But you are not yet old Cadenus if you love
— white dice, white ivory dice. (The old woman
sits up talking (Swifts Voice

There is that man again. Talk to ~~another woman~~ [?sees] squaw
that he the big chief has many squaws. They with him arguing
but not here at first – he is alone
Say feels old – Now is nobody
but strangers

1–13 Clued in to l. 9 on facing recto, 25r.
14–18 Apparently drafted for insertion at l. 24 on the facing recto, then canceled.

[NLI 13,582, 25r]

[NLI 13,582, 25r]

1 It is the uncertainty, that ~~keeps me them gambling~~.
2 ~~makes them throw the dice , draws them to the table~~. brings them to the table.
3 A man child perhaps – perhaps not perhaps no Cadenus.
4 I am the ivory dice, white – white ~~ivory~~ – white ivory
5 ~~Old Woman rises "I will not stay to be tortured~~
6 ~~Why do you talk~~ ~~but you would load~~
7 ~~I am not g~~ What ~~have~~ does intellect matter with its load dice
8 I am the common ivory dice – white – white – white ivory

9 ~~Sw~~ ~~Old woman rises~~ ~~"Swifts Voice"~~ ~~Jonathan~~ Swift

10 ~~will leave to mankind his intellect~~ – ~~intellect is~~ Go find
11 & find some young coxcomb – healthy blood – thats safe
12 ~~that~~ the very ful [?I] nothing [?have]. O god hear my prayer
13 grant to Jonathan Swift this afflicted man that he
14 may leave to posterity nothing but the intellect
15 that came to him from heaven – ~~(he~~ (. comes to door) who
(beats on door) who shut door. ~~It was open when I came~~ in
16 shut this door – I left it open My god I am
with Venessa who hates my soul, ~~my~~
17 shut in with my enemy‸ – (~~beats on d~~oor), ~~Voice of Silver~~-Cloud
[?~~still~~] crouches at door)
18 ~~Bad old man – big chief but once but~~ [?~~bad~~] does not
19 ~~know~~ ~~Old wo~~ Voice of Silver Cloud. Bad old man. Big
20 chief once ~~but~~ – bad old man – know he is dead. ~~Why~~
21 ~~used up~~ ~~Why is she standing up~~. Dont let him back –
22 used up power, & [?~~like~~] Silver Cloud can do ~~nothing~~ nothing – Cannot
23 find dear ones – ~~fath~~ fathers, husbands, sons. Tell them father is
24 if no power. (Some one leads old woman back to her chair)
25 Silver Cloud do another verse of hymn – Everybody. Sing.)

---

1 "me" begins "men," which is canceled in favor of "them."
9 Lines 1–13 on facing verso, 24v, are clued in to replace this line.

[NLI 13,582, 26r]

[NLI 13,582, 26r]

bring good influence. (Verse sung – Old Woman begins to speak during singing – singing falters & stops). Swifts Voice

The follows scene in which Swift speaks to Stella quoting her poem. He ~~do~~ has most wronged her. He asks her assurance. But no he has her poem. She has had had children – but she has her intellect – many friends – If she had married – where would she be now. Would her face give so much light. He begs to out live him – to close his eyes – ~~then it will be as though~~ His life has been always solitary – but for her – Many friends & yet solitary – begs her at the end. Repeats her poem—Yes that is right to come to [?her] soon.

Silver Cloud "Power all gone. Silver Cloud can do nothing more to night. Good by friends – Silver Cloud very sorry – bad old man –

–

The ~~people in sceance come to say good by~~ – Miss X — says were [?n't] [?but] you tried your best – puts down money

[NLI 13,582, 27r]

[NLI 13,582, 27^{r}]

Old Woman says cannot accept it after a sceance like that "No no – You must – Whether sceance is good or bad it exhausts you just the same. People who had put down money & take it up again "Now put it down –" They go one by one Young man says "I thought it a wonderful sceance Mrs P. You know I ~~am doing my~~ get my Doctorate by an essay on Swift – that is what brought me to Dublin. Old Woman "I should not take your money – I should not really." ~~He puts it~~ down – She (~~looks~~) I will not take anything. He says look I have given you twice as much as your regular fee now I will make it five times as much. They are all gone now – Wont you tell me how you know so much about Swift – Hardly any body knows anything about that poem of Stellas, & it is the best ~~poem by~~ a womans poem in the language – Dont you think it like Donne in places – though the begginning [?] comes from Eighteenth Century – – I wonder she read. Then too that about his Madness. I ~~could~~ never could accept the idea so many people hold that he hated Stella & Vanessa or he did because of what the biographers call a phisical defect. It is dead ~~at~~ against the

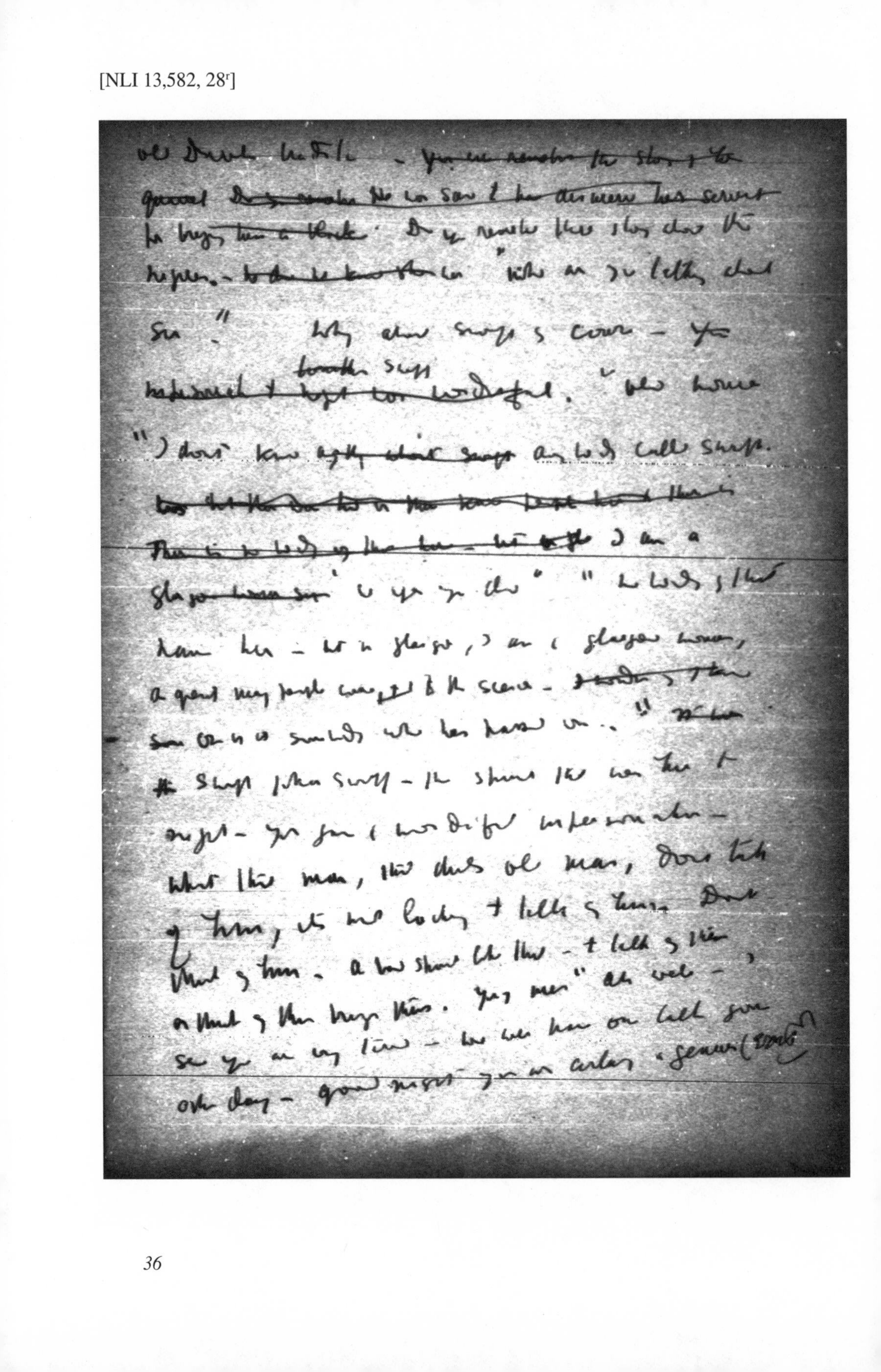

[NLI 13,582, 28r]

[NLI 13,582, 28r]

old Dublin tradition. ~~You will remember the story of the~~
~~quarrel~~ Do you remember He was said ~~to have dismissed his servant~~
for brin~~ging him a black~~. Do you remember that story about the
negress. – ~~He did not know she~~ was "Who are you talking about
Sir ." Why about Swift of course – ~~Your~~
~~Jonathan~~ Swift
~~impersonation to night was wonderful~~. "Old Woman
"I dont know ~~anything about Swift~~ any body call Swift.
~~was but there were two or three knew people here & there is~~
~~There is no body of that name – but~~ [~~? ?~~] I am a
Glas~~gow woman sir~~ "O yes you do" "Nobody of that
name here – but in Glasgow, I am a Glasgow woman,
a great many people come~~, t~~ to the sceances. ~~I wonder if I knew~~
~~som~~ Or is it somebody who has passed on. "~~It was~~
~~the~~ Swift Jonathan Swift – the spirit that was here to
night – You gave a wonderful impersonation –
What that man, that dirty old man, dont talk
of him, its not lucky to talk of him. Dont
think of him – A bad spirit like that – to talk of them
or think of them brings them. Young Man "Ah well – I
see you are very tired. We will have our talk some
other day – Good night You are certainly a genius (EXIT)

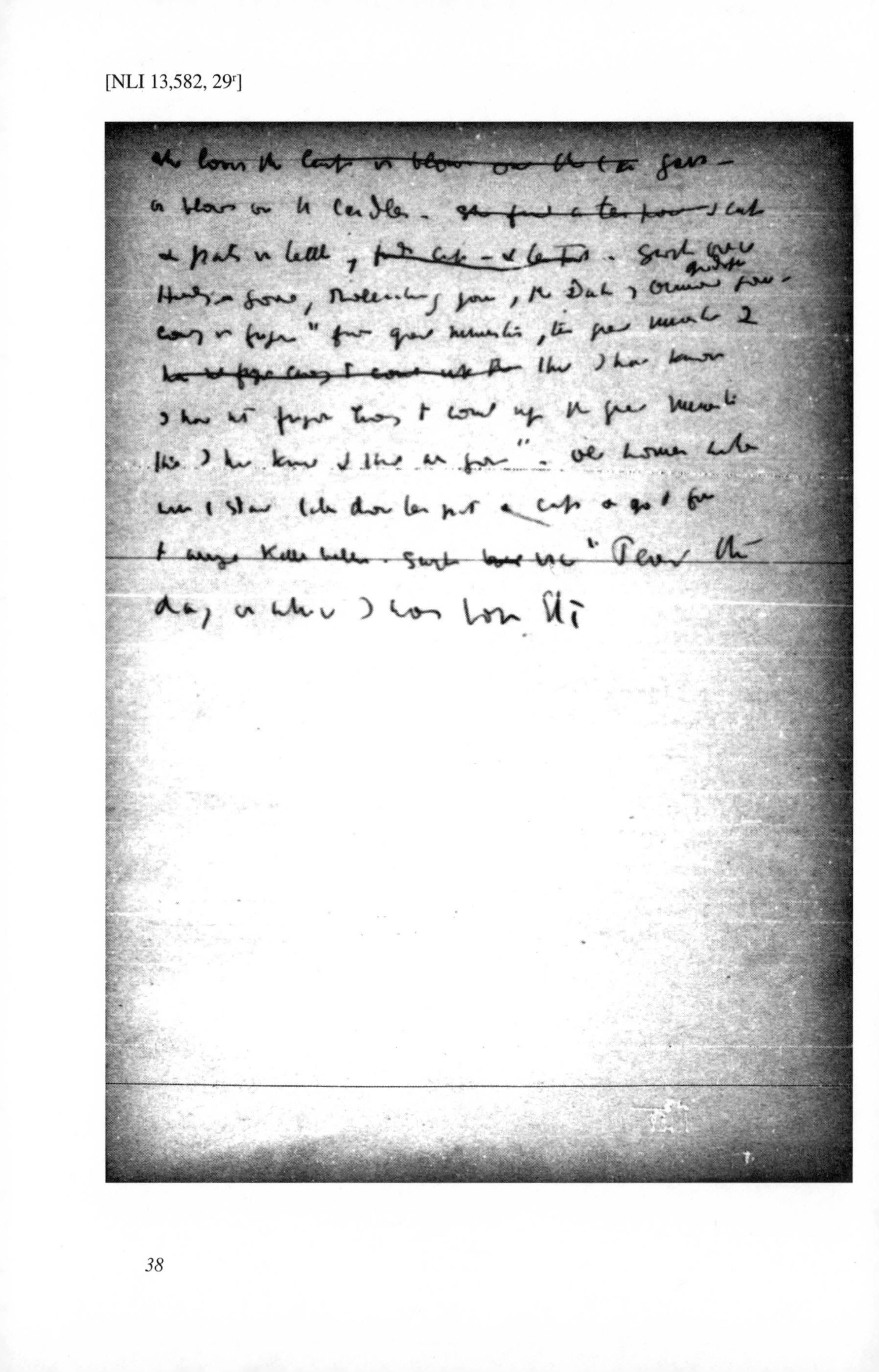

[NLI 13,582, 29r]

[NLI 13,582, 29^r]

she lowers the ~~lamp or blows out the lam~~ gass –
or blows out the candles. ~~She finds a tea pot~~ & cup
& puts on kettle ~~/~~ ~~finds cup – & tea pot~~. Swifts Voice
Godolphin
Hurley ~~/~~ gone, [?Boldenburg] gone, the Duke of Ormond gone –
Counting on fingers "five great ministers, ten great ministers ~~I~~
~~have not fingers enough to count up the~~ that I have known
I have not fingers enough to count up the great ministers
that I have known & that are gone". Old Woman wakes
with a start takes down tea pot & cup & go to fire
to arrange kettle better. Swifts ~~voic~~ voice "Perish the
day on which I was born Etc

[NLI 13,582, 29^{v}]

[NLI 13,582, 29v]

~~Scenario~~.

Characters.

~~Mack~~ McKnan
John ~~Lefanu~~ – man of ~~sixty~~ seventy

James Corbet – man of 25

Mary Duncan between 27 & 30 – not married

Rev Simon Mallet – man of 35

Mrs Hendeson – sixty, stout & common

Mrs James. woman of 45.

Scenario.

Lefanu & Corbet – discuss room & Swifts character.

Mallet & Mrs Duncan come up to complain of annoying spirit –
Mallet wants an exorcism.
Lefanu objects. – explains what spirits are.

Lefanu introduces Corbet to Mrs. Duncan.
Sc. places Conversation. She thinks spirits are transferseable
[?proved] by telepathy – but he thinks it all
juggling

Medium comes in.

[NLI 13,582, 30r]

[NLI 13,582, 30r]

A large room, ~~once a drawing room in a private house~~
~~furnished with~~ in a good many chairs – one arm chair ~~is~~
near center. A fire place, with a kettle on the hearth.
A cupboard where there are tea things.
Macken enter
~~Lefanu~~ & Corbet [?~~talk~~], ~~as they enter~~ they enter talking – one hears their voices
before they are on the stage
Mackenna
~~Lefanu:~~ ~~You~~ You have read his works.
Corbet – Only Uncle Silas – a first rate [?poetic] story.
Mackenna
Lefanu. You would understand what I mean if you had read
He
Through a glass darkly. ~~The Swedenborgian~~ The Spritualist
~~Both books are~~
& Swedenborgian interests are very marked. Both old fashioned
“Through a glass darkly” seems old fashioned now but Uncle Silas
~~now, but seemed very timely when it came out~~. reads as well as ever
~~Corbet. So Lefanu Sheridan Lefanu was your uncle~~.
Mackenna.
I did not quite hear
Corbet. ~~Did I understand your words~~. Did you say that the
Author of Uncle Silas, & Through a Glass Darkly was
your uncle.
Mackenna. Great uncle. Sheridan Lefanu was my great
~~uncle. I was often in his house as little~~ boy
~~& my parents talked a great deal about him~~.
Belonged to my mothers people – an interest in apparitions
ghosts omens & all ~~tha~~ kinds of things runs in the blood.
So you Sheridan Lefanus
Corbet. ~~You think that~~ You have inherited his interest ~~in spi~~ the apparition
~~of all kinds of~~
Mackenna. ~~Not so much that,~~ as ~~No not exactly that – he was only a~~
~~great uncle – he got his interests where I got mine~~
That kind of thing runs in my my mothers family
he was her uncle. I can just remember him.

[NLI 13,582, 30^{v}]

[NLI 13,582, 30^{v}]

If you had heard the talk I have heard from my mother & from my old aunts you would understand how in after life such things became an obsession, I have worked at my business, & ~~not had been~~ & have done well & yet I can honestly say that it has had very little of my thought. My great interest in life has been what people call apparitions – all that relation between man & the supernatur which philosophy & the Church ignore. Though my study has been mainly theoretical for there are no good mediums in Ireland –, & there are so few to share the expense, that we can very seldom ~~bring a medium~~ get one from across the water. Mrs Hendeson has come from Glasgow at her own ~~expense~~ risk We are all to give her what we can. She lives very economically & does not expect a great deal

---

This passage clued in to follow l. 10 on 31^{r}, the facing recto.

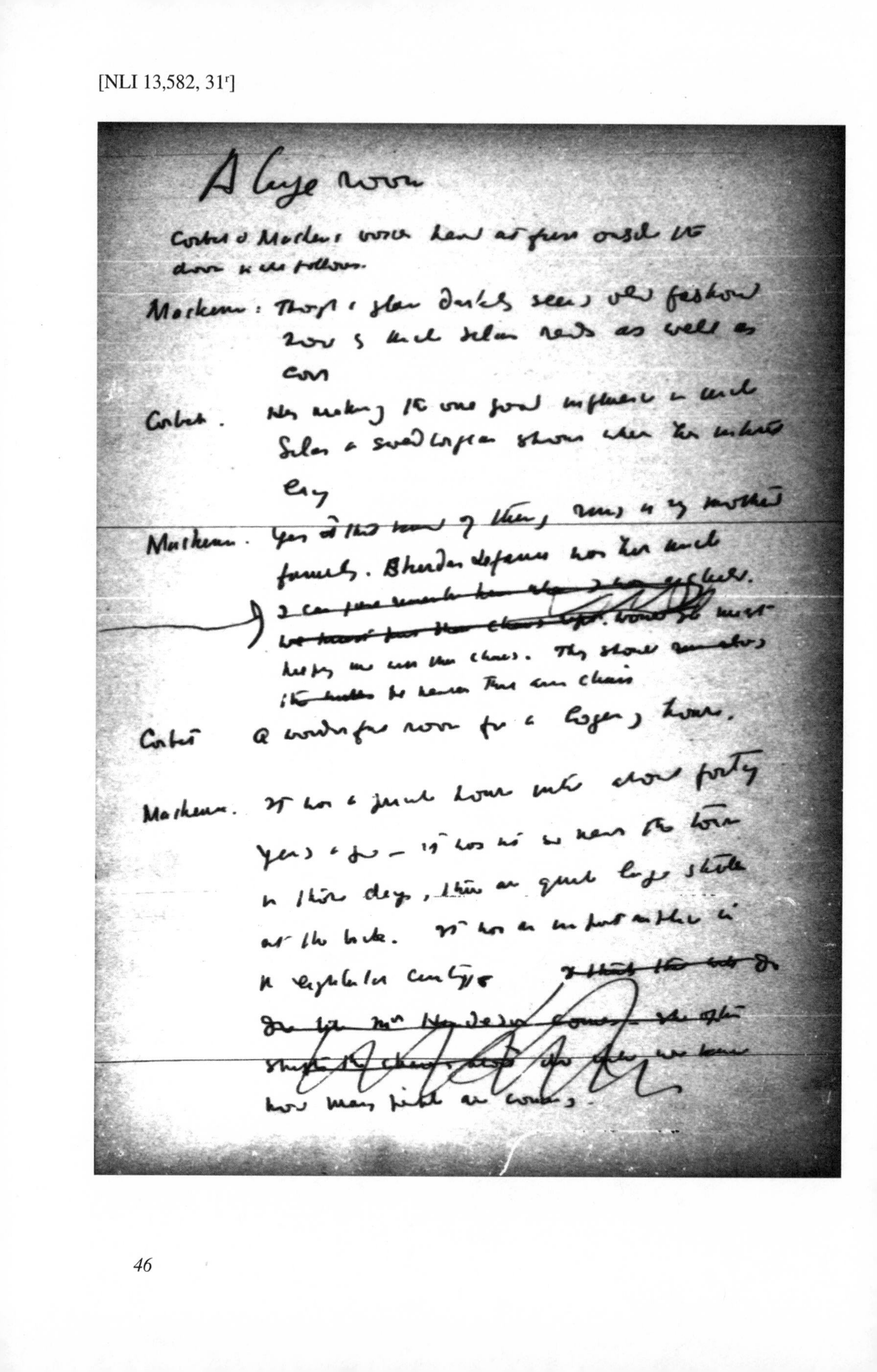

[NLI 13,582, 31r]

[NLI 13,582, 31^{r}]

A large room

Corbet & Mackennas voices heard at first outside the
door in what follows.

Mackenna: Through a glass darkly seems old fashioned
Most of Uncle Silas reads as well as
ever
Corbet. His making the one good influence in Uncle
Silas a Swedborgian shows where his interest
lay
Mackenna. Yes ~~it~~ that kind of thing runs in my mothers
S}
family. [?P]}heridan Lefanu was her uncle
——→ ~~I can just remember him when I was a child~~.
~~We must put the chairs right. Would you~~ must
helping me with these chairs. They should ~~run along~~
~~the walls~~ be nearer that arm chair
Corbet A wonderful room for a loging house.

Mackenna. It was a private house until about forty
years ago – it was not so near the town
in those days, there are quite large stables
at the back. It was an important place in
the Eighteenth Century, – ~~I think that will~~ do
~~do till Mrs Hendeson comes – She often~~
~~shifts the chairs about~~ do until we know
how many people are coming.

11 Passage on facing verso, 30^{v}, clued in here.

[NLI 13,582, 32r]

[NLI 13,582, 32^{r}]

~~st~~ enter & stand at door
Miss Duncan & Mr Mallet enter ~~and stand are seen talking~~ just
~~out side the d~~oor – Mr Mallet is taking off his coat
with Miss Duncan's help.

Mackenna. How many do you expect.

Miss Duncan Not more than seven or eight if as many.

Mackenna. We have enough chairs then. ~~Swift was often~~
Friends of John Swift lived here
~~in this room, & Stella~~ In ~~the first part~~ of the Eighteenth Century the house belonged
~~Swift was often here,~~ & Stella & her companion Tingley often
often sat at cards in this very room

Yes I think that should be enough. I do not expect many people –
In the early eighteenth century this house belonged to friends of Swift – its
mentioned in the Journal to Stella several times. Stella used to play cards here
& Swift ~~would chaff her about her lo~~ chaffed her about her losses
~~There are are lines on that window pane there someone~~ [~~?~~] ~~in writing~~ cut
There is something on this window pane, ~~which~~ [?was] cut with a diamond by Swift
after Stellas death. ~~The~~ Somebody else may have cut them there in memory
of them both for they are not the kind of ~~joclar thing Swift Sw~~ift
bitter jocular thing Swift cut in window panes.

Corbet. How exciting ~~I have taken Swift & Stella for the subject of~~ my doctor
~~for~~ I am hoping to get my doctorate at Oxford by an essay on Swift & Stella
That is what brought me to Dublin

from a poem of Stellas that
Mackenna. There are some lines of ~~Swifts~~ cut on ~~the~~ window with a diamond
~~but I dont think Swift them them there – not thing kind of thing he~~ cut on
windows. ~~They are from a poem Stella People say Swift cut them but~~ I dont
~~believe that~~ I wonder what Swift would think of our work to night
Corbet. Not much I think.

The facing verso, 31^{v}, contains a manuscript draft of the poem "For Anne Gregory," as do the pages immediately following this one, 32^{v}, 33^{r}, 33^{v}, and 34^{r}. A single line from the play—"how many do you expect Miss Duncan."—appears above the draft of the poem at the top of 33^{r}, apparently an afterthought improving l. 4 above.

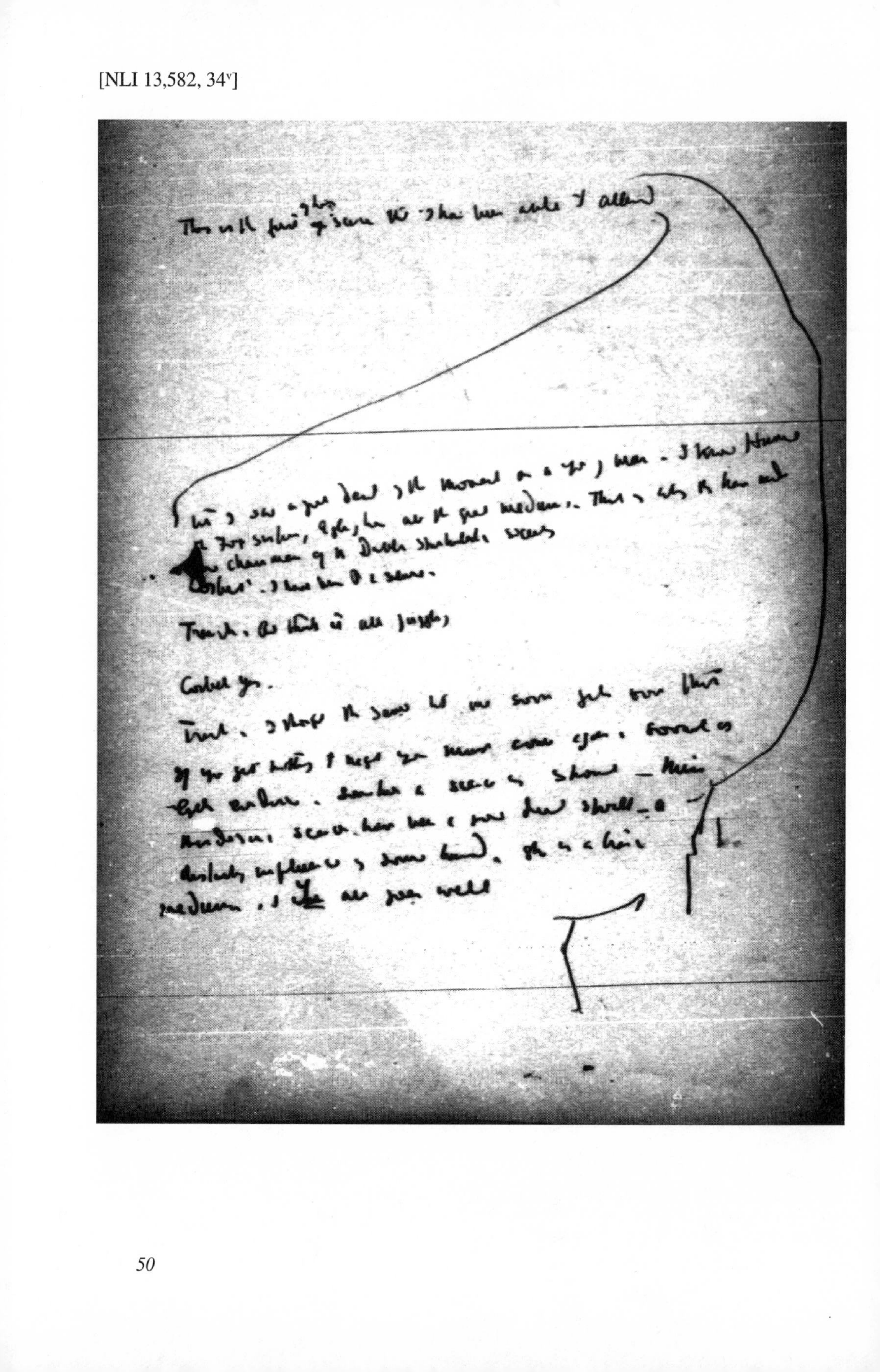

[NLI 13,582, 34v]

[NLI 13,582, 34v]

of her
This is the first ~~of~~ sceances that I have been able to attend
but I saw a great deal of the movement as a young man – I knew Hume
and Fox Simpson, [?Egleston] all the great mediums. That is why they have made
me chairman of the Dublin Spiritualists Society
Corbet. I have been to a sceance.

Trench. And think it all juggling

Corbet Yes.

Trench. I thought the same but one soon gets over that
If you get nothing to night you must come again. Several are
[?better] evidence. Sometimes a sceance is spoilt – Miss
Hendesons sceances have been a good deal spoilt – a
disturbing influence of some kind. She is a trance
if
medium, & ~~whe~~ all goes well

This passage clued in following l. 12 on 35r, the facing recto.

[NLI 13,582, 35r]

[NLI 13,582, 35r]

Swift.

Peter Trench & William Corbet enter.

Peter Trench: We have no good mediums in Ireland – ~~Mrs~~
~~Hendeson is from Glasgow~~ & we are so few that
we can seldom afford to bring a medium from the other
has come
side. Mrs Hendeson ~~is~~ from Glasgow. We all give what
we can. She lives very economically & does not expect a
great deal. This is her third sceance
Corbet. Have you had good results
Trench. I cannot tell you – My business keeps my nose to the grindstone
at this time of the year – Though I am chairman of "The Dublin
Spiritualists Association" this is the first of the sceances I have been
~~able to attend. I have no doubt you will~~ You may get [?some] [?good]
evidence to night ~~or you may get nothing – it is impossible to~~
say before hand. She is a trance medium, & somebody may come
~~that you can recognize. You may be given better first~~ some evidence
first, ^ or even recognize some mannerisms ^, some trick of phrase, or
even of movement shows who here. ~~(Voices out side~~ room door.
perhaps persons seen arriving) ~~some one perhaps~~ You might help
me with these chairs. ~~I want them in a semi-circle~~ round
~~They should be closer to the arm chair~~
Corbet. A wonderful room for a lodging house . (during
what follows two or three people enter – ~~one or two &~~
& ~~arrange things~~ but remain near the door as if listening to ~~th~~
what is going on outside).
fifty
Trench. ~~It was~~ This was a private house until about ~~forty~~ years ago
It was not so near the town in those days – there are quite
large stables at the back. People of some importance had lived

12 Lines 1–13 on facing verso, 34v, clued in here.

[NLI 13,582, 35v]

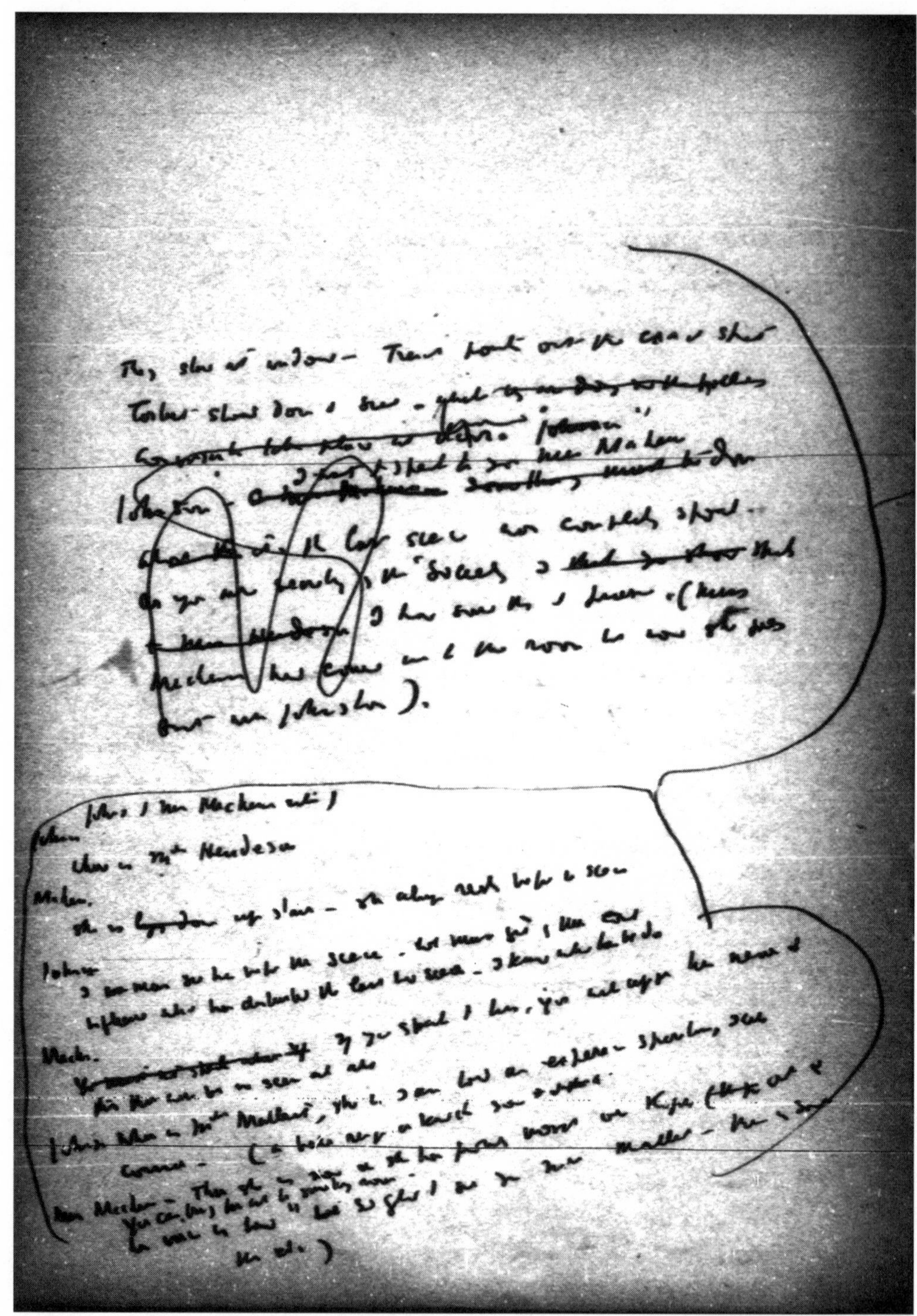

[NLI 13,582, 35^{v}]

They stare at window – Trench points out the exact spot
Corbet slows down & [? sees] – ~~While they are doing so the following~~
~~conversation takes place at door.~~ Johnson
I must speak to you Miss Mackenna
Johnson. ~~O Miss Mackenna. Something must be~~ done
about spirit. The last sceance was completely spoilt.
As your new secretary of the "Society ~~I think you should speak~~
~~to Mrs Hendeson~~ I have some thing to present. (Miss
Mackenna has come in to the room but now she goes
out with Johnston).

Johnson & Miss Mackenna entr)
Johnson
Where is Mrs Hendeson
Mackenna
She is ~~lying down~~ up stairs – she always rests before a sceance
Johnson
I ~~mu~~ must see her before the sceance. We must get of that evil
influence which has disturbed the last two sceances. I know what has to be done
Mackenna
~~You must not speak about it.~~ If you speak to her, you will upset her nerves &
then there will be no sceance at all
Johnson Where is Mrs Mallet, she is I am told an experienced spiritualist, I will
consult – . (A bell rings or knock sounds & [?] ~~th~~ a
Miss Mackenna. There she is now & she had probably noticed our thoughts (She goes out &
You can bring him into the smoking room.
her voice is heard "~~We~~ So glad to see you Mrs Mallet – here is some
[?tea] etc)

1–27 Clued in following l. 8 on 36^{r}, the following recto.

[NLI 13,582, 36r]

[NLI 13,582, 36r]

1 here in the Eighteenth Century. It once belonged to friends
2 of Swift – it is mentioned in the Journal to Stella several
3 times – Stella used to lose small sums at cards &
with a diamond
4 Swift chaffed her about them. Somebody cut ^ two lines from a
{e
5 poem of hers on th{is window ~~paine~~ pain. Trench says Swift
6 but ~~that is nonsense~~ – but ~~it is not~~ that is not likely as He never
7 anything that was not bitter in sentiment. ~~If you stoop down you may~~
8 ~~can see~~ them Here they are, but you can hardly see them in this light.
~~words~~
9 Corbet. I know those two lines well They are from a poem,
10 she wrote for his birth day. [?~~are~~] They might ~~have come out of~~ by some
11 seventeenth century poet – Donne or Crashaw. (He quotes

12 She was a much greater poet than Swift.

13 Trench. ~~Strange that you should~~ I have showed that writing to several people
14 but you are the first to recognize those lines.
15 Corbet. I am writing an essay on Swift & Stella— it is for my doctorate at
~~not~~
16 the university. ~~I dont think one of~~ [?~~hers for~~] ~~Swift would have ^ thought much~~
~~or of me for attending it.~~
17 ~~of our meeting to night, . He might even have written something bitter~~ & sarcastic
He would not think much of our occupation to night. {~~e~~
18 Trench. Is there something in Gulliver, about a Island where could {~~Gall~~ up
19 ~~any~~ call up any of the great dead they had a mind for

20 Corbet. There is

21 Trench. ~~A seeance.~~ A kind of sceance.

The Magicians Island. It ~~is dese~~
22 Corbet. ~~Yes a kind of sceance on~~ island
23 etc. It comes in the second [?~~vorly~~] voyage

8 Lines 1–25 on the facing verso, 35v, are clued in here.

[NLI 13,582, 36^{v}]

[NLI 13,582, 36v]

Spiritualists
Trench. ~~I cannot say that I agree~~ The founders of the ~~Spirituals~~
~~Movement–, I might admi~~ considered ~~as a religious movement~~
it enables
not as a [?sceinc] but as a religious movement, so ^ that ~~quite~~ ordinary
people to speak accross the great barrier, to other ordinary people
whom they had known & loved. In the first phase of the
a great many
~~Corbet~~ movement ^ people ~~deluded themselves~~ thought they could speak
& ~~have sent~~ call up just such spirits as Gulliver called up
They ran into every kind
on the Magicians Island. ~~But it led to nothing~~ but [?awkwardness] &
[?it]
delusion; ^ ~~but it~~ ~~But to day we discoverers attempt to call up no~~
~~Swift. Hat~~
Corbet. Swift hated the ordinary man. "I hate lawyers," I hate doctors' he was
accustomed to say though I love judge so & so Dr So & So.

1–11 Clued into l. 23 on 37r, the facing recto.

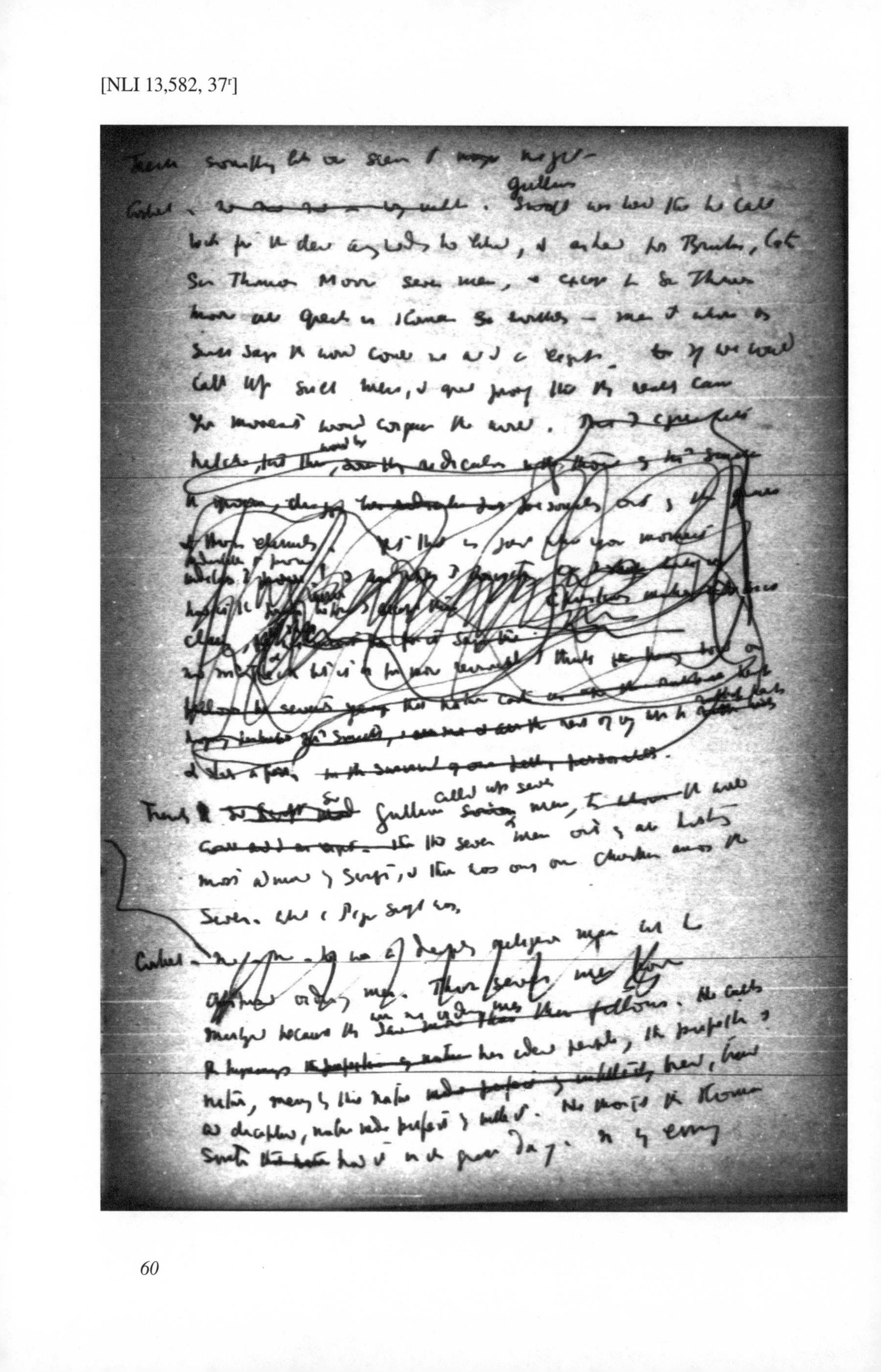

[NLI 13,582, 37^{r}]

[NLI 13,582, 37r]

1 Trench Something like our sceance to ~~nigh~~ night
Gulliver
2 Corbet – ~~No no no – very unlike~~. ~~Swift~~ was told that he call
3 back from the dead anybody he liked, & asked for Brutus, Cato
4 Sir Thomas Moore seven men, & except for Sir Thomas
5 Moore all Greek or Roman [?~~so~~] worthies – men to whom as
6 Swift says the world could not add an eighth. ~~We~~ If we could
7 call up such men, & give proof that they really came
8 your movement would conquer the world. ~~But I agree with~~
would be
9 [?Pilcher] , that there ^ something ridiculous in the thought of Mr Smith
10 the grocer, dragging ~~his ridiculous past~~ personality out of the grave
11 and through eternity. Yet that is just what your movement
undertakes to prove
12 undertakes to ~~prove!~~ I am open to [?correction] but I should look very
[?]
13 hard at the proofs before I accept them. Christianity makes no such
It says
14 claims, but ^ ~~we must~~ ~~be~~ for it says that
15 No Mr Trench but it is far more reasonable I think ~~that having told~~ our
16 ~~followers for seventy years,~~ that nature casts ~~us upon the rubbish~~ heap
~~rubbish heaps~~
17 ~~hoping perhaps Mr Smith, & all such & all the rest of every life~~ [?~~to~~] ~~rubbish heaps~~
18 & start a fresh, ~~in the survival of our petty personalities~~.
So called up seven
19 Trench ~~S~~ ~~So Swift made~~ Gulliver ~~sumen~~ ^ men, to ~~whom~~ the world
20 ~~could add an eighth. The~~ The seven men out of all history
21 most admired by Swift, & there was only one Christian among the
22 Seven. What a Pagan Swift was.
23 Corbet – ~~No – No. – he was a deeply religious man but he~~
24 ~~despised ordinary men. Those seven men were~~
were not ordinary men
25 martyred because they ~~saw more than their fellows~~. He calls
26 the hynamys ~~the perfection of nature~~ his ideal people, the perfection of
27 nature, merely by their nature ~~made perfect by intellect~~, bred, trained
28 and disciplined, nature made perfect by intellect. He thought the Roman
29 Senate ~~that natu~~ had it in its great day. In my essay

23 Lines 1–11 from the facing verso, 36v, clued in here.

[NLI 13,582, 37v]

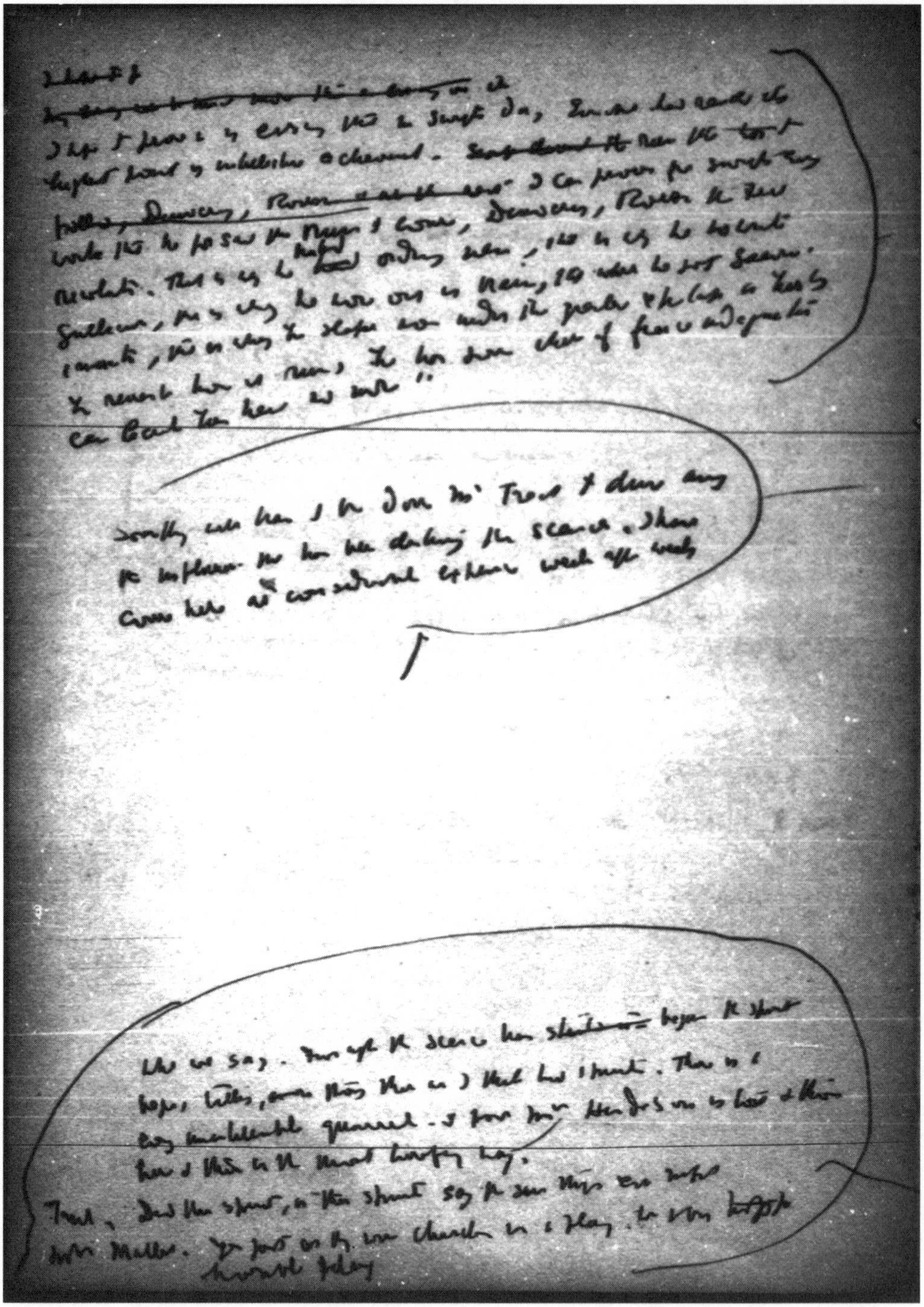

[NLI 13,582, 37^{v}]

~~I hope to~~ p
~~My essay will be much more than an essay on~~ the
I hope to prove in my essay that in Swifts day Europe had reached its
highest point of intellectual achievement. ~~Swift dreaded~~ the ruin that ~~was~~ to
~~follow, Democracy, Rousseau & all the rest~~. I can prove from Swifts every
work that he forsaw the ruin to come, Democracy, Rousseau, the French
hated
Revolution. That is why he ~~hated~~ ordinary men, that is why he ~~wo~~ wrote
Gulliver, that is why he wore out his brain, that where he got Saevio
[?in/nato], that is why he sleeps now under the greatest epitaph in history
You remember how it runs: He has gone where f fierce indignation
can lacerate his heart no more"

Something will have to be done Mr Trench to drive away
the influence that has been disturbing the sceances. I have
come here at considerable expence week after week

what we say. Just after the sceance has started it begins – the spirit
begins talking ~~as~~ as though there are I think two spirits. There is a
long unintelligible quarrel – & poor Mrs Hendeson is tost and thrown
here & there in the most horifying way.
Trench. Did this spirit, or these spirits say the same things every night
Mrs Mallet. Yes just as they were characters in a play but very [?~~horpile~~]
horible play

1–11 Clued in instead of ll. 1–8 on 38^{r}, the following recto.
9 "innato" is apparently a shortened version of "indignatio."
12–14 Clued in following l. 9 on 38^{r}.
15–21 Clued in following final line on 38^{r}.

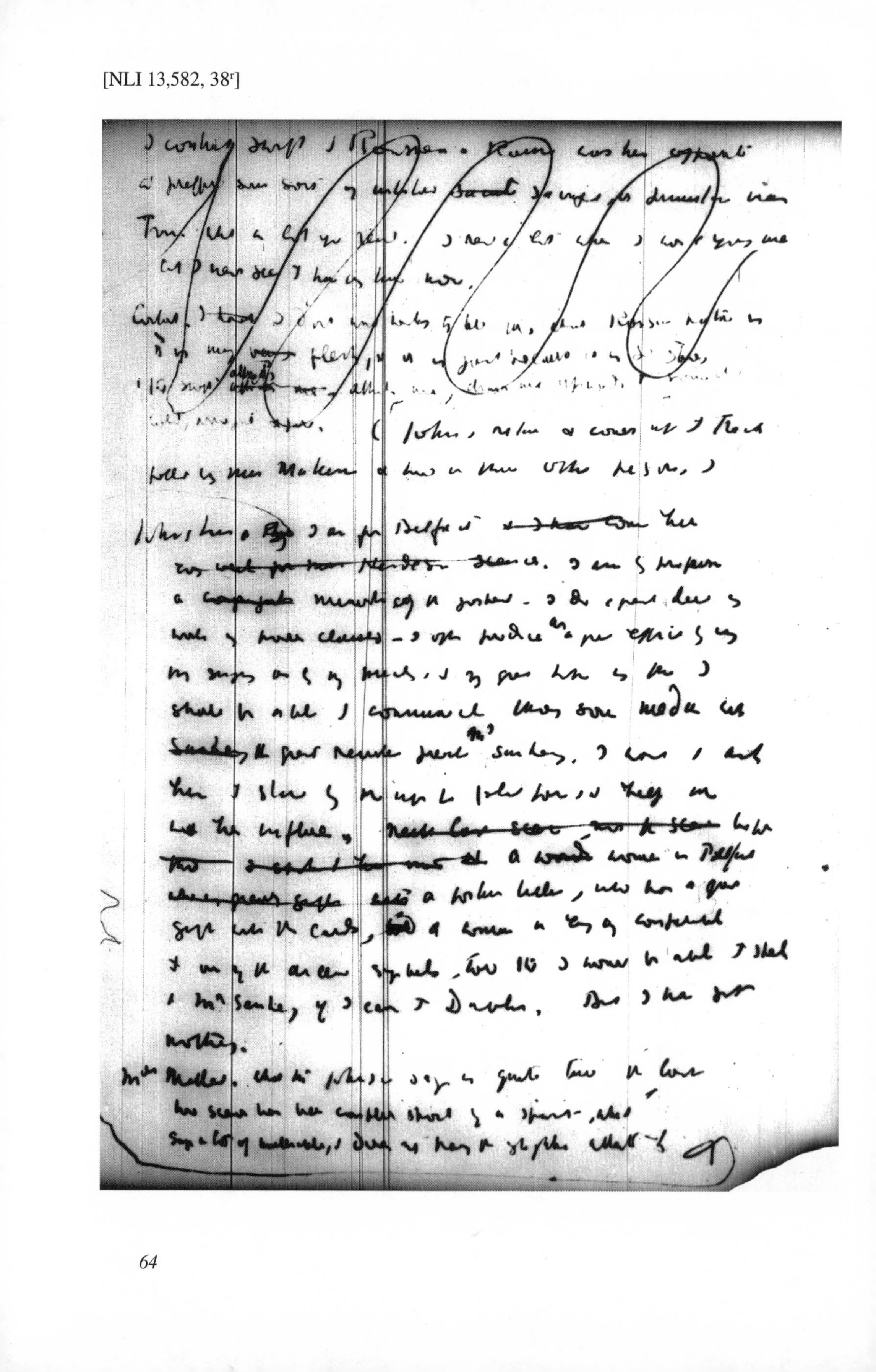

[NLI 13,582, 38r]

[NLI 13,582, 38r]

I contrast Swift & Rousseau. Rousseau was his opposite
& preffered some sort of untutored ~~savate~~ savage, or primitive man
Trench. What a lot you read. I read a lot when I was a young man
but I never seem to have any time now.
Corbet. ~~I have~~ I dont need books to tell me about Rousseau hatred is
it is my ~~very~~ flesh, & it is just because it is so strong
attracts
that Swift ~~attracts me~~ – attracts me, draws me upwards to some [?thing]
cold, arrogant & pure.
(Johnson returns & comes up to Trench
followed by Miss Mackenna & two or three other persons.)

Johnston. ~~This~~ I am from Belfast ~~& I have come~~ here
~~every week for Mrs Hendesons sceances~~. I am by profession
{of
~~a Congregation~~ minister {t the gospel – I do a great deal of
an
work [?by] poorer classes – I often produce a great effect by my
my singing [?as] by my preaching, & my great hope is that I
shall be able to communicate through some medium with
Mr
~~Sankey~~ the great revivalist preacher Sankey. I want to ask
him to stand by me upon the platform, & help me
with his influence. ~~Next last sceance, not the sceance~~ before
~~this I spoke to him more than~~ a ~~words~~ women in Belfast
~~who is greatly gifted with~~ a fortune teller, who has a great
gift with the cards, ~~told~~ a woman in every way comparable
to one of the ancient symbols, told that I would be able to speak
to Mr Sankey if I came to Dublin. But I have got
nothing.
Mrs Mallet. What Mr Johnson says is quite true the last
two sceances have been completely spoilt by a spirit, which
says a lot of unintelligible, & does not pay the slightest attention to

---

1–8 Cancelation replaced by ll. 1–11 on 37v, the preceding verso.
10 Lines 12–14 on 37v clued in here.
28 Lines 15–21 on 37v clued in after this line.

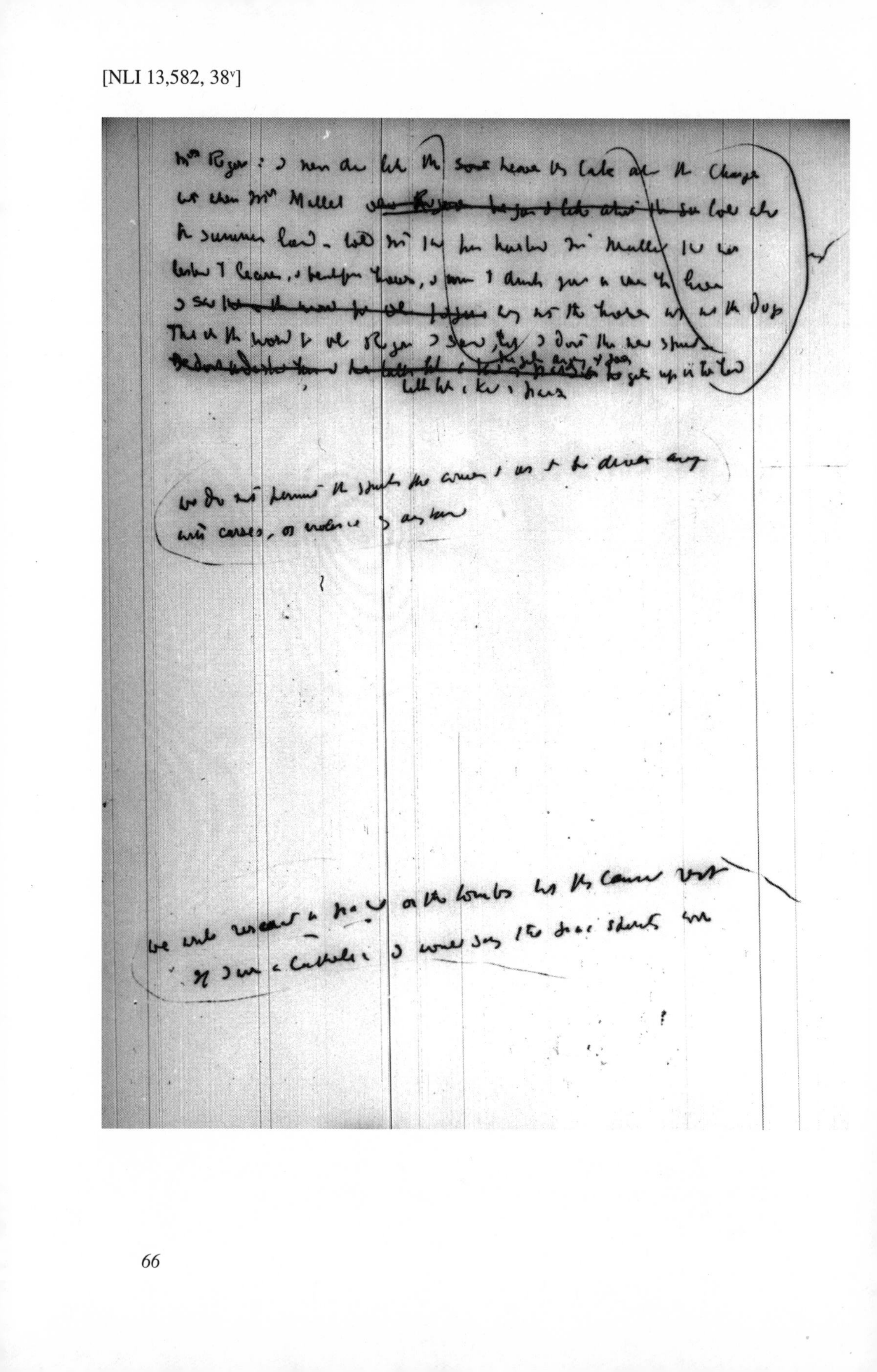

[NLI 13,582, 38v]

[NLI 13,582, 38^{v}]

Mr Rogers: I never did like the ~~sort~~ heaven they talk about the [?Churges]
but then Mrs Mallet ~~Old Rogers began to like about the su~~ told about
the summer land – told M^{r} that her husband Mr Mallet that was
asked to [?levers], & beautiful [?houses] & even to drink gin & [?ale] [?by] [?hours]
I said ~~that is the world for Old Rogers~~ only not the horses but with the dogs
That is the world for old Rogers I said, but I dont like new spirit –
he gets angry & goes
~~We dont understand him & he talks like a kind of parson he~~ gets up in her head
talks like a kind of parson

We do not permit the spirits that comes to us to be driven away
with curses, or violence of any kind

We write rescaet in pace on the tombs but they cannot rest
If I were a Catholic I would say that such spirits were

1–7 Clued in following l. 3 on 39^{r}, the facing recto, prior to cancelation.
8–9 Clued into l. 10 on 39^{r}.
10–11 Clued into l. 25 on 39^{r}.

[NLI 13,582, 39r]

[NLI 13,582, 39[r]]

~~what we say,~~. I have come here to consult my husband, who was
drowned at sea [?about] five years ago, but ~~he & I are as new comers~~, just
(I feel utterly lost when I cant speak to him)
→ as if he were still alive, & advises me about everything I do^
M[r] Johnson. I ask you as President of the Dublin Spiritualists Association
to permit me ~~to read through the ceremony~~ to go through a ceremony of exorcism
I have brought a book for the purpose. Such ceremonies are familiar to the
clergy of every Church, ~~up to~~ about up to modern times. They are most
~~M[r] Trench~~ effective against an evil spirit

M[r] Trench. We Spiritualists do not admit there are any evil spirits. The Spirits
are just ordinary people like ourself.^ Some spirits are what we call
earth bound – they think they are still living, they go over & over
they ~~what they~~ some action of their lives. We cannot keep dwelling on our
past actions, & if they were bad actions the thought is very painful. After we
are dead we do not really think of the past action, ~~but we repeat~~ it
~~and sometimes~~ but re enact. ~~The gambler reenacts the gambling brawl~~ in which
~~he was killed, we all when come back from the through~~ some medium
~~for the first time~~. When a spirit comes back through the medium for the first time
it reenacts the pains of death

M[rs] Mallet “When my husband came first, he seemed to gasp & struggle as he was
drowning – as the medium had to do the same it was most painful to watch

Trench. But some times & most spirits are of this kind a spirit
re-enacts some painful or passionate moment of its life. The murderer repeats
his murder, the robber his robbery, The lover seems to make love once
more, the soldier to hear the word of command.. ~~The spirit which muttered~~
~~unintelligible things~~^ such spirits do not often come to sceances unless those
sceances take place, in the house where the event reenacted took place
This spirit, who speaks unintelligible words, who does not answer when spoken to
if it was such a spirit, we can help it by patience & friendly thoughts.
It wears out its remorse, or passion by reenacting it

3 Lines 1–7 on facing verso, 28[v], were clued in here prior to cancelation.
10 Lines 8–9 on 28[v] are clued in here.
25 Lines 10–11 on 28[v] are clued in here, to replace the cancelation.

[NLI 13,582, 40r]

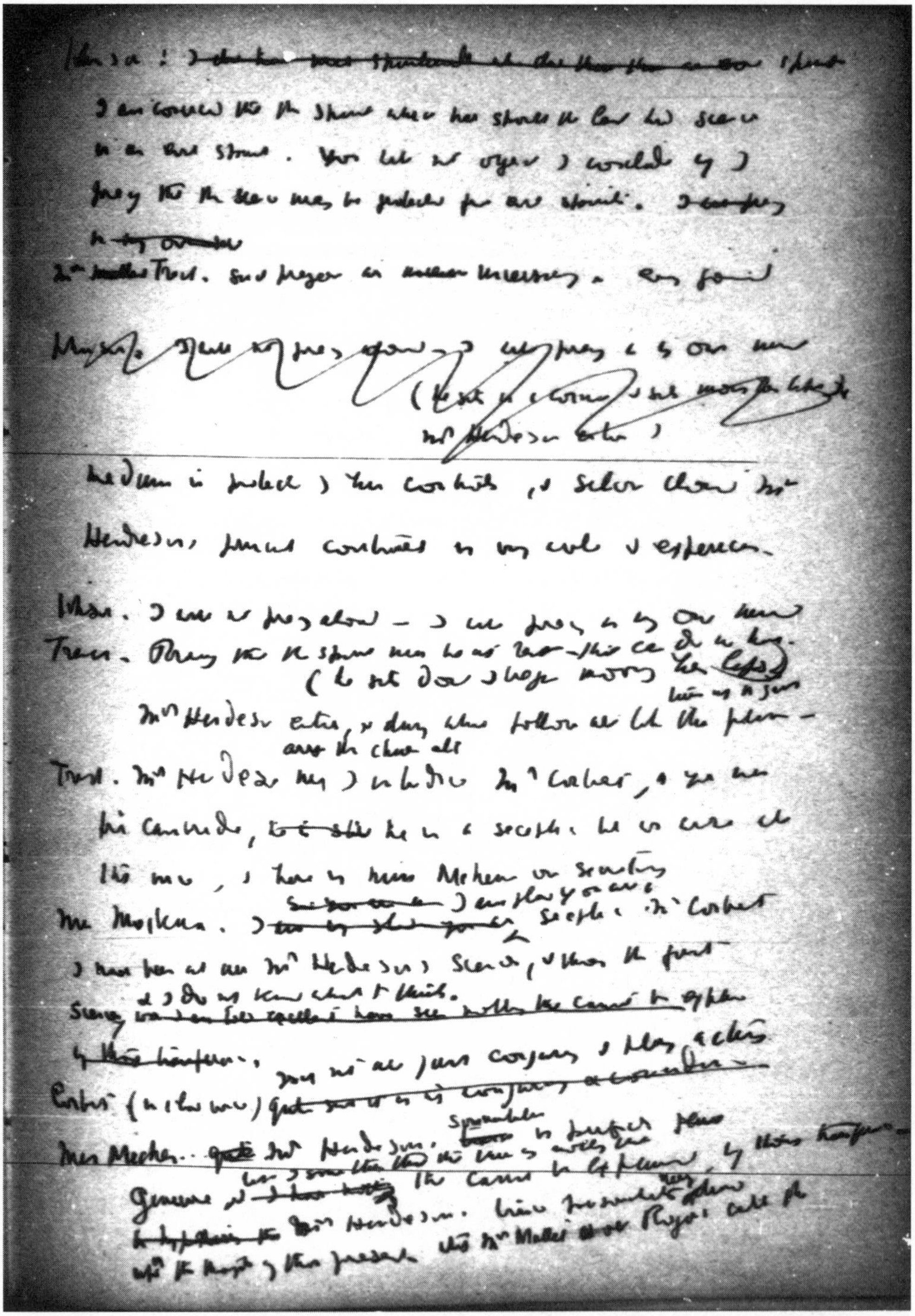

The facing verso, 39v, contains a single word: "Trench."

[NLI 13,582, 40r]

Johnson: ~~I do have met spiritualists who do think that there are evil~~ spirits
I am convinced that the Spirit which has spoilt the last two sceances
is an evil spirit. You will not object I conclude if I
prey that the sceance may be protected from evil spirits. ~~I will prey~~
in ~~my own mi~~
Mrs ~~Mallet~~ Trench. Such preyers are un~~nesse~~ unnecessary. Every good

Johnson: I will not prey aloud – I will prey in my own mind
(he sits in a corner & sits moving his lips)
Mrs Hendeson enters)

Medium is protected by her controls, & Silver Cloud Mrs
Hendesons personal controls is very able & experienced –

Johnson. I will not prey aloud – I will prey in my own mind
Trench. Prey that the spirit may be at rest – that can do no harm.
(he sits down & begins moving his lips.)
turns up th gass
Mrs Hendeson enters, & during what follows all take their places –
arrg the chairs etc
Trench. Mrs Hendeson, may I introduce Mr Corbet, a young man
from Cambride, ~~he is still~~ he is a seceptic but we were all
that once, & here is Miss Mackenna our secretary
~~Since you are a~~ I am glad you are a
Miss Mackenna. ~~I am very glad you are~~∧ secptic Mr Corbet
I have been at all Mrs Hendeson's sceances, & though the first
& I do not know what to think.
sceance∧ ~~was I am told excellent have seen nothing that cannot be explained~~
~~by thought transference~~.
Is it not all just conjuring & play acting
Corbet (in a low voice) ~~Quite sure it is not conjuring & [?coincidence]~~
somnambulance
Miss Mackenna. . . ~~Quite~~ Mrs Hendesons ~~trance~~ is perfectly ~~jenu~~
but I some times think that there is nothing that
Genuine, & ~~I heard nothing~~∧ that cannot be explained by thought transference.
may
~~A hypothesis that~~ Mrs Hendesons trance personality∧ draw
on
up the thoughts of those present. What Mrs Mallet and old Rogers call the

Lines from the verso of this leaf, 40v, are clued in to follow line 31 on its facing leaf, 41r (see p. 73):
Corbet – You said you are glad I am a sceptic

Miss Mackenna – It makes me feel safer, I came here
rather terrified – as if something might happen tonight

[NLI 13,582, 41r]

[NLI 13,582, 41r]

1 the summer land is just the kind of garden ~~one would expect the ordinary~~
some people desire
2 ~~expect half educated people to invent~~. ~~Perhaps we are all building up~~
3 ~~one man bring this one thing another something else~~ Everything they do here they
4 ~~Corbet. I prefer~~ they expect to do there – old Rogers lost every penny he
5 had on horses., ~~but~~ & expects to find a [?Bird] dogs & hares in the grave
6 where he can win back his money.
7 Corbet. I prefer the heaven of Botacheili ~~& the great~~.
[?Bottachel] heaven was as vulgar
8 Miss Mackenna. Perhaps ~~his heaven~~ was ~~much the same~~ before ~~poets & doctors~~
9 painters & poets refined it. I often wonder if we are not building up ~~a new~~
10 one adding this detail, another adding that detail, ~~When I think~~ I
11 ~~feel safer~~ ~~I do not want dreams come true to come [?]~~ a ~~new heaven~~.
12 ~~When I think that I feel safer, when I~~ [?~~sketic~~] a new heaven. The idea
say
13 rather terrifies me. That is why I ~~said~~ I am glad you are a skeptic.
14 I feel safer
15 Corbet. You are right. [?Aulgustine] ~~would not survive it~~ ~~another~~ it –
16 ~~We do not want another dread of~~ the sort.
17 Mrs Mackenna: Perhaps the heaven of Boccelli was not very different
18 before the painters & the doctors of the Church refined it

19 Corbet. You think that the Spiritualists
Old R
20 Miss Mackenna: ~~But~~ rogers & Mrs Mallet do not ~~understa~~
21 ~~Bocelli~~. They dont want be ~~transform into~~ Boccelli
or anything different from what they were
22 angels, ~~they want they are but to man do think~~, ~~but to do well~~
23 ~~Cor~~ ~~or any thing they cannot understand now~~.
proffeses to
think that the is because it proves
24 Corbet: You ~~thin that~~ Spiritualist ~~gets its~~ popular ~~from the fact~~
25 ~~that by its heaven it seems to prove the~~ the existence of heaven
26 ~~where every body crude desires & can sadisfy their crude desires~~
27 of an utterly impossible & preposterous heaven
~~Miss Mackenna: Some~~
28 Miss Mackenna: Sometimes I think that & then I dont mind, but at other
29 times I think just as Mr Trench does & then I am terrified
30 You remember the words of Job "A spirit passes before my face
31 The hair of my head stood up.
32 Corbet: That is why you are glad that I am a sceptic
33 Miss Mackenna. Yes I feel safer.

---

26 "desires" canceled twice, as first half of line canceled before second half.
31 Lines from preceding verso, 40v, clued in after this line; see the note on p. 71.

[NLI 13,582, 41v]

RESURRECTION

[NLI 13,582, 41v]

Were there actually spirits
"You have excited me by your words. ~~Spirits may have~~ ~~Were there spirits~~
~~perha~~ I have or did you as
~~Perhaps what I saw to night was~~ ~~I have seen~~ ~~a spirit, but~~ I prefer to think,
it all when
~~that it was you~~ created^~~either~~ awake or a sleep. I would like to compliment your scholarship
~~on your selection , of what I consider~~ of your explanation of Swifts [?the] celibacy, ~~that~~
an explanation ~~which I have [?advanced] myself~~ which I ~~shall~~ proved in my essay for my doctorate at
~~Cambridge~~ to the only plausible explanation, But there is something that I want to ask.
In Swifts day European intellect reached its climax, free from superstition at last –
~~no where of Swift~~ ~~If ever Swift thought himself~~ If regarded himself the intellect, &
forsaw its collapse he might ————————
~~arrogant~~
Swift was the chief representative of the intellect of his epoch – ~~the intellect~~ which
had ~~for the first time during the Christian Eara over superstition; he forsaw~~ the collapse
of ~~the intellect~~, the intellect arrogant its triumph over superstition, he for saw
its collapse. ~~Was that why~~ Did he refuse to beget children out of dread of
that
~~the~~ future. ~~Was that his madness or w~~ Was Swift mad or was it the
intellect it self that was mad.

2 "what I saw to night was" double canceled.

5 "have" double canceled.

16 Manuscript drafts toward *The Resurrection* begin on the bottom half of the page.

The Harvard Manuscript

H(1)

The words upon the window pane (1)

~~Jonathan~~ Swift.

a lodging house room, [an arm chair, a little table in front of it — chairs on either side] a fire place & window to right. a kettle on the hob & some tea things [on a shelf] ~~on a little table~~. a door to back & towards the left. Through the door one can see a entrance hall. The sound of a knocker. Miss Mackenna passes through hall & then she re-enters hall followed by John Corbet, a man of twenty two or twenty three, & ~~Walter~~ Dr Trench a man of between sixty & seventy

~~Walter~~ Dr Trench (in hall): May I introduce John Corbet, one of the ~~Knockroe~~ Corbets [of Ballymoney], but at present a Cambridge student. This is Miss Mackenna our energetic secretary. (They come into the room, take off their coats)

Miss Mackenna: I thought it better to let you in myself. This country is still sufficiently medieval to make spiritualism an undesirable theme for gossip. Give me your coats I will put them in my own room. It is just across the hall. Better sit down, [your watches must be too fast.] ~~nobody is very punctual~~ ~~even in punctual [illegible]~~ [Mrs Henderson is lying down, as she always does before a seance] (she goes out with hats & coats). [we must begin for [illegible] minutes yet.]

~~Walter~~ Dr Trench: Miss Mackenna does all the real work of the Dublin Spiritualistic associations. ~~[illegible]~~ She did all the correspondence with Mrs Henderson & persuaded the landlady to let her this big room & a small room upstairs. We are a poor society & cannot guarantee anything in advance. Mrs Henderson has come from Glasgow at her own risk. She lives very economically & does not expect a great deal. We all give what we can. ~~Mrs Henderson [illegible]~~ a poor woman with the soul of an apostle.

John Corbet. Have there been many seances?

~~Walter~~ Dr Trench. Only ~~two~~ three so far.

John Corbet. I hope she will not mind my scepticism. I have looked into Myers' "Human Personality" ~~[illegible]~~

[H(1), 1^{r}]

The words upon the window pane (1)
~~Jonathan Swift~~.
An arm chair, a little table in front of it – chairs on either side
A lodging house room.^ A fire place & window to right.
on a shelf
A kettle on the hob & some tea things ~~on a little table~~. A door
to back & towards the left. Through the door one can see an entrance
hall. The sound of a knocker. Miss Mackenna passes through hall &
then she reenters hall together with John Corbet, a man of twenty two or
D^{r}
twenty three, & ~~William~~ Trench a man ~~of~~ between sixty & seventy
D^{r} (in hall)
~~William~~ Trench ^: May I introduce John Corbet, one of the
of Ballymoney
~~Knock~~[?~~brune~~] Corbets^, but at present a Cambridge
student. This is Miss Mackenna our energetic
secretary. (They come into the room taking off their coats)
Miss Mackenna: I thought it better to let you in
myself. This country is still sufficiently medieval
to make spiritualism an undesirable theme for
gossip. Give me your coats I will put them
in my own room. It is just accross the
Your watches must ~~very~~ be fast.
hall. Better sit down. ~~Nobody is every punctual~~
Mrs Hendeson is lying down, as she always does before a sceance
~~ever very punctual~~, ~~in this country~~. (She goes out with
We wont begin for twenty minutes yet.
hats & coats).

Transcription continues on p. 81.

The words upon the window pane (1)

~~Jonathan~~ Swift.

an arm chair, a little table in front of it — chairs on either side

a lodging house room, ^ a fire place & window to right.

a kettle on the hob & some tea things ^or a shelf ~~on a little table~~. a door

to back & towards the left. Through the door one can see an entrance

hall. The sound of a knocker. Miss Mackenna passes through hall &

then she re-enters hall letting in John Corbet, a man of twenty two or

twenty three, & ~~Hallan~~ ^Dr Trench a man of between sixty & seventy

~~Hallan~~ ^Dr Trench ^(in hall): May I introduce John Corbet, one of the

~~[illegible]~~ Corbets, ^of Ballymoney but at present a Cambridge

student. This is Miss Mackenna our energetic

secretary. (They come into the room, take off their coats.)

Miss Mackenna: I thought it better to let you in

myself. This country is still sufficiently medieval

to make spiritualism an undesirable theme for

gossip. Give me your coats I will put them

in my own room. It is just across the

hall. Better sit down, ^Your hostess upstairs [illegible] ~~nobody is any further~~ ~~[illegible]~~ ^Mrs Henderson is lying down, as she always does before a seance ^we must begin in twenty minutes yet. (She goes out with hats & coats).

~~Hallan~~ ^Dr Trench: Miss Mackenna does all the real work

of the Dublin Spiritualists Association. ~~[illegible]~~ She

did all the correspondence with Mrs Henderson

& persuaded the landlady to let her this big

room & a small room upstairs. We are a

poor society & could not guarantee anything, in

advance. Mrs Henderson has come from Glasgow

at her own risk. She lives very economically

& does not expect a great deal. We all give what

can. ~~Mrs Henderson, is hardly~~ ^A poor woman ^has the soul of an

apostle.

John Corbet. Have there been many seances?

~~Hallan~~ ^Dr Trench. Only ~~two~~ ^three so far.

John Corbet. I hope she will not mind my scepticism

I have looked into ^this Myers' "Human Personality" ~~[illegible]~~

[H(1), 1r (continued)]

Dr
19 ~~William~~ Trench: Miss Mackenna does all the real work
20 of the Dublin Spiritualistes Assoceation. ~~It was~~ she
21 did all the correspondence with Mrs Henderson
22 & persuaded the landlady to let her this big
23 room & a small room upstairs. We are a
24 poor society & could not guarrantee anything in
25 advance. Mrs Henderson has come from Glasgow
26 at her own risk. She lives very economically
27 & does not expect a great deal. We all give what
A poor woman but the
28 can. ~~Mrs Hendeson~~ ^ ~~but has the~~ ~~^~~ soul of an
29 Apostle.
30 John Corbet. Have there been many sceances?
Dr three
31 ~~William~~ Trench. Only ~~three~~ so far.
32 John Corbet. I hope she will not mind my scepticism
into ~~thi~~
33 I have looked ^ Myers, "Human Personality" ~~& a book~~

(2)

~~[illegible]~~ is a wild book of Conan Doyle's, but an uncommon.

~~William~~ Dr Trench, we all have to find the truth for ourselves
~~my father~~ Lord Dunraven, then Lord Adare, introduced my father
to the famous David Home: my father often told me
that he saw David Home floating in the air in broad
daylight ~~but~~ I did not believe a word of it I had to investigate
for myself, & I was very hard to convince. Mrs Piper
~~John Corbet~~, an american trance medium, not unlike Mrs Henderson
~~[illegible]~~ convinced me.

John Corbet. A state of somnambulism & voices coming through
her lips that purport to be those of dead persons.

~~William~~ Dr Trench: Speaking quite the worst kind of mediumship of
you want I explained the identity of a spirit
but do not expect too much. There has been a
hostile influence.

John Corbet: You mean an evil spirit

~~William~~ Dr Trench, The poet Blake said that he never knew a bad
man who had not something very good about him.
All spirits are once ~~[illegible]~~ men. I say a hostile
influence, an influence that has disturbed the last seance
or seances. I cannot tell you what happened
~~for I was not at [illegible]~~ for I have not been
at any of Mrs Henderson's seances. Trance medium-
-ship has nothing new to show me ~~I have~~
I told the young people when they made me their president
that I would sleep at home, ~~[illegible] Swedenborg~~
that I would get more out of Emmanuel Swedenborg
~~than [illegible] spirits mediums & [illegible]~~
than out of any seance.
~~the [illegible]~~ (a knock) This is
probably old Cornelius Patterson; he thinks they race
horses & whippets in the other world & is so
anxious to find out if he is right that he is always
punctual. Miss Mackenna will keep him to the last
for some minutes. ~~She gets tips for the races~~
He gives her tips for Harold's Cross.

There is no writing on the facing verso, 1v. On page 2v is a single word in capitals, as though a title—"ASTRAY"—preceded by two numbers, "33" over "<u>21</u>."

[H(1), 2r]

(2)

~~by Ols~~ and a wilde book of Conan Doyles but am unconvinced.
D^r^
~~William~~ Trench. We all have to find the truth for ourselves
~~My father~~ Lord Dunraven, the Lord Adare, introduced my father
to the famous David Hume: My father often told me
that he saw David Hume floating in the air in broad
of it
daylight: & I did not believe a word.^ I had to investigate
for myself, & I was very hard to convince. Mrs Piper
~~John Corbet~~. an American trance medium, not unlike Mrs Hendeson
~~finally~~ convinced me.
John Corbet. A state of somnambulism & voices coming through
her lips that purport to be those of dead persons.
Dr Exactly –
~~William~~ Trench: Quite the best kind of mediumship if
you want to establish the identity of a spirit
but did not expect too much. There has been a
hostile influence.
John
^Corbet: You mean an evil spirit
D^r^
~~William~~ Trench: The poet Blake said that he never knew a bad
man who had not something very good about him.
All spirits were once ~~man~~ men. I say a hostile
influence, an influence that that disturbed the last sceance
very seriously. I cannot tell you what happened
~~for I was not at it~~ – ~~for I was~~ for I have not been
at any of Mrs Hendesons sceances. Trance medium -
- ship has nothing knew to show me – . ~~I had~~
told
I ~~warned~~ the young people when they made me their president
probably
that I would ^stay at home,. ~~& read Swedenborg~~
that I could get more out of Emmanuel Swedenborg
~~who denounced all spirit mediums & was himself~~
than out of any sceance
~~the greatest that ever lived~~. (a knock) That is
Cornelius Patterson he
probably old ~~Person~~ – ~~wh~~ ^thinks that ~~there~~ they race
world
horses & whippets in the ~~old~~ other ~~word~~ & is so
anxious to find out if he is right that he is always
punctual. Miss Mackenna will keep him ~~to s~~ to herself
for some minutes. ~~She gets tips for Harolds~~
He gives her tips for ~~har~~ Harold Cross.

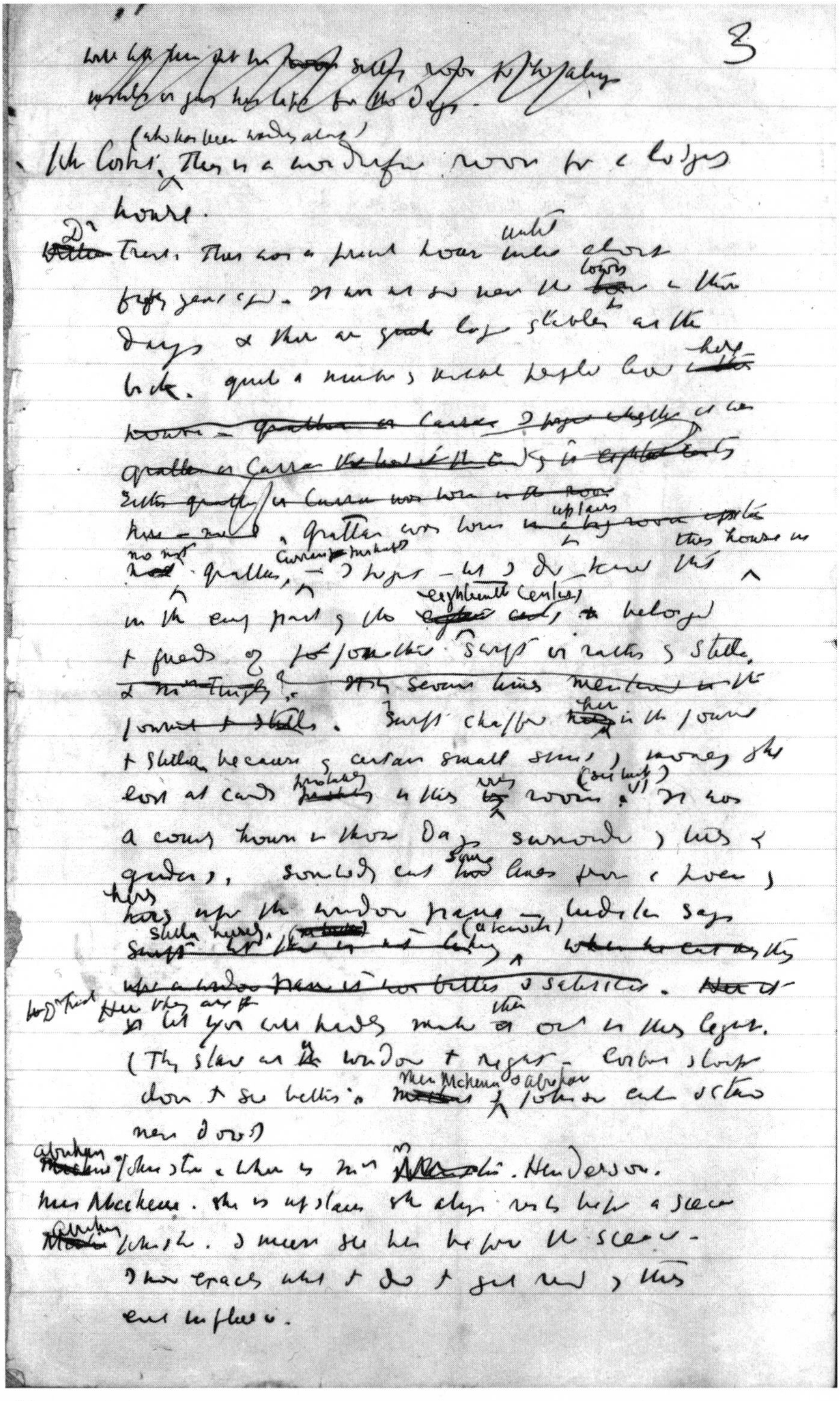
3

John Corbet (who has been wandering along). This is a wonderful room for a lodging house.

Dr Trench. This was a private house until about fifty years ago. It was not so near the town in those days & there are great long stables at the back. Quite a number of notable people have lived here. Grattan was born upstairs — no, not Grattan, Curran perhaps — I forget — but I do know that this house in the early part of the eighteenth century belonged to friends of Jonathan Swift or rather of Stella. Swift chaffed her in the Journal to Stella because of certain small sums of money she lost at cards probably in this very room. It was a country house in those days surrounded by trees & gardens. Somebody cut some lines from a poem of hers upon the window pane — tradition says Stella herself. (A knock) Here they are but you will hardly make them out in this light.

(They stand at the window & read. Corbet stoops down to see better. Miss McKenna & Abraham Johnson enter & stand near door)

Abraham Johnson. Where is Mrs Henderson?

Miss McKenna. She is upstairs. She always rests before a seance.

Abraham Johnson. I must see her before the seance. I know exactly what to do to get rid of this evil influence.

[H(1), 3r]

3

will take him into the ~~room~~ sitting room for he always
insists on giving her tips for the dogs.
(who has been walking about)
John Corbet: ^ This is a wonderful room for a lodging
house
Dr   until
~~William~~ Trench. This was a private house until about
town
fifty years ago. It was not so near the (~~house~~ in those
days & there are ~~quite~~ large stables at the ^
here
back. Quite a number of notable people lived ~~in this~~
house – Grattan or Curran I forget whether it was
Grattan or Curran that had in the Eit by the eighteenth century
Either Grattan or Curran was born in the room
upstairs
~~here – no~~ [?] Grattan was born ~~in a ^ big room upstairs~~
no not   Curran [?] perhaps   this house in
~~no I~~ ^ Grattan, ^ – I forget – but I do know that ^
eighteenth Century ^
in the early part of the ~~eighteenth~~ ~~century~~ ~~to~~ belonged
to friends of ~~Joh~~ Jonathan S^wift or rather of Stella.
~~& Mrs Tingly~~. ~~It is several times mentioned in~~ the
her
~~Journal to Stella~~. Swift chaffed ~~her~~ ^, in the Journal

Transcription continues on p. 87.

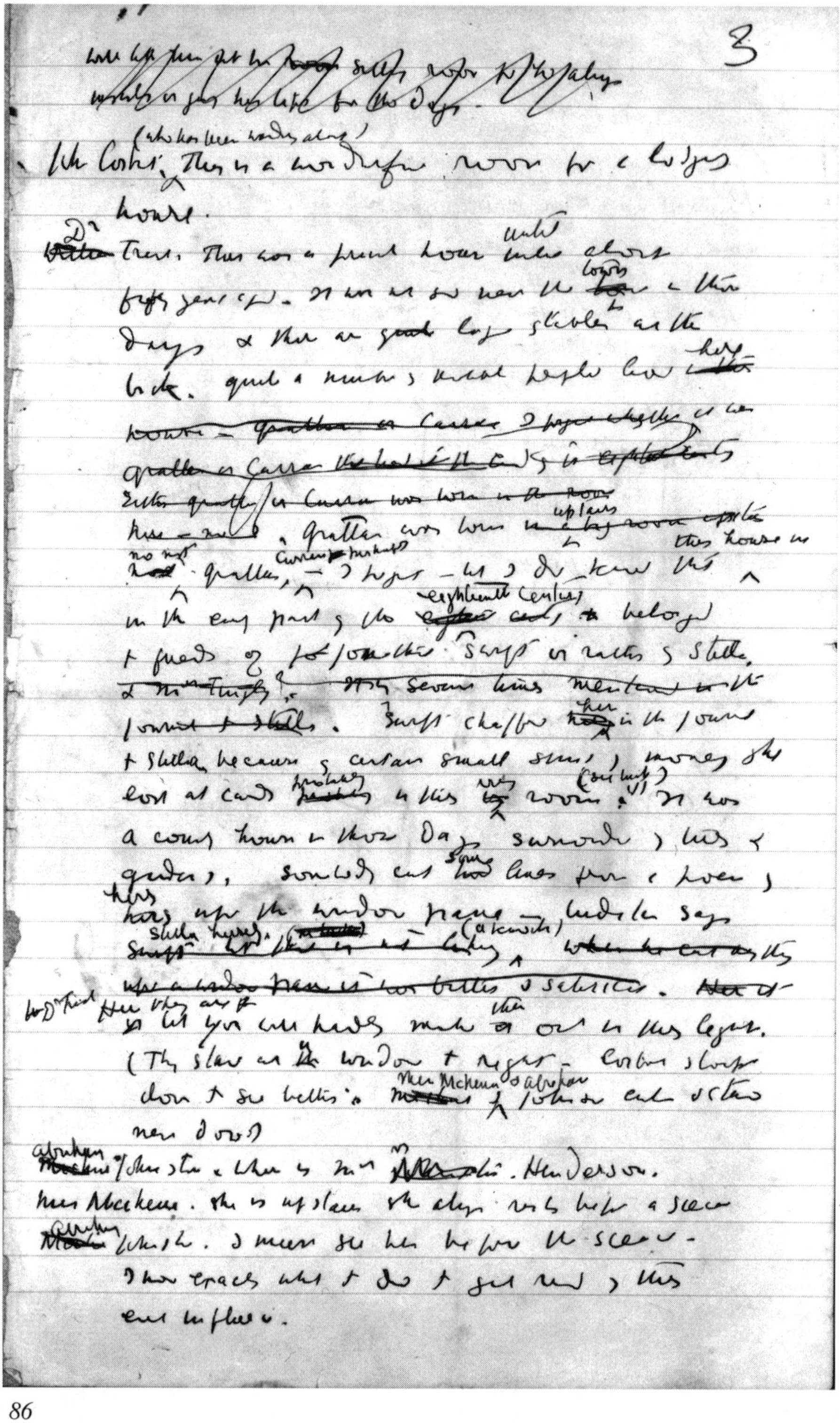

3

John Corbet (who has been reading along): There is a wonderful room for a lodging house.

Dr Trench. This was a private house until about fifty years ago. It was not so near the town in those days & there are great long stables at the back. Quite a number of notable people lived here. Grattan was born upstairs — no not Grattan, Curran perhaps — I forget — but I do know this house in the early part of the eighteenth century belonged to friends of Jonathan Swift or rather of Stella. Swift chaffed her in the Journal to Stella because of certain small sums of money she lost at cards probably in this very room (Corbet looks at it). It was a country house in those days surrounded by trees & gardens. Somebody cut some lines from a poem of hers upon the window pane, tradition says Stella herself (a Kewish[illegible]). [illegible] Here they are but you will hardly make them out in this light. (They stand at the window & Corbet stoops down to see better. Miss McKenna & Abraham Johnson enter & stand near door)

Abraham Johnson. Where is Mrs Henderson.

Miss McKenna. She is upstairs. She always rests before a seance.

Abraham Johnson. I must see her before the seance. I know exactly what to do to get rid of this evil influence.

[H(1), 3r (continued)]

to Stella, because of certain small sums of money she
(see back)
probably very \II
lost at cards ~~possibly~~ in this [?~~very~~] room. It was
a country house in those days surrounded by trees &
some
gardens. Somebody cut ~~word~~ lines from a poem of
hers
~~hers~~ upon the window pane — tradition says
Stella herself. ~~(see back)~~ (a knock)
~~Swift but that is not likely.~~ ~~When he cut any~~thing
~~W~~ Dr Trench upon a window pane it was bitter & satirical. Here it
Here they are ~~b~~ them
is but you will hardly make ~~it~~ out in this light.
a
(They stare at ~~the~~ window to right. Corbet stoops
Miss Mackenna & Abraham
down to see better. ~~Michael~~ & Johnson enter & stand
near door.)
Abraham M
~~Michael~~ Johnston. Where is Mrs ~~Johnston~~. Henderson.
Miss Mackenna. She is upstairs She always rests before a sceance
Abraham
~~Michael~~ Johnston. I must see her before the sceance.
I know exactly what to do to get rid of this
evil influence.

---

18 Roman numeral "II" refers to the passage on 3v to be inserted here.
23 The period after "likely" is canceled by the caret.

[H(1), 3v]

[H(1), 3^{v}]

(I)

That was before Vanessa had appeared upon the scene
Stran~~ge that an austere~~ & grey scholar should have been loved by two such women
Stran~~ge that Swift a an austere aging scholar should have~~
loved by two such women.

II

Before they were cut ~~Stella~~ Vanessas ~~nine years love~~ had
come & gone.
~~John~~
John Corbet: Vanessa met Swift in London at the height of
his ~~powers~~ political powers, followed him to Dublin
~~& m~~ & died there, her death hastened perhaps
by his fierce rejection of her love. Stella wrote those
lines a few months after her death.. Strange
that an austere aging ~~scholars~~ scholar should have
been loved by two such women. Vanessa
loved him for nine years & Stella ~~all her~~
~~from~~ all her life.

Dr Trench. I suppose the problem of Swifts celebacy will
never be ~~queried~~ solved.
John Corbet.

These passages were probably meant for insertion at l. 19 or l. 23 on 4^{r}, facing.

[H(1), 4r]

[H(1), 4^{r}]

Miss Mackenna: If you you up set her there will no 4
~~As Dr Trench says we should not~~
stet sceance at all. ~~She says it dangerous~~ even to think
much less speak of an evil influence.
Abraham
Michael Johnson ÷ Then I will speak to the president
Miss Mackenna: Better talk the whole thing over first
in my room. Mrs Hendeson says there must
be perfect harmony
Abraham
~~Michael~~ Johnson: Something must be done. The last
sceance was completely spoilt.
(a knock)
Miss Mackenna
~~That sounds must be M^{rs}~~
That may be Mrs Mallet She is a very experienced
spiritualist. Come to my room. Old Paterson
is there already. (They go out)
John Corbet: I know those lines well – they are part of a poem
fifty fourth
Stella wrote for Swifts ^ birthday. ~~There are only~~ {O / only}
two poems of hers – & some lines she added to a poem of
Swifts have come down to us, but they are enough to prove
her a better poet than Swift. Even those few words on
a
the window make me think of ^ Seventeenth Century poet Donne or
~~They were written a few months after the death of Vanessa~~
Crashaw. (~~See back~~)

You taught ~~me~~ how
I might youth prolong
By knowing what is right or wrong
How from the heart to
bring supplies
Of luster from my
fading eyes

Transcription continues on p. 93.
Before it was canceled, the passage in the right margin was clued in to follow l. 22.

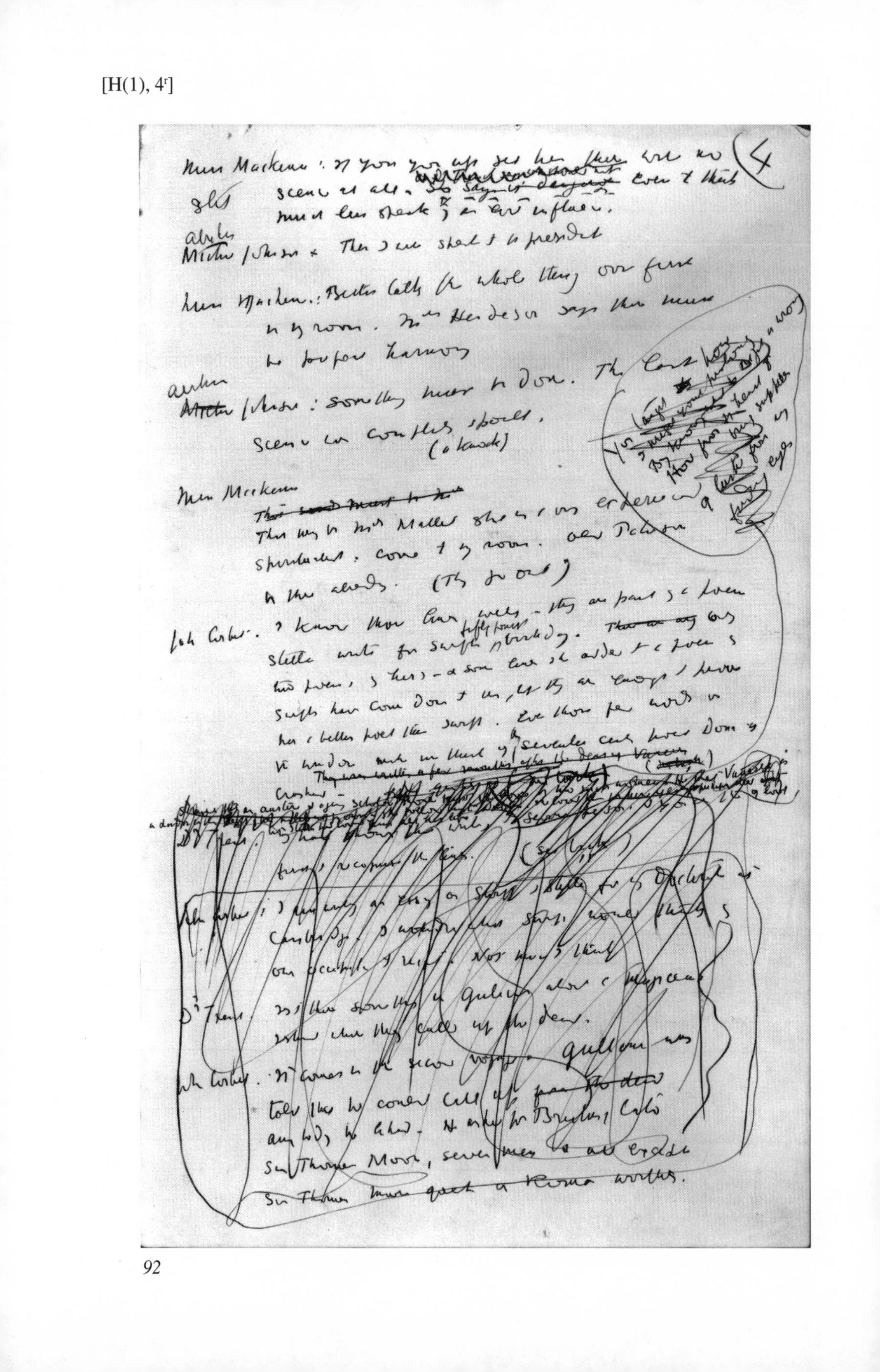

[H(1), 4^{r}]

[H(1), 4r (continued)]

[?] [?questions] (See back) (~~See back~~)
Strange that an austere & aging scholar should kept the love of two such women. I He met
Vanessa in
London in the height of his political power. She followed him to Dublin. She loved him for
nine years perhaps died ~~of it~~
but Stella had loved him all her life. of love
Dr Trench. I have shown this writing several persons, & you are the
first to recognise the lines. ~~(See back)~~

II

John Corbet: I am writing an essay on Swift & Stella for my Doctorate at
Cambridge. I wonder what Swift would think of
our occupation to night. Not much I think
Dr Trench. Isnt there something in Guliver about a Magicians
Island where they called up the dead.
John Corbet. It comes in the second voyage. Gulliver was
told that he could call up ~~from the dead~~
anybody he liked. He asked for Brutus, Cato
Sir Thomas Moore, seven men & all except
Sir Thomas Moore Greek or Roman worthies.

23–34 This passage was apparently developed on 4v, and then canceled there and revised on 5r.

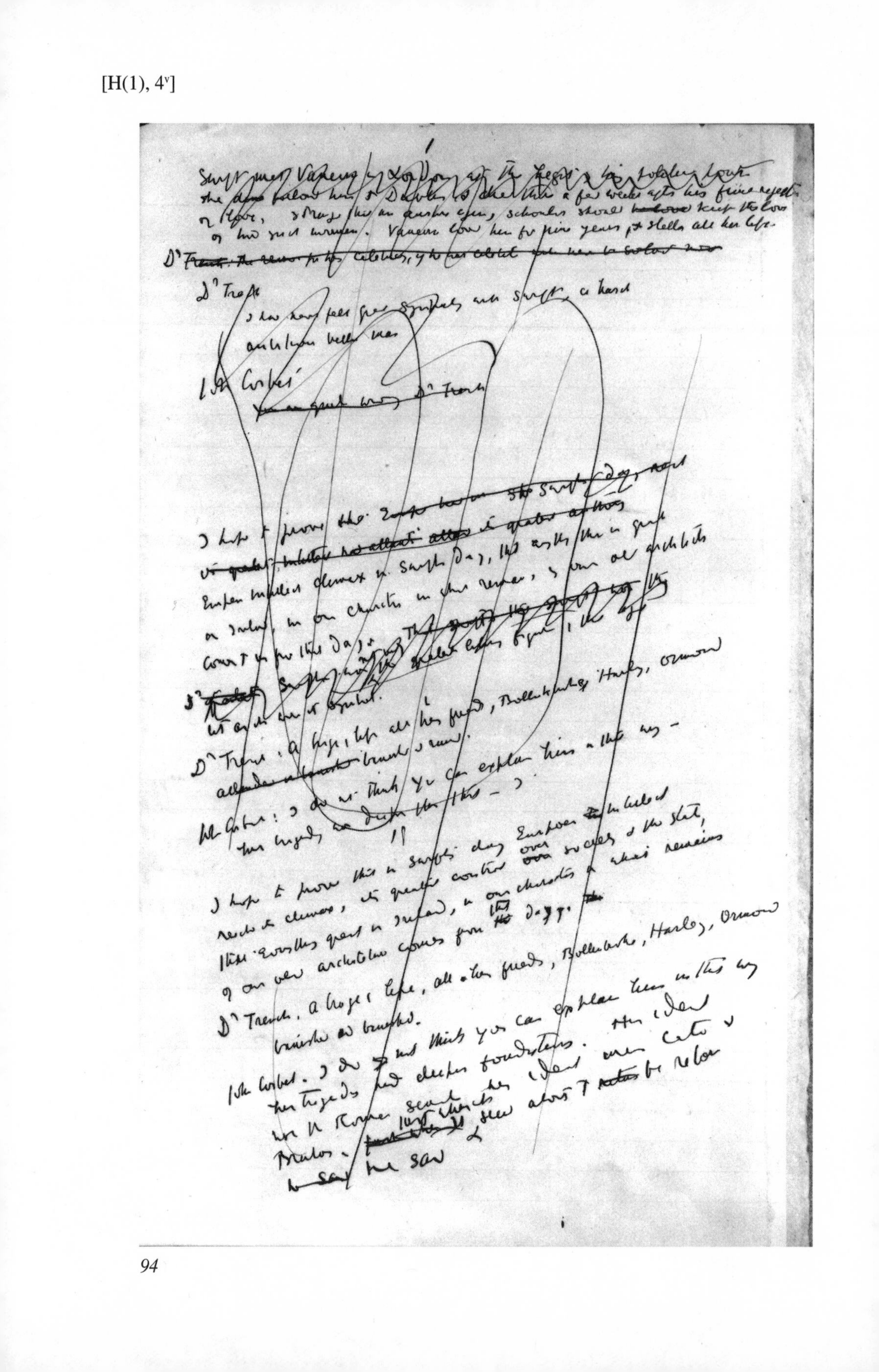

[H(1), 4v]

[H(1), 4v]

I

1 Swift met Vanessa in London at the hegit of his political power.
2 She ~~dine~~ followed him to Dublin, & died there a few weeks after his fierce rejection
3 of love. Strange that an austere ageing scholar should ~~be loved~~ keep the love
4 of two such women. Vanessa loved him for nine years, & Stella all her life.
5 ~~Dr Trench: The reason for his celebacy, if he was celebate will never be solved now~~
6 Dr Trench
7 I have never felt great sympathy with Swift, a hard
8 ambitious bitter man
9 John Corbet
10 ~~You are quite wrong Dr Trench~~

11 I hope to prove that ~~Europe had in Sh Swifts day, reached~~
12 ~~its greatest~~ Intellect ~~had attainet attained~~ its greatest as though
13 European intellect climax in Swifts day, that everything that is great
14 in Ireland, in our character in what remains of our old architects
15 comes to us from those days ~~That Swifts that Swift was~~ the
not only
16 ~~Dr Trench~~ Swift was ^ the greatest literary figure of the age
17 but as it were its symbol.

I

18 Dr Trench: A tragic life all his friends, Bollenbrooke, Harley, Ormond
~~all ended as banished~~ banished or ruined.
19 John Corbet: I do not think you can explain him in that way—
his tragedy was deeper than that – I

II

20 I hope to prove that in Swifts day Eurpoen In intellect
over
21 reached its climax, its greatest control ~~ovre~~ society & the State,
22 that everything great in Ireland, in our character in what remains
that
23 of our old architecture comes from ~~tho~~ day~~s~~. ~~The~~
24 Dr Trench. A tragic life, all his friends, Bollenbroke, Harley, Ormond
banished and [?banished].
25 John Corbet. I do ~~y~~ not think you can explain him in that way
his tragedy had deeper foundations. His ideal
26 was the Roman Senate his ideal men Cato &
Just when its
27 Brutus. ~~Just when It~~ ^ seemed about to ~~retur~~ be reborn
28 ~~he saw~~ he saw

Canceled in three main stages. These passages are developed on 5r, facing.

5

(he quotes)

You taught how I might youth prolong
By knowing what is right or wrong
How from the heart to bring supplies
Of lustre for my fading eyes

How strange that a celibate scholar, well on in life should keep the love of two such women. He met Vanessa in London in the height of his political power. She followed him to Dublin. She loved him for nine years, perhaps died of love but Stella had loved him all her life.

Dr Trench. I have shown that writing to several persons & you are the first who has recognised the lines.

John Corbet. I am writing an essay on Swift & Stella for my doctorate at Cambridge. I hope to prove that in Swift's day men of intellect reached the height of their power – the greatest position they have ever attained in society & the state, that everything great in Ireland, in our character, in what remains of our architecture comes from that day; that we have kept its seal longer than England.

Dr Trench: A tragic life, Bolingbroke, Harley, Ormond, all those great ministers that were his friends, banished & broken.

John Corbet: I do not think you can explain him in that way – his tragedy had deeper foundations. His ideal order was the Roman senate, his ideal men Brutus & Cato; such an order & such men had seemed possible once again, but the movement passed & he foresaw

[H(1), 5r]

[~~?~~]
5

(he quotes)
You taught how I might youth prolong
By knowing what is right or wrong
How from the heart to bring supplies
Of lustre for my fading eyes

How strange that a celebate scholar, well on in life
should keep the love of two such women. He met
Vanessa in London in the height of his political power. She
followed him to Dublin. She loved him for nine years,
perhaps died of love but Stella had loved him all her
life.
Dr Trench. I have shown that writing to several persons
and you are the first ~~tha~~ who has recognised the lines.

John Corbet. I am writing an essay on Swift
& Stella for my doctrinat at Cambridge. I hope
men of reached the height of their
to prove that in Swifts day ~~European~~ ^ intellect ^ power
~~their greatest power~~ – the greatst position they have ever attained in
in
~~reached its~~ ^ ~~climax~~ , – ~~its greatest control~~ of ^ society & ^ the state,
that everything great in Ireland & in our character, in what remains
of our architecture comes from those days, that we have kept its seal
longer than England
Dr Trench: A tragic life, ~~all his friends~~, Bolingbroke, Harley
all those great ministers that were his friends
Ormond, ^ banished and broken
John Corbet: I do not think you can explain him in that
way – his tragedy had deeper foundations. His ideal order
was the Roman Senate, his ideal men Brutus & Cato
~~just when~~ such an order & such men had seemed
again
possible once ~~more~~, but the moment passed & he forsaw

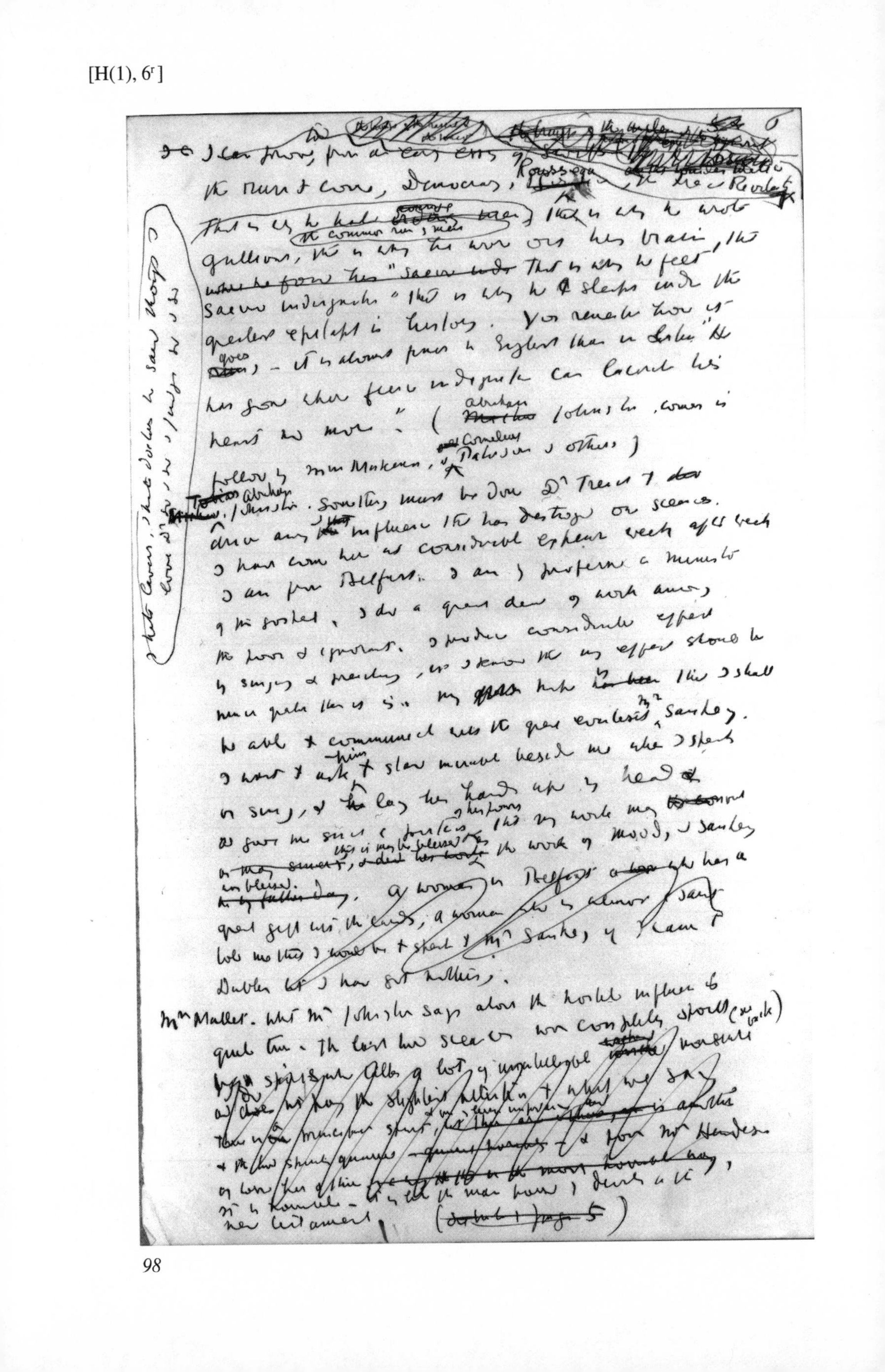

[H(1), 6r]

~~5~~ ^ 6

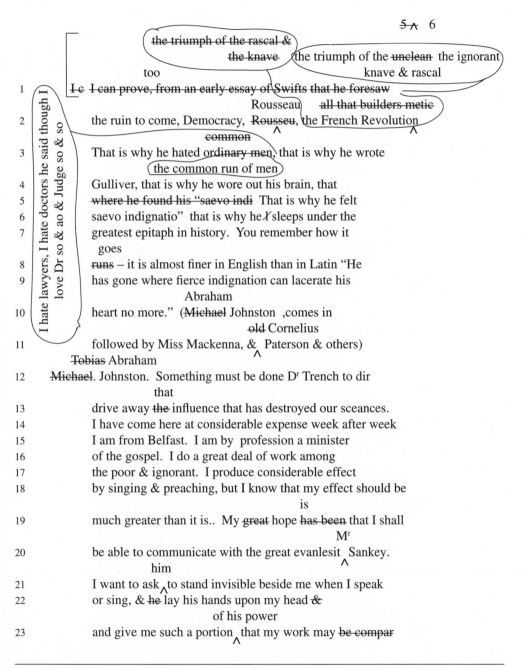

~~the triumph of the rascal &~~
~~the knave~~ the triumph of the ~~unclean~~ the ignorant
too knave & rascal
~~I c~~ ~~I can prove, from an early essay of Swifts that he foresaw~~
Rousseau ~~all that builders metic~~
the ruin to come, Democracy, ~~Rousseu~~, ^ the French Revolution ^
~~common~~
That is why he hated ~~ordinary men~~, that is why he wrote
the common run of men
Gulliver, that is why he wore out his brain, that
~~where he found his "saevo indi~~ That is why he felt
saevo indignatio" that is why he ✗ sleeps under the
greatest epitaph in history. You remember how it
goes
~~runs~~ – it is almost finer in English than in Latin "He
has gone where fierce indignation can lacerate his
Abraham
heart no more." (~~Michael~~ Johnston ,comes in
~~old~~ Cornelius
followed by Miss Mackenna, & ^ Paterson & others)
~~Tobias~~ Abraham
~~Michael~~. Johnston. Something must be done Dr Trench to dir
that
drive away ~~the~~ influence that has destroyed our sceances.
I have come here at considerable expense week after week
I am from Belfast. I am by profession a minister
of the gospel. I do a great deal of work among
the poor & ignorant. I produce considerable effect
by singing & preaching, but I know that my effect should be
is
much greater than it is.. My ~~great~~ hope ~~has been~~ that I shall
Mr
be able to communicate with the great evanlesit ^ Sankey.
him
I want to ask ^ to stand invisible beside me when I speak
or sing, & ~~he~~ lay his hands upon my head ~~&~~
of his power
and give me such a portion ^ that my work may ~~be compar~~

[Left margin, written vertically:] I hate lawyers, I hate doctors he said though I love Dr so & so & Judge so & so

Transcription continues on p. 101.

20 "evanlesit" is meant to stand for evangelist, spelled better elsewhere.

23 "a portion" apparently proved so difficult for the typist to transcribe that it was left blank in the typescript—NLI(2)—and was filled in by WBY in clearer handwriting. See p. 153 below.

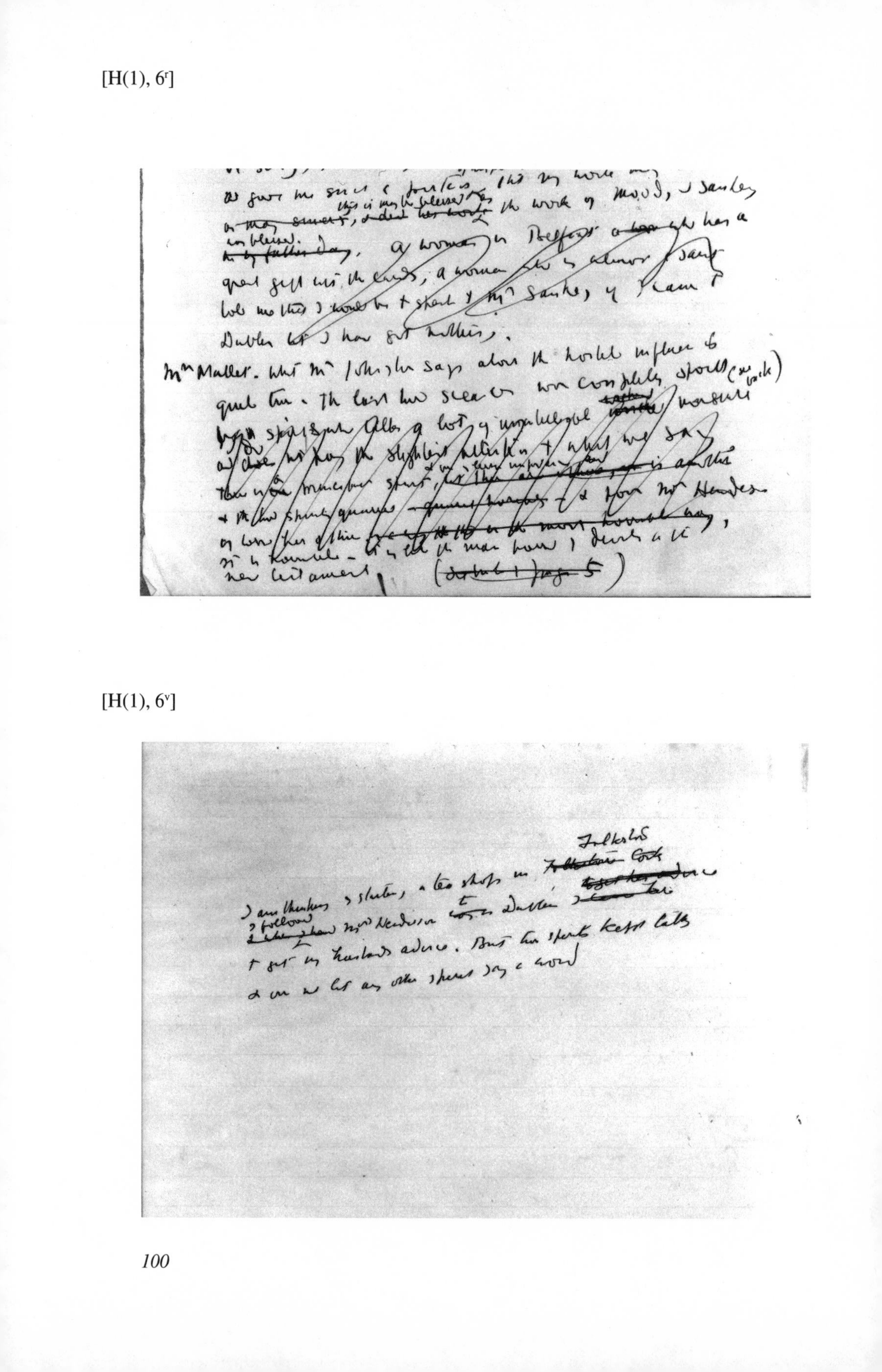

[H(1), 6^{r}]

[H(1), 6^{v}]

[H(1), 6^r (continued)]

that it may be blessed as
24 ~~or may succeed~~ , ~~as did~~ ~~his work~~ ^ the work of Moody & Sankey
was blessed.
25 ~~in my fathers day~~. A woman in Belfast ~~a wise~~ who has a
26 great gift with the cards, a woman who is almost a saint
27 told me that I would [?try] to speak to Mr Sankey if I came to
28 Dublin but I have got nothing.
29 Mrs Mallet. What Mr Johnston says about the hostile influence is
30 quite true. The last two sceances were completely spoilt (see
~~wicked~~ back)
32 by ~~a~~ spirit s who talks a lot of unintelligible ~~nonseen~~ nonsense
did
33 and ~~does~~ not pay the slightest attention to what we say
a & there is every unfortunate kind
34 There is ~~one~~ principal spirit, ~~but there are others, one~~ is another
35 & the two spirits quarrel – ~~quarrel horribly~~ – & poor Mrs Hendeson
36 is tossed here & their ~~this way & that in the most horrible way~~,
37 It is horrible—it is like the man possessed by devils in the
38 New Testament. (~~See back~~ [?~~to~~] ~~page 5~~)

[H(1), 6^v]

Folkestone
1 I am thinking of starting a tea shop in ~~Folkestone~~ ~~Cork~~
I followed to ~~to get her advice~~
2 ~~& when~~ ^ ~~I heard~~ Mrs Hendeson ~~was in~~ Dublin, ~~I came here~~
3 to get my husbands advice. But two spirits kept talking
4 & would not let any other spirit say a word

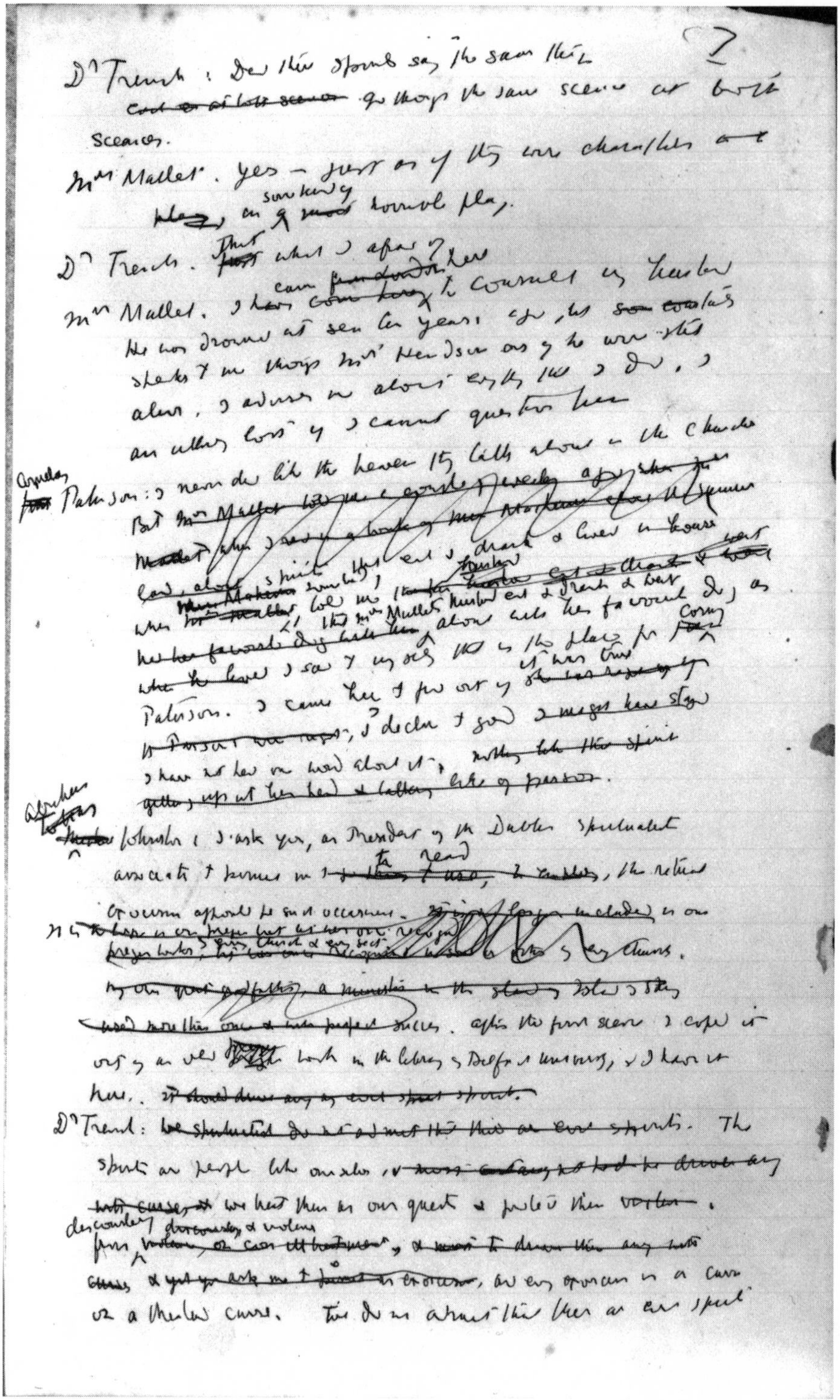
Dr Trench: Does this spirit say the same thing [illegible] goes through the same scene at both
seances.

Mrs Mallet. Yes — just as if they were characters [illegible]
[illegible], in a sickening horrible play.

Dr Trench. That what I after?

Mrs Mallet. I came here to counsel my husband
He was drowned at sea ten years ago, [illegible]
[illegible] Mrs Henderson as if he were [illegible]
alive, I advise me about everything that I do, I
am utterly lost if I cannot question him

Patterson: I never did like the heaven they talk about in the Church
[illegible]
[illegible]
[illegible] spirits [illegible] drink & lived [illegible]
when [illegible] told me [illegible] Mrs Mallet's husband ate & drank & went
about with his favourite dog, as
[illegible] I saw that [illegible] that is the place for [illegible]
Patterson. I came here to find out if it was true
[illegible], I declare to God [illegible]
I have not heard one word about it, [illegible]
[illegible] like of [illegible].

[illegible]: I ask you, as President of the Dublin Spiritualist
association to permit me to read [illegible], the ritual
of [illegible] appropriate to such occasions. [illegible] in our
[illegible]
[illegible] of [illegible] churches.
[illegible]
[illegible] success. after the first seance I copied it
out of an old [illegible] book in the library of Belfast University, & I have it
here. [illegible]

Dr Trench: [illegible]. The
spirits are people like ourselves, [illegible]
[illegible] we treat them as our guests & protect them [illegible].
from [illegible], discourtesy & violence [illegible]
[illegible] any exorcism, or any opinion in a curse
or a [illegible] curse. [illegible] about [illegible] spirit

[H(1), 7r]

Dr Trench: Did these spirits say the same things (7
~~end~~ ~~en at both seances~~ go through the same scenes at both
sceances.
Mrs Mallet. Yes – just as if they were characters in a
some kind of
~~play,~~ in ~~a most~~ horrible play.
That ^
Dr Trench. ~~Just~~ what I afraid of
came ~~from London~~ here
Mrs Mallet. I ~~have come here~~ ^ to consult my husband
He was drowned at sea ten years ago, but ~~som comforts~~
speaks to me through Mrs Hendson as if he were still
alive. I advises me about everything that I do. I
am utterly lost if I cannot question him
[?Cornelius]
Mrs Paterson: I never did like the heaven they talk about in the Churches
But ~~Mrs Mallet told me a couple of weeks ago~~ ~~When Mrs~~
~~Mallet~~ When I ~~read in a book of Miss Mackennas about the summer~~
~~land, about~~ spirits that eat & drank & lived in houses
~~Miss Mackenna~~ somebody ~~husband~~ ~~went~~
When ~~Mrs Mallet~~ /told me ~~that her husband eat & drank & went~~
^/ that Mrs Mallets husband eat & drank & went
~~had his favourite dog with him~~ ^ about with his favourite dog as
Corny
~~when he lived~~ I said to myself that is the place for ~~James~~
it was true
Paterson. I came here to find out if ~~she was right or if~~
I
~~the Parsons were right~~, & declare to god ~~I might have stayed~~
I have not heard one word about it. ~~Nothing like that spirit~~
~~getting up into her head & talking like any parson~~.

Transcription continues on p. 105.
16 The slash after "Mrs Mallet" seems to serve as an insertion mark for the words below the line.

[H(1), 7[r]]

[H(1), 7r (continued)]

Abraham
~~Tobias~~
23 ~~Michael~~ Johnston: I ask you, as President of the Dublin Spiritualists
to read
24 Association to permit me ~~to go through~~ ~~to use,~~ ~~to employ,~~ the ritual
25 exorcism appropriate for such occurrences. ~~It is no longer included~~ in our
~~It is no longer in our prayers but was once recognised~~
by every Church & every sect.
26 ~~prayer books, but was once recognised in some~~ or other by every Church.
27 My own great grandfather, a minister in the Stanley Islands & they
28 ~~used more than once & with perfect~~ succes. After the first sceance I copied it
~~prayer~~
29 out of an old ~~prayer~~ book in the library of Belfast University, & I have it
30 here.. ~~It should drive away any evil spirit spirit.~~
31 Dr Trench: ~~We Spiritualists do not admit that there are evil spirits.~~ The
32 spirits are people like ourselves, & ~~must certainly not be dr be driven away~~
33 ~~with curses, &~~ we treat them as our guests & protect them ~~violence~~.
discourtesy ~~discourtesy~~ & violence
34 from ^ ~~violence, or even ill treatment,~~ ~~& must to drive them away with~~
e
35 ~~curses~~ & ~~yet you ask me to purmit an exorcism~~, and every exorcism is a curse
36 or a threatened curse. We do not admit that there are evil spirits

(8)

some spirits are earth bound — they think they are still living, and go over & over some action of their past lives, just as we go over & over some painful thought except that where they are thought is reality. When a spirit which has died a violent death comes to a medium for the first time, for instance, it relives all the pains of death.

Mrs Mallet: when my husband came for the first time the medium gasped & struggled as if she were drowning. It was terrible to watch.

Dr Trench. Sometimes a spirit re-lives ~~the the moment of its death~~ not ~~the hour~~ of the pain of death, but some passionate or tragic moment of its life. Swedenborg describes this & gives the reason for it, there is an incident of the kind in the Odyssey, & many in earlier literature: the murderer repeats his murder, the robber his robbery, the lover his serenade, the soldier hears the trumpet once again. If I were a Catholic, I would say that such spirits were in Purgatory. In vain do we write requiescat in pace upon their tombs for they must suffer, & we in our turn must suffer until God gives peace. Such spirits ~~[illegible]~~ do not often come to seances unless those seances are held in houses where those spirits lived or where the event took place. This spirit which speaks such unintelligible words & does not answer when spoken to is such a spirit. The more patient we are, the more quickly will it wear out its passion, & its remorse.

Abraham Johnson. I am still convinced that the spirit which disturbed the last two seances is evil. If I may not exorcise it ~~may I not pray [illegible] to send [illegible]~~.

Dr Trench. I will certainly pray for protection for it.

Dr Trench: ~~[illegible]~~. Mrs Henderson's control is able & experienced & can protect both medium & sitters, but it may help Lulu [illegible] if you pray that the spirit find rest.

(Abraham Johnson sits down & prayer silently, moving his lips

[H(1), 8r]

8

some spirits are earthbound—they think they are still living
and go over & over some action of their past lives, just as
we go over & over some painful thought except that where they
are thought is reality. When a spirit which has died a violent
death comes to a medium for the first time, it for instance, it
relives all the pains of death.
Mrs Mallet: When my husband came for the first time the medium
gasped & struggled as if it she were drowning. It was terrible to
watch.
{D
{Mr Trench. Sometimes a spirit re-lives ~~just the moment of its death~~
not ~~the pain of~~ the pain of death, but some passionate or tragic
moment of its life. Swedenborg describes this & gives the reasons
for it, ~~&~~ there is an incident of the kind in the Odessey,
and many in earlier literature: The murderer repeats his murder,
the robber his robbery, the lover his serenade, the soldier
hears the trumpet once again. If I were a Catholic, I ~~would~~
say that In vain do we
~~describe~~ such spirits ~~as in pur~~ were in Purgatory. ~~We~~ ^ write
requesat in pace upon the tombs for they must suffer, & we
in our ~~m~~ turn must suffer until God gives peace. Such spirits,
~~though often seen re-enacting their past lives in where those lives were~~

Transcription continues on p. 109.

13 The misspelling of Odyssey survives in the Cuala Press printing.

(8)

some spirits are earth bound — they think they are still living, & go over & over some action of their past lives, just as we go over & over some painful thoughts except that where they are thought is reality. When a spirit which has died a violent death comes to a medium for the first time, for instance, it relives all the pains of death.

Mrs Mallet: When my husband came for the first time the medium gasped & struggled as if ~~she~~ she were drowning. It was terrible to watch.

Dr Trench. Sometimes a spirit re-lives ~~the moments of its death~~ not ~~the pain~~ of the pain of death, but some passionate or tragic moment of its life. Swedenborg describes this & gives the reason for it, ~~&~~ there is an incident of the kind in the Odyssey, & many in eastern literature: The murderer repeats his murder, the robber his robbery, the lover his serenade, the soldier hears the trumpet once again. If I were a Catholic, I ~~would~~ ~~describe~~ say that such spirits ~~are in purgatory~~ were in Purgatory. ~~but~~ [illegible] write requiescat in pace upon their tombs for they must suffer, & we in our turn must suffer until God gives peace. Such spirits, ~~they often seem to revisit their past lives when those lives were lived~~ & do not often come to séances unless those séances are held ~~took place~~, in houses where those spirits have lived or where, ~~the memorable event~~ the [illegible] event ~~first happened~~ the event took place. ~~for the first time~~. This spirit which speaks such unintelligible words & does not answer when spoken to is such a spirit. ~~we can help it by patience~~ The more ~~[illegible]~~ patient we are, ~~[illegible]~~, the more quickly will it wear out its passion, its remorse.

~~Patrick~~ ~~Mallet~~ Abraham Johnson. I am still convinced that the ~~[illegible]~~ spirit which disturbed the last two séances is evil. If I may not exorcise it ~~may I not pray for the seance to be saved from destruction~~.

~~Dr Trench~~. Mr I will certainly pray for protection for it.

Dr Trench: ~~Such prayer is unnecessary~~. Mrs Henderson's control Silver Cloud is able & experienced & can protect ~~the~~ both medium & sitters, but it may help Silver Cloud if ~~pray that the~~ ~~spirit~~ ~~God to give the [illegible]~~ you pray that the spirit find rest

(~~Tuppence~~ Abraham Johnson sits down & prays silently, moving his lips

[H(1), 8^{r} (continued)]

are held
21 ~~lived~~ ~~tend~~ do not often come to sceances unless those sceances ~~is held~~
in houses where those spirits have lived, or where
22 ~~take place~~ ^where ~~the re-enacted event~~ ~~the ever renewed event~~
23 ~~first happened~~ the event took place. ~~for the first time~~. This spirit
which
24 ~~who~~ speaks such unintelligible words & does not answer when spoken to
25 is such a spirit. ~~We can help it by patience~~ The more ~~painent~~ patient
26 we are ~~perhaps~~, the more quickly will it wear out its passion, ~~or~~ its
27 remorse.

~~Tobias~~
28 ~~Matthew~~ Johnston. I am still convinced that the ~~spirit~~ spirit which disturbed
(Abraham)
29 the last two sceances is evil. If I may not ~~use~~ exorsise it
30 ~~may I not prey prey that the sceance be saved from distractions~~.
from
31 ~~Dr Trench~~. ~~It~~ I will certainly pray for protection ~~for~~ it.
Silver Cloud
32 Dr Trench: ~~Such prayers are unnecessary~~. Mrs Hendesons control ^is
33 able & experienced & can protect ~~the me~~ both medium &
it
34 sitters, but ~~yo~~ may help Silver Cloud if ~~prey that the~~
35 ~~spirit~~ ~~God to give the spirit peace~~ you prey that the spirit find rest
~~Tobias~~ Abraham
36 (~~Michael~~ Johnston sits down & preyers silently, moving his lips

[H(1), 9r]

with Miss Mackenna ~~10~~
Mrs Hendeson – a fat vulgar woman comes ^ in with 9
perhaps some others.
Dr Trench: Mrs Henderson may I introduce to you Mr
Corbet, a ~~Cambridge student~~ a young man from Cambridge
& a sceptic, who hopes you will be able to convince him.
Mrs Henderson. ~~We are all sceptics when we beg~~
~~He must not expect f to mu~~ We w ~~al~~ were all sceptics once
{He
~~I hope I may be able to, but~~ {he must not expect
to much from a first sceance. He must persevere
{S
({The ~~takes~~ sits in the arm chair & others begin to seat
themselves. ~~Robert &~~ ~~John Corbet~~ & Miss Mackenna
~~remain standing.)~~ comes up to John Corbet & they remain
standing).
Miss Mackenna: I am glad you are a sceptic.
John Corbet. I thought you were a spiritualist.
Miss Mackenna: I have seen a good many sceances, & I sometimes think
it is all coincidence & thought transference. ^ . (She says this in
a low voice) Then at other times I think as Dr
Trench does, & then I feel as Job. You know the
quotation – The hair of my head stands up. A spirit
passes before my face.
John ~~Corbet. You feel that way to~~ night?
Mrs Mallet
~~Mackenna~~.. Come & sit here Miss Mackenna.
beside
Miss Mackenna. No I am going to sit ~~beide~~ Mr Corbet.
John Corbet. You feel that way to night. ^
Miss Mackenna. I feel that something is going to happen
That is why I am glad you a sceptic.
John Corbet. You feel safer.
Miss Mackenna Yes, safer.
~~Dr Trench~~. ~~Hush – Hush~~ – ~~It is time to begin~~

10

Mrs Henderson: I am glad to meet all my dear friends again and to welcome Mr Corbet amongst us. As he is a stranger I must explain that we do not call up spirits. We make the right conditions & they come. I do not know who is going to come. Sometimes there are a great many & the guides try to choose. We do not always succeed. If you want to speak to some dear friend who has passed over do not be discouraged. If your friend cannot come this time maybe he can next time. My control, is a little dear girl called Lulu, who died when she was seven or eight. She describes the spirits present, & tells us what spirits want to speak. Miss Mackenna a verse of a hymn please, the same we had last time & will everybody join in the singing. They sing the following lines

(Mrs Henderson leans back in her chair asleep)

Miss Mackenna (to John Corbet) She always snores like this when she is going off.

Mrs Henderson (in child's voice) Lulu glad to see everybody.

Mrs Mallet: And we are glad you have come Lulu.

Mrs Henderson (in child's voice) Lulu glad to see strange man.

Miss Mackenna (to John Corbet) She is speaking to you

John Corbet. Thank you Lulu.

Mrs Henderson (in child's voice) You must not laugh at the way I speak

John Corbet: I am not laughing Lulu

Mrs Henderson (in child's voice) Nobody must laugh. Lulu does her best but cannot speak queer words & make sounds that fill up mouth. Tall man here, lots of hair on face, and not much light up, not much

[H(1), 10r]

~~11~~
10

Mrs Henderson: I am glad to meet all my dear friends again
and to welcome Mr Corbet amongst us. As he is a stranger I must
explain that we do not call up spirits. We make the right
conditions & they come. I do not know who is going to come.
there are
Sometimes^ a great many ~~want to come~~ and the guides [~~?~~] choose
amongst them. The guides try to send somebody ~~to~~ for everybody
but do not always succeed. If you want to speak to some dear
friend
friend who has passed over do not be discouraged. If your^ ~~frend~~
can
cannot come this time may be he ~~will come~~ next time
dear
My control, ~~Mr Corbet~~, is a ^little girl called Lulu, who
died when she was seven or eight. She describes the
spirits present, & tells us what spirit wants to speak.
Miss Mackenna a verse of a hymn please, the same
we had last time & will everybody join in the
singing. They sing the following lines

(Mrs Hendeson ~~is seen~~ leaning back in her chair asleep)
Miss Mackenna (to John Corbet) She always snores like that
when she is going of see
~~meet~~
Mrs Hendeson (in childs voice) Lulu glad to ~~see~~^ everybody.
you have come
Mrs Mallet: And we are glad ~~to meet you~~ Lulu
(stranger)
Mrs Hendeson (in childs voice) Lulu glad to see ~~strange~~ man.
Miss Mackenna (to John Corbet) She is speaking to you
John Corbet. Thank you Lulu.
~~Mrs Hendeson (in childs voice~~)
Mrs Hendeson (in childs voice) You must not laugh at the
way I speak
John Corbet: I am not laughing Lulu
Mrs Hendeson (in childs' voice) Nobody must laugh. Little
~~but~~
but ← does her best^ cannot speak
girl ~~cannot speak~~^ queer words & make sounds that
fill up mouth. Tall man here, lots
of hair on face, not much high up, not much

her (Mrs Henderson touches top of her head) ~~Rev~~ neckties
funny sort of his. 4

Mrs Mallet. Yes. yes.

Mrs Henderson (in child's voice). Then like a horse-shoe.

Mrs Mallet. It's my husband.

Mrs Henderson (in child's voice) He has a message.

Mrs Mallet. Yes.

Mrs Henderson (in child's voice). ~~Cannot hear~~ Lulu cannot hear ~~cannot~~.
He is too far off, He has come near. Lulu
can hear now. He says — he says 'Drive that man
away!' He is pointing to a ~~coloured~~ lady in the corner
— ~~corner~~. That corner over there. He says it is
the bad man who spoiled everything last time.
If they won't drive him away Lulu will
scream.

Miss Mackenna. That horrible spirit again

Abraham Johnson. Last time he monopolised the séance

Mrs Mallet. Won't he let anybody speak but himself.

Mrs Henderson (in child's voice) They have driven bad man
away. Young lady here.

Mrs Mallet: Is not my husband here.

Mrs Henderson (in child's voice) [illegible] man with [illegible]
young lady here — [illegible]
funny [illegible] [illegible] [illegible]
green clothes, — [illegible]
[illegible]
funny dress clothes, hair all curls. [illegible]
[illegible]
crouched in floor near the
old man with glasses.

Dr Trench. ~~I~~ do not recognise her. Pale, looks as if she had been crying [illegible]

Mrs Henderson (in child's voice) May be for Young lady there. [illegible]

Miss Mackenna: No I do not recognise her.

Mrs Henderson (in child's voice) ~~it has now~~. That bad man
This bad man in the corner. ~~[illegible]~~ They have let him back,

[H(1), 11^{r}]

11

here (Mrs Henderson touches top of her head) Red necktie
funny sort of pin.
M^{rs}. Mallet. Yes. Yes.
Mrs Hendeson (in child's voice). Pin like a horse-shoe.
Mrs Mallet. It's my husband.
voice
Mrs Hendeson (in child's ~~vice~~) He has a message.
Mrs Mallet. Yes. cannot hear
Mrs Hendeson (in child's voice). ~~Cant here~~ Lulu ~~can here~~.
He is too far off. He has come near. Lulu ^
can hear now. He says – he says 'Drive that man
away.' He is pointing to ~~cor~~ somebody in the corner
– - ~~corner s~~. That corner over there. He says it is
the bad man who spoilt everything last time.
If they wont drive him away Lulu will
scream.
Miss Mackenna. That horrible spirit again
Abraham Johnson. Last time he monopolised the sceance
Mrs Mallet. Would not let anybody speak but himself.
Mrs Hendeson (in childs voice) They have driven bad man
Young
away. ~~Old~~ ^ lady here.
my
Mrs Mallet: Is not ^ husband here. Man with
Mrs Henderson (in child's ~~voce~~ voice) ~~Not here~~ ~~Man~~ ^ ~~with queer~~
Young
funny pin gone away. ~~Old~~ Lady here – looks
queer clothes – ~~Lulu never saw &~~ ~~hair all frizzed up~~.
~~pale~~ ~~looks week – cant move much – face~~ pale.
fancy dress clothes, hair all curls. ~~Is crouchi~~ Or ~~stands beside~~ that
~~grey hair, frizzled all over head~~. ~~Cowers from~~
crouched on floor near that
old man with glasses.
^ No
Dr Trench. ^ I do not recognise her.
Pale, looks as if she had been crying
~~Excited, crying. Lulu never saw spirit cry before~~ ~~Says she passed away~~
young ~~last~~ year
Mrs Henderson (in child's voice) ^ May be for ~~young~~ lady there.
Miss Mackenna: No I do not recognise her. ~~A~~
bad
Mrs Hendeson (in childs voice) ~~Not here now~~. That ~~bad~~ ^ man
That bad man in the corner. ~~Lullu~~ They have let him back.

12

Lulu goes, & scream. Oh-Oh. (then in a man's voice)
How dare you write to her. How dare you ask if we
were married. How dare you question her.

Dr Trench: A soul in its agony — it cannot see us or
hear us

Mrs Henderson (upright & rigid, only her lips moving & still in man's voice)
You sit crouching there. Did you not hear what I said.
How dared you question her. I found you an ignorant little girl
without intellect, without moral ambition. How many times
did I not stay from great men's houses, how
many times forsake the Lord Treasurer, how many
times neglect the business of the state that we might
read Plutarch together. I taught you to think in every situation
of life not as Hester Van Homrigh would think
[illegible]
in this situation but as Cato or Brutus would & now
you behave like some common slut, some
[illegible] with her ear against the key hole.
tavern slut

John Corbet (to Miss Mackenna) It is Swift, Jonathan Swift speaking,
to the woman he called Vanessa. She was christened Hester
Van Homrigh.

Mrs Henderson (in Vanessa's voice) I questioned her Jonathan because
I love. Why have you let me spend hours in your
company if you did not want me to
love you (in Swift's voice) When I rebuilt Rome
in your mind it was as though I walked its
streets. (in Vanessa's voice) Was that all Jonathan. Was
I nothing but a painter's canvas.
(in Swift's voice) My God do you think it
was easy. I was a man of strong passions & I
had sworn never to marry (in Vanessa's voice)
If you & she are not married why should we not
marry like other men & women.

[H(1), 12r]

12

then
Lulu going to scream. Oh. Oh. (^in a man's voice)
How dare you write to ~~a~~ her. How dare you ask if we
were married. How dare you question her.
Dr Trench: A soul in its agony – it cannot see us or
hear us
Mrs Hendeson (upright & rigid, only her lips moving & speaks in mans voice)
You sit crouching there. Did you not hear what I said.
dared you little
How ~~dared you~~ question her. I found you an ignorant^girl
without^intellect, without moral ambition. How many^times
did I not stay from great mens houses, how
many times forsake the Lord Treasurer, how many
times neglect the business of the state that we might ~~be~~
taught you to think situation
read Plutarch together. I^~~thought~~ ~~you~~^in every ~~situation~~
of life ~~to think~~ not as Hester Van Homrigh ~~would~~ ^
~~think (Corbet draws Miss Mackennas attention) to the name~~ would think
in that situation— but as Cato or Brutus would & now
~~you peep & peer like any common slut like any tavern~~
you behave like
~~slut~~., ~~You take for model~~^some common slut, some
tavern slut her ear against the key hole.)
John Corbet (to Miss Mackenna) It is Swift, Jonathan Swift speaking
to the woman he called Vanessa. She was christened Hester
Van Homrigh.
Mrs Hendeson (in Vanessas voice) I questioned her Jonathan because
I love. ~~If~~ Why have you let me spend hours in your
company, [~~?if y &] hours~~ if you did not want me to
love you (in Swift's voice) When I rebuilt Rome
walked
in your mind it was as though I ~~walked~~ its
streets. (in Vanessas voice) Was^that all Jonathan
~~a canvas to point upon~~. a painters' canvas
~~(in S~~ was I nothing but ~~canvas~~, ~~under the brush~~ ^
(in Swift's voice) My God do you think it
was easy. I was a man of strong passions &
I had sworn never to marry. (in Vanessas voice)
married
If you & she are not ~~married~~ why should we not
marry like other men & women. ~~(in Swift's voice~~)
~~You came to my mothers house & began to teach me~~

[H(1), 13^{r}]

When you came to my mothers house & 13
began to teach me
1 I loved you from the first moment.^ I thought it would
2 be enough to look at you, to speak to you, to hear you speak.
3 I followed you to Ireland five years ago & I can bear it no
4 longer. It is not enough to look, to speak, to hear.
5 Jonathan, Jonathan I am a woman The women Brutus
6 & Cato loved were not different. (in Swifts voice)
7 I have ~~that~~ something in my blood that no child must ~~inher~~
8 ~~in herrit~~ inherit. I have constant attacks of dizziness. I
9 ~~had them in London~~ pretend ~~they come~~ they come from a surfeit
10 of fruit when I was a child. I had them in London.
Arbuthnot
11 There was a great doctor there — D^{r} ~~Arbunott~~ ^ – I told him
dizziness
12 of those attacks of ~~dissiness~~^, I told him of worse things. It was he
14 who explained. Pope knew – ~~I to~~ there is a line of his. (in Vanessas voice)
15 O I know 'great ~~witt~~ Wit to madness near alleid.' If
16 you had children Jonathan my blood would make them
will will
17 healthy. ~~Where is your hand~~ I ^ take your hand. I ~~will~~ lay it
18 upon my heart – upon the Van Homrigh blood that has been
19 healthy for generations (Mrs Hendeson slowly raises her left hand
That is the first time you have touched my body Jonathan (She stands up & remains rigid, ~~in Swift's voice~~
20 until is resting upon heart)) (^ – in Swifts voice) ~~What do I~~

Transcription continues on p. 121.

I loved you from the first [when you came to my mother's house & began to teach my] moment, I thought it would
be enough to look at you, to speak to you, to hear you speak.
I followed you to Ireland five years ago & I can bear it no
longer. It is not enough to look, to speak, to hear.
Jonathan, Jonathan I am a woman the women Brutus
& Cato loved were not different. (in Swift's voice)
I have ~~that~~ something in my blood that no child must ~~inherit~~
~~inherit~~ inherit. I have constant attacks of dizziness. I
~~had them in London~~ pretend ~~they come~~ they come from a surfeit
of fruit when I was a child. I had them in London.
There was a great doctor there — Dr ~~Arbuthnot~~ [Arbuthnot] — I told him
of these attacks of ~~dizziness~~ [dizziness], I told him of worse things. It was he
who explained. Pope knew — ~~it is~~ there is a line of his. (in Vanessa's voice)
O Jonathan 'great wits to madness near allied'. If
you had children Jonathan my blood would make them
healthy. ~~there is your hand~~ I [will] take your hand. I ~~will~~ [will] lay it
upon my heart — upon the Vanhomrigh blood that has been
healthy for generations (Mrs Henderson slowly raises her ~~left hand~~ ~~[illegible]~~
[This is the first time you have touched my body Jonathan] [Mrs Henderson stands up & remains rigid] ~~[illegible]~~
until it rests upon her heart) (in Swift's voice) ~~What do~~ I
~~care if it be healthy~~ — what do I care if it would be
healthy [slut]
more healthy — am I to add another to the healthy
rascaldom & knavery of the world (in Vanessa's voice)
Look at me Jonathan — your arrogant intellect separates us
give me both your hands. I will put them upon
my breast. (Mrs Henderson raises her right hand
to the level of her left & then raises both to her breast — in
Vanessa's voice) O it is white — white as the gamblers
dice — white ~~[illegible]~~ [ivory] dice. Think of the uncertainty
Perhaps a ~~[illegible]~~ mad child — perhaps a rascal,
perhaps a knave — perhaps not Jonathan. The
dice of the intellect are loaded but I am the
common ivory dice. ~~[illegible]~~ (Her hands are
~~[illegible]~~ ~~[illegible]~~ ~~[illegible]~~ or though drawing
[struck] out ~~[illegible]~~ towards her) Not my hands
~~[illegible]~~ [my hands are weak] they could
not draw you back — ~~you are strong~~
not draw you back if you did not love me I
love. You said that you had strong hardness in

[H(1), 13r (continued)]

it
stet ~~care if it be healthy~~ – What do I care if ~~is~~ could make
mine healthy. Am I to add another to the healthy
rascaldom & knavery of the world (in Vanessas voice)
Look at me Jonathan – Your arrogant intellect separates us
Give me both your hands. I will put them upon
my breast. (Mrs Hendeson raises her right hand
to the level of her left & then raises both to her breast – in
Vanessa's voice) O it is white – white as the gamblers
ivory
dice – white ~~ivory~~ dice. Think of the uncertainty
Perhaps a ~~rascal~~ mad child — perhaps a rascal,
perhaps a knave – perhaps not Jonathan. The
dice of the intellect are loaded but I am the
common ivory dice. ~~It is not~~ (Her hands are
stretched
~~streched~~ out ~~as pulling at some one)~~ as though drawing
some one towards her) It is not my hands
My hands are weak
that draw you back – ~~You are strong~~ They could
not draw you back if you did not love as I
love. You said that you have strong passions.

28–29 On the cover of a prompt copy of the play are written what appear to be two alternate titles: "Perfect Harmony" and "White Dice." See NLI(4) in the Census, p. xii, above.

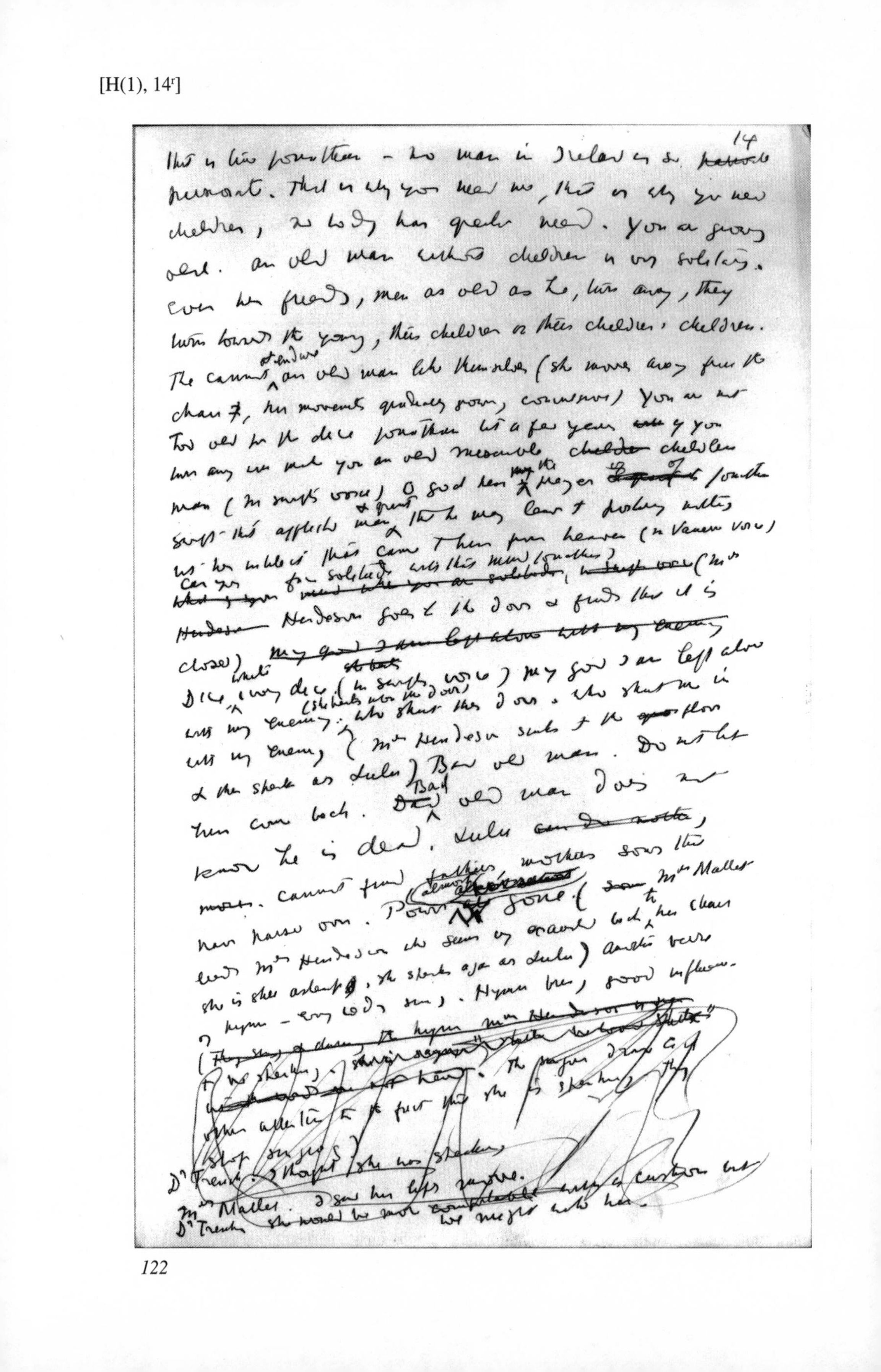

[H(1), 14r]

[H(1), 14r]

14

That is true Jonathan. No man in Ireland is so ~~passonate~~
passionate. That is why you need me, that is why you need
children, no body has greater need. You are growing
old. An old man without children is very solitary.
Even his friends, men as old as he, turn away, they
turn towards the young, their children or their childrens children.
~~ab~~ endure
They cannot ^ an old man like themselves .(She moves away from the
chair~~)~~, her movements gradually growing convulsive) You are not
too old for the dice Jonathan but a few years ~~will~~ if you
turn away will make you an old miserable ~~childre~~ childless
~~my~~ the ~~of~~ of
man (In Swifts voice) O god hear ^ a prayer & ~~grant to~~ ^ Jonathan
& grant
Swift that afflicted man ^ that he may leave to posterity nothing
but his intellect that came to him from heaven (in Vanessas voice)
Can you face solitude with that mind Jonathan?
~~What of your mind when you are solitude~~ (~~in Swifts voice~~ (Mrs
~~Hendeson~~ Hendeson goes to the door & finds that it is
closed) ~~My god I am left alone with my enemy~~
white ~~She beats~~
Dice, ^ ivory dice. (in Swifts voice) My god I am left alone
(She beats upon the door)
with my enemy.. ^ Who shut this door. Who shut me in
with my enemy (Mrs Hendeson sinks to the ~~grou~~ floor
& then speaks as Lulu) Bad old man. Do not let
Bad
him come back. (~~Dad~~ old man does not
know he is dead. Lulu ~~can do nothing~~
~~more~~. Cannot find fathers, mothers sons that
(almost)
~~almost used~~
have passed over. Power ^^ all gone. (~~Some~~ Mrs Mallet
to
leads Mrs Hendeson who seems very exausted back ^ her chair
She is still asleep~~)~~. She speaks again as Lulu) Another verse
of hymn – everybody sing. Hymn bring good influence.

Transcription continues on p. 125.

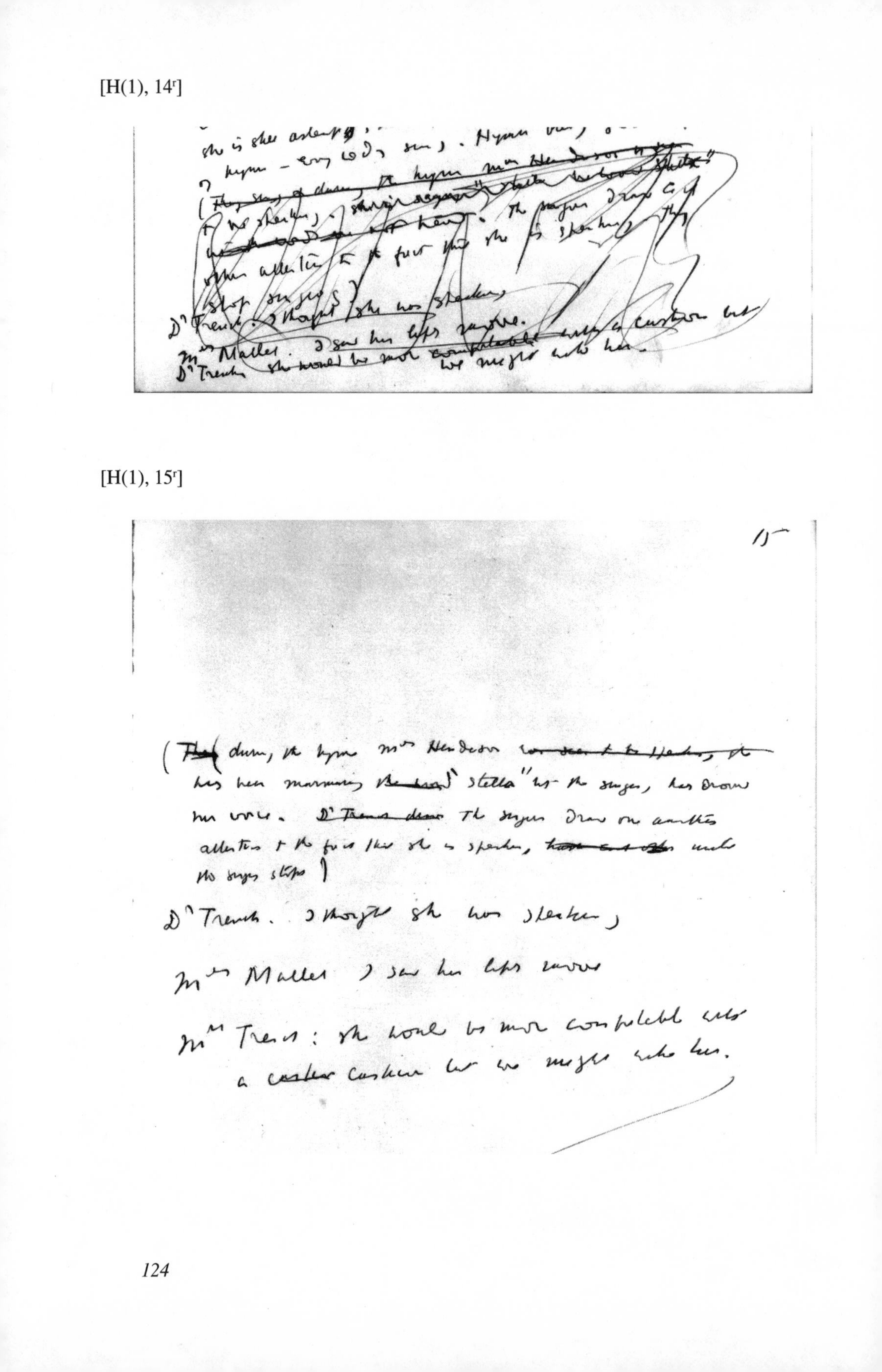

[H(1), 14r]

[H(1), 15r]

[H(1), 14r (continued)]

(~~They sing & during the hymn Mrs Hendeson is seen~~
to be speaking. ~~She is saying "Stella beloved Stella"~~
~~but her words are not heard~~. The singers draw each
others attention to the fact that she is speaking. They
stop singing)
Dr Trench. I thought she was speaking
Mrs Mallet. I saw her lips move.
Dr Trench. She would be more comfortable with a cushion but
we might wake her.

[H(1), 15r]

15

(~~They (~~during the hymn Mrs Henderson ~~was seen to be speaking She~~
has been murmuring ~~the word~~ "Stella" but the singing has drowned
her voice. ~~Dr Trench draws~~ The singers draw one anothers
attention to the fact that she is speaking, ~~hush each other~~ until
the singing stops)

Dr Trench. I thought she was speaking
Mrs Mallet I saw her lips move
Mrs Trench: She would be more comfortable with
a ~~cushon~~ cushion but we might wake her.

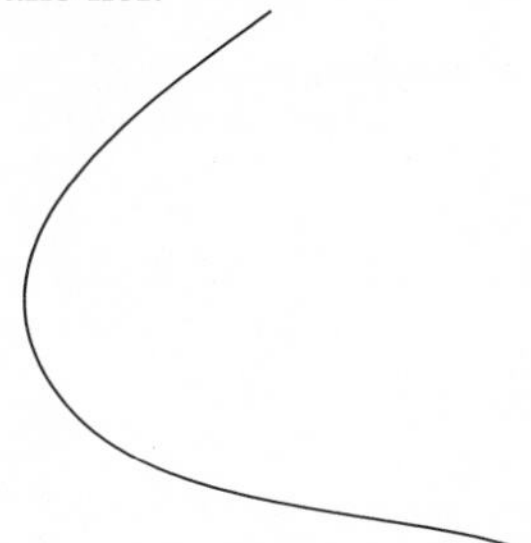

15r These lines replace ll. 28–36 on 14r. The curved line indicates continuation to 16r.

16

Mrs Mallet: Nothing can wake her out of a trance like that until she wakes of herself. (She brings a cushion & she & Dr Trench put Mrs Henderson during what follows into a more comfortable position)

Mrs Henderson (in Swift's voice) Stella

Miss Mackenna (to John Corbet) Did you hear that. She saw Stella.

John Corbet. Vanessa has gone Stella has taken her place.

Miss Mackenna. Did you notice the change while we were singing. The new influence in the room

John Corbet, I thought I did but it must have been fancy

Miss Mackenna! It was as though we came suddenly out of a crowded lighted room into stillness & darkness.

John Corbet. Hush.

Mrs Henderson (in Swift's voice) Have I wronged you beloved Stella. Are you unhappy. You have no children. You have no lover, You have no husband. A cross and ageing man for friend – nothing but that. But no do not answer – you have answered already in that poem you wrote for my last birthday, my fifty fourth birthday. With what scorn you speak there of the common lot of women – "women with no endowments but a face
"Before the thirtieth year of life.
Maid forlorn or hated wife.
It is the thought of the great Chrysostom, who wrote in a famous passage the women loved according to the soul, loved as saints can love, keep their beauty longer have greater happiness than women loved according to the flesh. That thought has comforted me but it is a terrible thing to be responsible for another's happiness. There are moments when I doubt, when I think Chrysostom may have been wrong. But now I have your poem to drive doubt away. You have addressed me in these noble words.

"You taught how I might youth prolong
By knowing what is right or wrong;
How from my heart to bring supplies
Of lustre to my fading eyes,
How soon a beauteous mind repairs
The loss of changed or fading hairs,
How wit & virtue from within
Can spread a smoothness o'er the skin."

[H(1), 16^{r}]

16

Mrs Mallet: Nothing can wake her out of a trance like
that until she wakes up herself.. (She brings a cushion
during what follows
& she and Dr Trench put Mrs Hendeson ^ into a more
comfortable position.)
Mrs Henderson (in Swifts voice) Stella
{id
Miss Mackenna (to John Corbet) D{o you hear that. She said Stella
John Corbet. Vanessa has gone Stella has taken her place.
Miss Mackenna. Did you notice the change while we were singing.
The new influence in the room
John Corbet. I thought I did but it must have been fancy
Miss Mackenna: It was as though we came suddenly out of crowded
lighted room into stillness & darkness.
John Corbet. Hush.
Mrs Hendeson (in Swifts voice) Have I wronged you beloved Stella
Are you unhappy. You have no children. You have no lover.
You have no husband. A cross and ageing man for friend
– nothing but that. But no do not answer – you have answered
already in that poem you wrote for my last birthday, my
~~forty fo~~ fifty fourth birthday. With what scorn you
speak there of the common lot of women – "women
~~as~~ with no adornment but a face"
"Before the thirtieth year of life
Maid forlorn or hated wife."

Transcription continues on p. 129.

16

Mrs Mallet: Nothing can wake her out of a trance like
that until she wakes of herself. (She brings a cushion
& she & Dr Trench put Mrs Henderson [during what follows] into a more
comfortable position)

Mrs Henderson (in Swift's voice) Stella

Miss Mackenna (to John Corbet) Did you hear that. She said Stella.

John Corbet. Vanessa has gone Stella has taken her place.

Miss Mackenna. Did you notice the change while we were singing.
The new influence in the room

John Corbet. I thought I did but it must have been fancy

Miss Mackenna: It was as though we came suddenly out of a crowded
ugly room into stillness & darkness.

John Corbet. Hush.

Mrs Henderson (in Swift's voice) Have I wronged you beloved Stella
Are you unhappy. You have no children.. you have no lover,
you have no husband. a cross and ageing man for friend
– nothing but that. But no do not answer – you have answered
already in that poem you wrote for my last birthday, my
~~foot for~~ fifty fourth birthday. With what scorn you
speak then of the common lot of women – "women
~~so~~ with no endowment but a face"
"Before the thirtieth year of life,
Maid forlorn or hated wife."
It is the thought of the great Chrysostom, who wrote in a famous
passage that women loved according to [the] soul, loved as ~~they~~
Saints [can] ~~to~~ love, as Saints can be loved keep their beauty longer
have greater happiness than women loved according to the flesh.
That ~~passage~~ thought has comforted me but it is a terrible
thing to be responsible for another's happiness. There are moments
when I doubt, when I think Chrysostom may have been wrong.
But now I have your poem to drive doubt away.
You [have] ~~have~~ addressed me in these noble words.
"You taught how I might youth prolong,
By knowing what is right or wrong;
How from my heart to bring supplies
Of lustre to my fading eyes,
How soon a beauteous mind repairs
The loss of changed or fading hairs,
How wit & virtue from within
Can spread a smoothness o'er the skin."

[H(1), 16r (continued)]

24 It is the thought of the great Crisostum, who wrote in a famous
the
25 passage that women loved according to ^ soul, loved as ~~only~~
can
26 Saints ~~co~~ love, as Saints can be loved keep their beauty longer,
27 have greater happiness than women loved according to the flesh.
28 That ~~passage~~ thought has comforted me but it is a terrible
29 thing to be responsible for anothers happiness. There are moments
30 when I doubt, when I think Crisostum may have been wrong.
31 But now I have your poem to drive doubt away.
have
32 ⁄ You ~~have~~ addressed me in these noble words.
33 "You taught how I might youth prolong
34 By knowing what is right or wrong;
35 How from my heart to bring supplies
36 Of lustre to my fading eyes,
37 How soon a beauteous mind repairs
38 The loss of changed or fading hairs,
39 How wit & virtue from within
40 Can spread a smoothness o'er the skin."

24, 30 "Cristostum" phonetically renders the honorific for St. John Chrysostom ("golden mouth").

John Corbet: The words on the window pane.
Mrs Henderson (in Swift's voice)
Then because you understand that I am afraid of solitude 17
afraid of outliving my friends — and myself — you comforts
me in the last [illegible], you own place my moral nature
when you allude to it a rich mantle, oh how touching those words which describe your love.

Late dying may you cast a shred
Of that rich mantle o'er my head;
To bear with dignity my sorrow,
One day alone then die to-morrow.

Yes you will close my eyes dear Stella
But you will live long after me for you are still a young
woman. But you will close my eyes. (Mrs Henderson
sinks back in chair & speaks as Lulu) Bad old man gone.
Power all used up. Lulu can do no more. Good
by friends. Lulu sorry. Bad old man. (in her own voice)
go away — go away. (she wakes) I saw him a moment ago. Has he spoilt
the scene again.

Mrs Mallet. Yes Mrs Henderson — my husband came but
was driven away.

Dr Trench: Mrs Henderson is very tired. We must leave her to rest. (to
You did your best & nobody can do more than that (he
takes out money)

Mrs Henderson. No — no — I cannot take any money, not
after a scene like that.

Dr Trench. Of course you must take it Mrs Henderson. gives a hurried glance
(He puts money on table & Mrs Henderson does the same as each sitter
& sees how much it is. She
lays down his or her money.)

Mrs Mallet. A bad scene is just as exhausting as a good
scene, and you must be paid.

Mrs Henderson. No — no — please don't. It is very wrong to
take money for such a failure. (Mrs Mallet lays down money)

Cornelius Patterson. A jockey is paid whether he wins or not. (lays down money)

Miss Mackenna. That spirit rather upset me. (lays down money)

Mrs Henderson. If you insist I must take it.

Abraham Johnson. I shall pray for you to night. I shall ask God to bless
and protect your seances. (lays down money. All go out
except John Corbet & Mrs Henderson)

[H(1), 17^{r}]

John Corbet: the words on the window pane.
M^{s} Henderson (in Swift's voice)
^Then because you understand that I am afraid of solitude 17
comfort
afraid of outliving my friends – and myself – you ~~comfort~~
moral nature
me in that last ~~touching~~ verse – You overpraise my ~~soul~~^
when you attribute to it oh ~~describe~~
~~when conscient~~ ^ a rich mantle, but^how touching~~ly you speak~~^
~~of yourself~~ ~~of your love for me~~ those words which describe your love.
Late dying may you cast a shred
Of that rich mantle o'er my head,
To bear with dignity my sorrow,
One day alone then die to-morrow.
Yes ~~dear~~
~~You~~ You will close my eyes ~~my eyes Stella~~
dear Stella
But you will live long after me, ^ for you are still a young
will
women.. But you^ close my eyes. (Mrs Hendeson
sinks back in chair & speaks as Lulu) Bad man gone.
~~B~~ Power all used up. Lulu can do no more. Good
by friends. Lulu sorry. Bad old man. (in her own voice)
go away – go away. (She wakes) I saw him a moment ago. Has he spoilt
the sceance again.
Mrs Mallet. Yes Mrs Hendeson – My husband came but ~~he drove~~
~~him away~~ ~~my husband away~~. was driven away.

Transcription continues on p. 133.

John Corbet: The words on the window pane.
Mrs Henderson (in Swift's voice)
Then because you understand that I am afraid of solitude 17
afraid of outliving my friends — and myself — you comfort
me in the last [illegible], you overpraise my moral nature
[illegible] when you attribute to it a rich mantle, ah how touching those words which describe your love.

Late dying may you cast a shred
Of that rich mantle o'er my head;
To bear with dignity my sorrow,
One day alone then die to-morrow.

Yes you will close my eyes ~~with~~ dear Stella
But you will live long after me for you are still a young
woman. But you will close my eyes. (Mrs Henderson
sinks back in chair & speaks as Lulu) Bad man gone.
Power all used up. Lulu can do no more. Good
bye friends. Lulu sorry. Bad old man. (in her own voice)
go away – go away. (she wakes) I saw him a moment ago. Has he spoilt
the seance again.

Mrs Mallet. Yes Mrs Henderson – my husband came but ~~[illegible]~~
~~[illegible]~~ was driven away.

Dr Trench: Mrs Henderson is very tired. We must leave her to rest. (to her)
You did your best & nobody can do more than that (he
takes out money)

Mrs Henderson. No – no – I cannot take any money, not
after a seance like that.

Dr Trench. Of course you must take it Mrs Henderson. Mrs Henderson gives a hurried glance
(He puts money on table & Mrs Henderson does the same as each sitter
& sees how much it is. She does the same as each sitter
lays down his ~~money~~ or her money.)

Mrs Mallet. A bad seance is just as exhausting as a good
seance & and you must be paid.

Mrs Henderson. No – no – please dont. It is very wrong to
take money for such a failure. (Mrs Mallet lays down money)

Cornelius Patterson. A jockey is paid whether he wins or not. (lays down money)

Miss Mackenna. ~~But as the seance~~ That spirit rather upset me.
(lays down money)

Mrs Henderson. If you insist I must take it.

Abraham Johnson: I shall pray for you to-night. I shall ask God to bless
and protect your seances. (lays down money. All go out
except John Corbet & Mrs Henderson)

[H(1), 17r (continued)]

Dr Trench: Mrs Hendeson is very tired. {W / Se} must leave her to rest. You did your best & nobody can do more than that (he takes out money

Mrs Hendeson. No – no – I cannot take any money, not after a sceance like that.

Dr Trench. Of course you must take it Mrs Hendeson. (He puts money on table & Mrs Hendeson gives a hurried glance to see how much it is. She does the same as each sitter lays down his ~~money~~ or ^ her money.)

Mrs Mallet. A bad sceance is just as exausting as a good seance, and you must be paid.

Mrs Henderson. No – no – please dont. It is very wrong to take money for such a failure. (Mrs Mallet lays down money.)

Cornelius ^Patterson ~~Johnson~~. A jockey is paid whether he wins or not. (lays down money

Miss Mackenna. ~~Bad as the sceance was~~ That spirit rather thrilled me. (lays down money)

Mrs Hendeson. If you insist I must take it.

Abraham Johnson: I shall prey for you to night. I shall ask god to bless and protect your sceances. (lays down money)~~.~~ All go out except John Corbet & Mrs Hendeson)

John Corbet: I know you are tired Mrs Henderson but I must (18
thank you. I have been deeply moved by what I have
heard. This is my ~~explanation~~ contribution & proves that I am ~~deeply~~
satisfied — completely satisfied. (He puts a note on the
table)

Mrs Henderson: A pound note — nobody ~~ever~~ ~~before~~ ever gives me more
than ten shillings & yet the seance was a failure.

John Corbet (sitting down near medium) When I say I am satisfied
I do not mean that I am convinced it was the words of spirits.
I prefer to think that you created it all whether ~~awake~~ or
awake or asleep, that you are an accomplished actress and
scholar. In my essay for my Cambridge doctorate I
examine all the explanations of Swift's celibacy offered by
~~his~~ his biographers, & prove that the explanation you
selected is the only plausible one. But there is something
I must ask you. Swift was the chief representative
of the intellect of his epoch, that arrogant intellect free
at last from superstition. He foresaw its collapse. He
He must have dreaded the future.
foresaw Democracy, & did he refuse to beget children
because of that dread? Was Swift mad? or was it
the intellect itself that was mad?

Mrs Henderson. Who are you talking of, sir.

John Corbet. Swift of course.

Mrs Henderson. Swift. I do not know anybody called
Swift.

John Corbet: Jonathan Swift whose spirit seemed
to be present ~~tonight~~.

Mrs Henderson: What! That dirty old man.

John Corbet: He was neither old nor dirty when
Stella & Vanessa loved him.

Mrs Henderson. I saw him just as I woke up — I saw him
very clearly. His clothes were dirty, his face dirty.
His face covered with boils. It was horrible. Some
disease ~~that~~ had made one of his eyes swell up.
It stood out from his face like a hens-egg.

John Corbet: He looked like that in his old age.
Stella had been dead a long time. His brain
~~had begun to go~~ had gone, his friends had deserted
him. ~~He was in the charge of a man~~ The man

[H(1), 18r]

John Corbet: I know you are tired Mrs Hendeson but I must 18
speak to you. I have been deeply moved by what I have
contribution ~~completely~~
heard. There is my ~~explanation~~ to prove that I am ~~deeply~~
satisfied – completely satisfied. (He puts a note on the
table)
gives
Mrs Henderson: A pound note – nobody ~~ever before~~ ever ~~gave~~ me more
than ten shillings & yet the sceance was a failure.
John Corbet (Sitting down near medium) When I say I am satisfied
I do not mean that I am convinced it was the work of spirits.
I prefer to think that you created it all whether ~~awake or~~
awake or asleep, that you are an accomplished actress and
scholour. In my essay for my Cambridge docternate I
examine all the explanations of Swifts celebacy offered by
~~schol~~ his biographers, & prove that the explanation you
selected is the only plausible one. But there is something
I must ask you. Swift was the chief representative
of the intellect of his epoch, that arrogant intellect freed
at last from superstition. He forsaw its collapse. He
He must have dreaded the future.
forsaw democracy. ^ Did he refuse to beget children
because of that dread? Was Swift mad? Or was it
the intellect itself that was mad?
Mrs Henderson. Who are you talking of sir.
John Corbet. Swift of course.
Mrs Henderson. Swift. I do not know anybody called
Swift
John Corbet: Jonathan Swift whose spirit seemed
to be present tonight.
Mrs Hendeson: What! That dirty old man.
John Corbet: He was neither old nor dirty when
Stella & Vanessa loved him.
Mrs Hendeson. I saw him just as I woke up. I saw him
very clearly. His clothes were dirty, his face dirty,
his face covered with boils. It was horrible. Some
disease ~~what~~ had made one of his eyes swell up.
It stood out from his face like a hens-egg.
John Corbet: He looked like that in his old age.
Stella had been dead a long time. His brain
~~had begun to go.~~ had gone, his friends had deserted
him. ~~He was in the charge of a man~~ The man

[H(1), 19r]

apothecary to take charge of him beat him to keep him quiet.

Mrs Henderson. ~~Sometimes~~ now they are old, ~~sometimes~~ now they are young: they change all in a moment as their thoughts change. It is sometimes a terrible thing to be out of the body. God help us all.

Dr Trench (at door) Come Mrs Corbet, Mrs Henderson is tired out.

John Corbet. ~~Goodbye~~, good by Mrs Henderson (He goes out with Dr Trench). Mrs Henderson counts the money. Finds her purse which is in a vase on the mantle piece & puts the money in it.

Mrs Henderson. How tired I am. I'd be the better of a cup of tea. (She finds tea pot & puts it on a little & puts kettle on fire & as she ~~speaks in Swift's voice~~, winds down by hearth & counts her fingers & speaks in Swift's voice) Five great ministers that were my friends are gone. Ten great ministers that were my friends are gone. I have not fingers enough to count the great ministers that were my friends & that are gone. (She wakes with a start & speaks in her own voice) Where did I put the tea caddy — ah there it is and there should be a cup & saucer (she finds the saucer) but where is the cup. (She moves aimlessly ~~about~~ about stage & then her arms drop suddenly & the saucer falls & she speaks in Swift's voice "Perish the day on which I was born."

Oct 1930

W B Yeats.

Coole Park,

[H(1), 19r]

19

appointed to take charge of him beat him to keep
him quiet.
now now
Mrs Hendeson. ~~Sometimes~~ ^ they are old, ~~sometimes~~ they are
young. The change ^ all in a moment as their
thoughts change. It is sometimes a terrible thing to be out
of the body, God help us all.
Dr Trench (at door) Come Mr Corbet, Mrs Hendeson is tired out.
John Corbet. ~~Good by~~, good by Mrs Hendeson (He goes out
with Dr Trench)~~.~~ Mrs Hendeson counts the
money. Find her purse which is in a vase on the
mantlepiece & puts the money into it.
Mrs Hendeson. How tired I am. Id be the better of a cup
of tea. (She finds tea pot & puts it on table & puts
and then
Kettle on fire ~~&~~ ~~then~~ ~~speaks in Swifts voice~~, crouching down
by hearth ~~&~~ counts ^ her fingers & speaks in Swifts voice)
Five great ministers that were my friends are gone.
Ten great ministers that were my friends are gone.
I have not fingers enough to count the great
Ministers that were my friends & that are gone. X
(she wakes with a start & speaks in her own voice)
Where did I put the tea cady – ah there it is
and their should be a cup & saucer (she finds the saucer)
about
but where is the cup. (she moves aimlessly ~~accross~~
stage & then her arms drop suddenly & the saucer falls
& she speaks in Swifts voice "Perish the day
on which I was born."

Oct 1930
W B Yeats.
Coole Park.

The Earliest Typescript

NLI(2)

As the photographs and transcriptions of NLI(2) reveal, errors attributable to the typist are silently corrected; these include overstrikes, inaccurate spacing, and mistakes of spelling, accents, capitalization, and punctuation. Similarly, in the apparatus beneath the text, variants in the three typescripts, two proofs, and two printed texts that are clearly attributable to the typist or printer are generally omitted, whether corrected or not.

[NLI(2), p. 1]

The Words Upon the Window Pane.

A lodging house room, an armchair, a little table ~~in~~ front of it, chairs ~~at~~ on either side . A fireplace and window ~~to right~~. A kettle on the hob and some tea things on a shelf. A door to back ~~and towards the left~~. Through the door one can see an entrance hall . The sound of a knocker. Miss MacKenna passes through hall and then she re-enters hall together with John Corbet a man of twenty two or twenty three, and Dr.Trench, a man of between sixty and seventy.

Dr. Trench. (in hall) May I introduce John Corbet, one of the Corbet's of Ballymoney, but at present a Cambridge student. This is Miss MacKenna our energetic secretary. (They come into the room, take off their coats)

Miss MacKenna. I thought it better to let you in myself. This country is still sufficiently mediaeval to make spiritualism an undesirable ~~indescribable~~ theme for gossip. Give me your coats and hats and I will put them in my own room . It is just across the hall. Better sit down, your watches must be fast. Mrs Henderson is lying down, as she always does before a seance. We won't begin for twenty minutes yet. (She goes out with hats and coats)

Dr Trench, Miss Mackenna does all the real work of the Dublin Spiritualists Association . She did all the correspondence with Mrs Henderson and persuaded the landlady to let her this big room and a small room upstairs. We are a poor society and could not guarantee anything in advance. Mrs Henderson has come from London ~~Glasgow~~ at her own risk.

title On *revised to* Upon *LCP; NLI(4) has two alternate titles written on cover in pencil, both crossed out:* Perfect Harmony *and* White Dice *(see NLI(2), typescript p. 5, l. 2 and typescript p. 17, ll. 9–10, pp. 149, 173, below)*

4 at the] at *NLI(5)* to *restored NLI(3), NLI(4), H(2)* ~~and towards the left~~] and towards the right *NLI(3); so NLI(4), LCP, H(2), NLI(5)*

6 through hall] through *NLI(3), NLI(4), LCP, H(2)* *marginal stage direction:* from L x R *NLI(4)*

6–7 through hall . . . together with] the door, returns bringing with her *NLI(5)*

[NLI(2), p. 1]

The Words Upon the Window Pane.

a dresser o

A lodging h^use room, an armchair, a little table in front of it, chairs ~~at~~ on either side . **A fireplace and window ~~to right~~. A kettle on the hob and some tea things on ~~a shelf~~. A door ~~to~~** at the **back ~~and towards the left.~~ Through the door one can see an entrance hall. The sound of a knocker. Miss MacKenna passes through hall and then she re-enters hall together with John Corbet a man of twenty two or twenty three, and Dr.Trench, a man of between sixty and seventy.**

Dr.Trench. **(<u>in hall</u>) May I introduce John Corbet, one of the Corbet's of Ballymoney, ~~but~~ at present a Cambridge student. This is Miss MacKenna** but^ **our energetic secretary. (<u>They come into the room, take off</u>** their^ **<u>coats</u>)**

Miss MacKenna. **I thought it better to let you in myself. This country is still sufficiently mediaeval to make spiritualism an ~~inde cribable~~** undesirable **theme for gossip. Give me your coats and** hats^ **I will put them in my /**own **room. It is just across the hall. Better sit down, your watches must be fast. Mrs Henderson is lying down, as she always does before a seance. We won't begin for twenty minutes yet. (<u>She goes out with hats and coats</u>)**

Dr Trench, **Miss Mackenna does all the** real **work of the Dublin/ Spiritualists Association. She did all the correspondence with Mrs Henderson and persuade{d/s} the landlady to let her this big room and a small room upstairs. We are a poor society and could not guarantee anything in advance. Mrs Henderson has come from ~~Glasgow~~** London **at her own risk**

---

8 a man *omitted NLI(3), NLI(4)*

9–10 Good evening *in margin, pencil, LCP*

10–12 *marginal stage direction showing location of speakers:* T. C. Miss McC *NLI(4)*

12 energetic *revised to* enthusiastic *LCP; revisions retained H(2), NLI(5)* energetic *restored in NLI 30,185*

13 the room] room *NLI(3), NLI(4), LCP, H(2), NLI(5)* and take *NLI(5)*

20 twenty] ten *NLI(3), NLI((4), LCP, H(2), NLI(5)*

21 *added stage direction:* x L *with marginal stage direction* standing back to fire *NLI(4)*

27 *added:* She was born in Dublin and wants to spread the movement here. *NLI(3), NLI(4), LCP, H(2), NLI(5)*

2

(Dr. Trench.ctd.) She lives very econonically and does not expect a great deal. We all give what we can. A poor woman with the soul of an apostle.

John Corbet — Have there been many seannes?

Dr Trench — Only three so far.

John Corbet — I hope she will not mind my scepticism. I have looked into Myers' "Human Personality", and a wild book by Conan Doyle, but am unconvinced.

Dr Trench — We all have to find the truth for ourselves. Lord Dunraven, then Lord Adare, introduced my father to the famous David Home. My father often told me that he saw David Home floating in the air in broad daylight, and I did not believe a word of it. I had to investigate for myself, and I was very hard to convince. Mrs Piper, an American trance medium, not unlike Mrs Henderson, convinced me.

John Corbet — A state of sonnambulism and voices coming through her lips that purport to be those of dead persons?

Dr. Trench — Exactly: quite th best kind of mediumship if you want to establish the identity of a spirit, but do not expect too much. There has been a hostile influence.

John Corbet — You mean an evil spirit?

[NLI(2), p. 2]

2

(Dr. Trench.ctd.) **She lives very economically and ~~down~~** does **not expect a great deal. We all give what we can. A poor woman with the soul of an apostle.**

John Corbet **Have there been many seances?**

Dr Trench **Only three so far.**

John Corbet **I hope she will not mind my scepticism. I have looked into Myers' "Human Personality", and a wild book by Conan Doyle, but am unconvinced.**

Dr Trench **We all have to find the truth for ourselves. Lord Dunraven, ~~the Lord~~** then Lord Adare, **introduced my father to the famous David H~~u~~**o**me. My father often told me that he saw David H~~u~~**o**me floating in the air in broad daylight, and I ~~do~~** did **not believe a word of it. I had to investigate for myself, and I was very hard to convince. Mrs Piper, an American trance medium, not unlike Mrs Henderson, convinced me.**

John Corbet **A state of sonnambulism and voices coming through her lips that purport to be those of dead persons** ?

Dr. Trench **Exactly: quite the best kind of mediumship if you want to establish the identity of a spirit** [~~?~~] **but do not expect too much. There has been a hostile influence.**

John Corbet **You mean an evil spirit?**

---

9 for *omitted H(2)*
11, 12 Home] Hume *H(2)*
13 and] but *NLI(3), NLI(4), LCP, H(2), NLI(5)*

[NLI(2), p. 3]

3

Dr Trench The poet Blake said that he never knew a bad man that had not something very good about him. I say a hostile influence, an influence that disturbed the last seance very seriously. I cannot tell you what happened for I have not been at any of Mrs Henderson's seances. Trance mediumship has nothing new to show me - I told the young people when they mademe their President that I would probably stay at home, that I could get more out of Emmanuel Swedenborg than out of any seance. (a knock) That is probably old Cornelius Pattison, he thinks that they race horses and whippets in the other world and is so anxious to find out if he is right that he is always punctual. Miss MacKenna will keep him to herself for some minutes. He gives her tips for Harold's Cross.

John Corbet (Who has been wandering about) This is a wonderful room for a lodging house.

Dr Trench. This was a private house until about fifty years ago. It was not so near the town in those days and there are large stables at the back. Quite a number of notable people lived here. Grattan was born upstairs, no, not Grattan, Curran perhaps - I forget - but I do know that this house in the early part of the Eighteenth century belonged to friends of Jonathan Swift, or rather of Stella.

[NLI(2), p. 3]

3

Dr Trench **The poet Blake said that he never knew a bad man that**
had not something very good about him. I say a
disturbed
hostile influence, an influence that ~~destroyed~~ the last
seance very seriously. I cannot tell you what
happened for I have not been at any of Mrs Henderson's
seances. Trance mediumship has nothing new to show
me – I told the young people when they made me their
{t {me
President that I would probably stay a{n ho{ur, that I
could get more out of Emmanuel Swedenborg than out of
any seance. (<u>a knock</u>) That is probably old
Cornelius Pattison, he thinks ~~that~~ they race horses
they tell me
and whippets in the other world and is ^ so anxious to
find out if he is right that he is always punctual.
Miss MacKenna will keep him to herself for some minutes.
He gives her tips for Harold's Cross.

John Corbet **(<u>Who has been wandering about</u>) This is a wonderful**
room for a lodging house.

It
Dr. Trench. **~~This~~ was a private house until about fifty years ago.**
It was not so near the town in those days and there are
large stables at the back. Quite a number of notable
people lived here. Grattan was born upstairs, no, not
Grattan, Curran perhaps – I forget – but I do know that
this house in the early part of the Eighteenth century
belonged to friends of Jonathan Swift, or rather of Stella.

---

7 me – *revised to* me. *NLI(5)*

12 Pattison] Patterson *NLI(3), NLI(4), LCP, H(2), NLI(5)* they tell me] so they tell me *NLI(3), NLI(4), H(2) with* so *inserted, NLI(5)*

15/16 *stage directions:* (Miss Mackenna crosses to hall door and admits Cornelius Patterson. She brings him to her room across the hall) *NLI(3), NLI(4), LCP, H(2), NLI(5)* *inserted stage direction:* C. behind table *NLI(4)*

Dr T.(td.) Swift chaffed her in the Journal to Stella because of certain small sums of money she lost at cards probably in this very room. That was before Vanessa had appeared upon the scene. ~~Strange that an austere and grey [illegible] should have been loved by two such~~ women. It was a country house in those days surrounded by trees and gardens. Somebody cut some lines from a poem of hers upon the window pane - tradition says Stella herself. (a knock) Here they are but you will hardly make them out in this light. (They stand in the window ~~to right~~. Corbet stoops down to see better. Miss MacKenna and Abraham Johnson enter and and stand near door.)

A.Johnson Where is Ms Henderson?

Miss Mackenna She is upstairs, she always rests before a seance.

A.Johnson I must see her before the seance. I know exactly what to do to get rid of this evil influence.

Miss Mackenna If you go up to see her there will be no seance at all. She says it is dangerous even to think, much less to speak of an evil influence.

Abraham Johnson Then I shall speak to the President.

[NLI(2), p. 4]

4

Dr T.Ctd.) **Swift chaffed her in the Journal to Stella because of certain small sums of money she lost at cards probably in this very room. That was before Vanessa had appeared upon the scene. ~~Strange that an austere and grey scholar should have been loved by two such women~~. It was a country house in those days surrounded by trees and gardens. Somebody cut some lines from a poem of hers upon the window pane - tradition says Stella herself. (a knock) Here they are but you will hardly make them out in this light. (They stand in the window ~~to right.~~ Corbet stoops down to see better. Miss MacKenna and Abraham Johnson enter and and stand near door.)**

A.Johnson **Where is Mrs Henderson**

Miss Mackenna **She is upstairs, she always rests before a seance.**

A.Johnson **I must see her before the seance. I know exactly what to do to get rid of this evil influence.**

Miss Mackenna **If you go up to see her there will be no seance at all. She says it is dangerous even to think, much less to speak of an evil influence.**

Abraham Johnson **Then I shall speak to the President.**

---

1 Journal to Stella *in quotes H(2) italics NLI(5)* because *revised to* because of *H(2)*

3–4 had appeared] appeared *NLI(3), NLI(4), H(2), NLI(5)*

4 (knock) *following* scene *in pencil LCP* (a knock) *NLI(4), retained H(2)*

7–9 *marginal stage direction:* X to window front of table *NLI(4)*

9 (a knock) *deleted NLI(4)*

13–14 *marginal note showing locations NLI(4):*

McK Johnson C T

5

Mis Mackenna Better talk the whole thing over first in my room. Mrs Henderson says that there must be perfect harmony.

Abraham Johnson Something must be done. The last seance was completely spoilt.

(a knock)

Miss Mackenna That may be Mrs Mallet, she is a very experienced Spiritualist. Come to my room, old Peterson is there already.

(they go out)

John Corbet I know those lines well - they are part of a poem Stella wrote for Swift's fifty fourth birthday. Only two poems of hers - and some lines she added to a poem of Swift's have come down to us, but they are enough to prove her a better poet than Swift. Even those few words on the window make me think of a seventeenth century poet , Donne or Crashaw. (he quotes)

"You taught how I might youth prolong
By knowing what is right or wrong,
How from the heart to bring supplies
Of lustre from my fading eyes."

How strange that a celibate shholar, well on in life, should keep the love of two such women. He met Vanessa in London at the height of his political power. She followed him to Dublin. She loved him for nine years, perhaps died of love, but Stella had loved him all her life.

[NLI(2), p. 5]

5

<u>Miss Mackenna</u> Better talk the whole thing over first in my room. Mrs Henderson says that there must be perfect harmony.

<u>Abraham Johnson</u> Something must be done. The last seance was completely spoilt.

(<u>a knock</u>)

<u>Miss Mackenna</u> That may be Mrs Mallet, she is a very experienced

a

Spiritualist. Come to my room, old P~~e~~terson is there already. ^

(<u>they go out</u>)

<u>John Corbet</u> I know those lines well – they are part of a poem Stella

three

wrote for Swift's fifty fourth birthday. Only ~~two~~ poems of hers – and some lines she added to a poem of Swift's have come down to us, but they are enough to prove her a better poet than Swift. Even those few words on the window make me think of a seventeenth century poet, Donne or Crashaw. (<u>he quotes</u>)

"You taught how I might youth prolong
By knowing what is right or wrong,
How from the heart to bring supplies
for/ ~~to~~ / **Of lustre ~~from~~ my fading eyes."**

How strange that a celibate scholar, well on in life, should keep the love of two such women. He met Vanessa in London at/ **~~in~~ the height of his political power. She followed him to Dublin. She loved him for nine years, perhaps died of love, but Stella ~~had~~ loved him all her life.**

---

1 Better] That might start a discussion. Better *NLI(4)* first *deleted NLI(4)*

3 done *entered as revision in ink LCP*

7 room *revised to* room, *LCP* is *revised to* and some others are *NLI(3) and NLI(4); LCP, H(2), NLI(5) as revised*

9–10 (<u>they go out</u>) *replaced by* (<u>she brings him to the other room and later crosses to hall-door to admit Mrs. Mallet</u>) *NLI(3), NLI(4), LCP, H(2), NLI(5)*

10 those] these *NLI(5)*

10–13 *marginal stage direction:* Trench has come to R. of Corbet *NLI(4)*

18 or] and *LCP, H(2), NLI(5)*

19 the *revised to* my *BL(2)*

20 lustre for *revised to* lustre to *NLI(3), LCP; H(2), NLI(5) as revised*

6

Dr Trench I have shown that writing to several persons and you are the first who has recognised the lines.

John Corbet I am writing an essay on Swift and Stella for my doctorate at Cambridge. I hope to prove that in Swift's day men of intellect reached the height of their power - the greatest position they ~~can~~ attain in society and in the State, that everything great in Ireland and in our character, in what remains of our architecture, comes from ~~those~~ day~~s~~; that we have kept its ~~secret~~ longer than England.

Dr Trench A tragic life, Bolin broke, Harley, Ormond, all those great ministers that were his friends, banished and broken.

John Corbet I do not think you canexplain him in ~~this~~ way - his tragedy had deeper foundations, his ideal order was the Roman Senate, his ideal men Brutus and Cato, such an order and such men had seemed possible once ~~again~~, but the moment passed and he foresaw the rain to come, Democracy, Rousseau, the French Revolution, ; that is why he wrote Gulliver, that is why he wore out his brain, that is why he felt "saevo indignatio" that is why he sleeps under the greatest epitaph in history. You remember how it goes? It is almost finer in English than in Latin:— "He has gone where fierce indignation can lacerate his heart no more.".

[NLI(2), p. 6]

6

<u>Dr Trench</u> **I have shown that writing to several persons and you are the first who has recognised the lines.**

<u>John Corbet</u> **I am writing an essay on Swift and Stella for my doctorate at Cambridge. I hope to prove that in Swift's day men of intellect reached the height of their power – the greatest position they ~~can~~** ever **attain**ed **in society and in the State, that eveything great in Ireland and in our character, in what remains of our architecture, comes from ~~those~~** that **day~~s~~; that we have kept its ~~secret~~** seal **longer than England.**

<u>Dr Trench</u> **A tragic life, Bolingbroke, Harley, Ormond, all those great ministers that were his friends, banished and broken**

<u>John Corbet</u> **I do not think you can explain him in ~~this~~** that **way – his tragedy had deeper foundations, his ideal order was the Roman Senate, his ideal men Brutus and Cato, such an order and such men had seemed possible once ~~again~~,** more **but the moment passed and he foresaw the ruin to come, Democracy, Rousseau, the French Revolution, ; that is why he wrote Gulliver, that is why he wore out his brain, that is why he felt "saevo indignatio" that is why he sleeps under the greatest epitaph in history. You remember how it goes? It is almost finer in English than in Latin: ,— "He has gone where fierce indignation can lacerate his heart no more.".**

---

6 they *revised from* that *BL(2)* and in] and *NLI(3), NLI(4), LCP, H(2), NLI(5)*

10 Bolingbroke . . . Ormonde] Ormonde, Harley, Bolingbroke *NLI(5)*

11 great] tragic *revised by typist to* great *NLI(3), NLI(4)*

15 moment] movement *LCP, H(2), NLI(5)*

17–18 Revolution, that is why he wrote Gulliver] Revolution, that is why he hated the common run of men , – "I hate lawyers, I hate doctors" he said "though I love Dr so and so and Judge so and so," – That is why he wrote Gulliver *NLI(3), NLI(4), LCP, H(2), NLI(5)*

[NLI(2), p. 7]

7

(Abraham Johnson comes in followed by Miss Mackenna Cornelius Paterson and others)

Abraham Johnson Something must be done, Dr Trench, to drive away the influence that has destroyed our seances. I have come here week after week at considerable expense. I am from Belfast. I am by profession a Minister of the Gospel, I do a great deal of work among the poor and ignorant. I produce considerable effect by singing and preaching, but I know that my effect should be much greater than it is. My hope is that I shall be able to communicate with thegreat Evangelist ~~Mr.~~ Sankey. I want to ask him to stand ~~immovable~~ invisible beside me when I speak or sing and lay his hands upon my head and give me such a portion of his power that my work ~~may continue, that it~~ may be blessed as the work of Moody and Sankey was blessed.

Mrs Mallet What Mr. Johnson says about the hostile influence is quite true. The last two seances were completely spoilt. I am thinking of starting a teashop in Folkestone. I followed Mrs Henderson to Dublin to get my husband's adivce, but two spirits kept talking and would not let any other spirit say a word.

[NLI(2), p. 7]

7

<u>(Abraham Johnson comes in followed by Miss Mackenna Cornelius Paterson and others</u>

<u>Abraham Johnson</u> Something must be done, Dr Trench, to drive away the influence that has destroyed our seances. I have come here week after week at considerable expense. I am from Belfast. I am by profession a Minister of the Gospel, I do a great deal of work among the poor and ignorant. I produce considerable effect by singing and preaching, but I know that my effect should be much greater than it is. My hope is that I shall be able to communicate with the great Evangelist ~~Dr.~~ Sankey. I

invisible

want to ask him to stand ~~immovable~~ beside me when I speak or sing and lay his hands upon^ my head and give me such

a portion **of his power that my work ~~may convince that it~~ may be blessed as the work of Moody and Sankey was blessed.**

<u>Mrs Mallet</u> What Mr. Johnson says about the hostile influence is quite true. The last two seances were completely spoilt. I am thinking of starting a teashop in Folkestone. I followed Mrs Henderson to Dublin to get my husband's advice, but two spirits kept talking and would not let any other spirit say a word.

1–2 followed by Miss Mackenna . . . and others *revised to* followed by Miss Mackenna & Cornelius Patterson *NLI(3); revised to* Cornelius Patterson and Mrs Mallet *NLI(4)* followed by Mrs. Mallet and Cornelius Patterson *LCP, H(2), NLI(5)*

stage direction expanded in NLI(4) to:

Enter Johnson / Mallet / McK / Pattison *with diagram for placement added at foot of page:*

McK

Pat Mallet John Trench Corbet

11 Sankey *revised to* Moody *BL Add. MS 55885*

[NLI(2), p. 8]

8

Dr Trench Did the spirits say the same thing and go through the same ~~scene~~ drama at both seances?

Mrs Mallet Yes - just as if they were characters in some kind of horrible play.

Dr Trench That is what I was afraid of.

Mrs Mallet I came here to consult my husband. He was drowned at sea ten years ago but constantly speaks to me through Mrs Henderson as if he were still alive. He advises me about everything I do, and I am utterly lost if I cannot question him.

Cornelius Patterson I never did like the Heaven they talk about in the Churches, but when somebody told me that Mrs Mallet's husband ate and drank and went about with his favourite dog I said to myself 'that is the place for Corn~~elius~~ey Patterson'. I came here to find out if it was true and I declare to God I have not heard one word about it.

Abraham Johnson I ask you, as President of the Dublin Spiritualists Association, to permit me to read the ritual of exorcism appointed for such occasions. After the ~~first~~ last seance I copied it out of an old book in the Library of Belfast University. I have it here. (He takes a paper out of his pocket)

[NLI(2), p. 8]

8

<u>Dr Trench</u> **Did the spirits say the same thing and go through the**
drama
same scene~~s~~ at both seances?

<u>Mrs Mallet</u> **Yes – just as if they were characters in some kind of horrible play.**

<u>Dr Trench</u> **That is what I was afraid of.**

<u>Mrs Mallet</u> **I came here to consult my husband. He was drowned at sea ten years ago but constantly speaks to me through Mrs Henderson as if he were still alive. He advises me about everything I do, and I am utterly lost if I cannot question him.**

<u>Cornelius Patterson</u> **I never did like the Heaven they talk about in the Churches, but when somebody told me that Mrs Mallet's husband ate and drank and went about with his favourite**
y
dog I said to myself 'that is the place for Corn~~elius~~ Patterson'. I came here to find out if it was true and I declare to God I have not heard one word about it.

<u>Abraham Johnson</u> **I ask you, as President of the Dublin Spiritualists Association , to permit me to read the ritual of exorcism**
last
appointed for such occasions. After the first seance I copied it out of an old book in the Library of Belfast University. I have it here. (He takes a paper out of his pocket)

---

6 I came here to consult my husband *deleted NLI(3) omitted LCP, H(2), NLI(5)* He *revised to* My husband *NLI(3); LCP, H(2), NLI(5) as revised*

12–13 *marginal stage direction:* (his back to the fire) *NLI(4)*

12 the Churches] church *H(2)* churches *NLI(5)*

17 you, as] you, Dr Trench, as *NLI(3), NLI(4), LCP, H(2), NLI(5)* Spiritualist *NLI(5)*

21 a paper] paper *NLI(3), NLI(4), LCP, H(2), NLI(5)*

9

Dr Trench The spirits are people like ourselves, we treat them as our guests and protect them from discourtesy and violence, and every exorcism is a curse or a threatened curse. We do not admit that there are evil spirits. Some spirits are earth-bound - they think they are still living and go over and over some action of their past lives, just as we go over and over some painful thought, except that where they are thought is reality. When a spirit which has died a violent death comes to a medium for the first time, (for instance,) it re-lives all the pains of death.

Mrs Mallet When my husband came for the first time the medium gasped and struggled as if she were drowning. It was terrible to watch.

Dr Trench Sometimes a spirit re-lives not the pain of death but some passionate or tragic moment of life. Swedenborg describes this and gives the reason for it. There is an incident of the kind in the Odessey, and many in Eastern literature: the murderer repeats his murder, the robber his robbery, the lover his serenade, the soldier hears the trumpet once again. If I were a Catholic I would say that such spirits were in Purgatory. In vain do we write requiscat in pace upon the tomb for they must suffer, and we in our turn must suffer until God gives peace. Such spirits do not often

[NLI(2), p. 9]

9

<u>Dr Trench</u> **The spirits are people like ourselves, we treat them as our guests and protect them from discourtesy and violence, and every exorcism is a curse or a threatened curse. We do not admit that there are evil spirits. Some spirits are earth-bound – they think they are still living and go over and over some action of theirs past lives, just as we go over and over some painful {thought / things}, except that where they are thought is reality. ^ When a spirit which has died a violent death comes to a medium for the first time, (for instance,) it re-lives all the pains of death.**

<u>Mrs Mallet</u> **When my husband came for the first time the medium gasped and struggled as if she were drowning. It was terrible to watch.**

<u>Dr Trench</u> **Sometimes a spirit re-lives ^not the pain of death but some passionate or tragic moment of life. Swedenborg describes this and gives the reason for it. There is an incident of the kind in the Odessey, and many in Eastern literature: the murderer repeats his murder, the robber his robbery, the lover his serenade, the soldiers hear ^s the trumpet once ~~ag[???]~~ again. If I were a Catholic I would say that such spirits were in Purgatory. In vain do we write <u>requiescat in pace</u> upon the tombs for they must suffer, and we in our turn must suffer until God gives peace. Such spirits do not often**

6–7 some action . . . painful thought] some painful thought *H(2)*
9 death *omitted then inserted LCP*
13 were] was *LCP*, *H(2)*, *NLI(5)*
15 a] the *H(2)*
17 the *omitted H(2)*

10

come to seances unless those seances are held in houses where those spirits have lived, or where^ the event took place. This spirit which speaks ~~such unintelligible~~ [those incomprehensible] words and does not answer when spoken to ~~is~~ [is] such ~~a spirit~~ [nature]. The more patient we are, the more quickly will it pass out of its passion and its remorse.

Abraham Johnson I am still convinced that the spirit which disturbed the last seance is evil. If I may not exorcise it, I will certainly pray for protection ~~from it~~.

Dr Trench Mrs Henderson's control Lulu is able and experienced and can protect both medium and sitters, but it may help Lulu if you pray that the spirit find rest.

(Abraham Johnson sits down and prays silently, moving his lips. Mrs Henderson, ~~[illegible]~~, comes in with Miss Mackenna and perhaps some others)

Dr Trench Mrs Henderson, may I introduce to you Mr Corbet, a young man from Cambridge and a sceptic, who hopes that you will be able to convince him.

Mrs Henderson We were all sceptics once. He must not expect too much from a first seance. He must persevere.

gous/ (She sits in the armchair and the others begin to seat themselves. Miss Mackenna ~~comes up~~ to John Corbet and they remain standing)

When paging the typescript, the typist struck a capital "I" in place of the number "1"; the arabic numeral was intended and is used in the transcription of NLI(2).

[NLI(2), p. 10]

10

come to seances unless those seances are held in houses where those spirits have lived, or where the event took place. This spirit which speaks ~~such unintelligible~~ [those incomprehensible] **words and does not answer when spoken to ~~is~~** [of] **such a ~~spirit~~** [~~mind~~] [nature]**. The more patient we are, the more quickly will it pass out of its passion and its remorse.**

Abraham Johnson **I am still convinced that the spirit which disturbed the last seance is evil. If I may not exorcise it , I will certainly pray for protection ~~from it~~.**

Dr Trench **Mrs Henderson's control Lulu is able and experienced and can protect both medium and sitters, but it may help Lulu if you pray that the spirit find rest.**

(Abraham Johnson sits down and prays silently, moving his lips. Mrs Henderson, ~~a fat vulgar woman~~, comes in with Miss Mackenna and perhaps some others)

Dr Trench **Mrs Henderson, may I introduce to you Mr Corbet, a young man from Cambridge and a sceptic, who hopes that you will be able to convince him.**

Mrs Henderson **We were all sceptics once. He must not expect too much from a first seance. He must persevere.**

(She sits in the armchair and the others begin to seat themselves. Miss Mackenna ~~comes up~~ [goes/] **to John Corbet and they remain standing)**

---

1 come *inserted in ink LCP*

2 have *omitted LCP, H(2), NLI(5)*

4 to of] to is of *NLI(3), NLI(4), LCP, H(2), NLI(5)*

13–15 *marginal stage direction:* Johnson sits in chair above window. Mallet joins Pattison at fire. *NLI(4)*

14 with *deleted to* to *then restored with* stet *NLI(3)*

15 perhaps some *deleted NLI(3), omitted LCP, H(2), NLI(5)* *added to stage direction:* Miss McKenna shuts the door *NLI(3), NLI(4), LCP, H(2), NLI(5)*

18–19 *NLI(4) has marginal stage direction showing locations:* Hend Trench Corbet *accompanied by inserted page of stage directions, with diagram, beginning* Pattison sits R end of sofa with women and 2 other men Trench sits behind table

19 must not *revised to* mustn't *NLI(4)*

II

Miss Mckenna	I am glad you are a sceptic.
John Corbet	I thought you were a spiritualist.
Miss Mackenna	I have seen a good many seances and sometimes think it is all coincidence and thought transference. (She says this in a low voice) Then at other times I think as Dr Trench does, and then I feel as Job – you know the quotation – the hair of my head stands up. A spirit passes before my face.
Mrs Mallet	Come and sit here, Miss Mackenna.
Miss Mackenna	No, I am going to sit beside Mr Corbet (Mr Corbet & Miss Mackenna sit down)
John Corbet	You feel like Job tonight?
Miss Mackenna	I feel that something is going to happen, that is why I am glad you are a sceptic.
John Corbet	You feel safer?
Miss Mackenna	Yes, safer.
Mrs Henderson	I am glad to meet all my dear friends again and to welcome Mr Corbet amongst us. As he is a stranger I must explain that we do not call up spirits, we make the right conditions and they come. I do not know who is going to come, sometimes there are a great many and the guides choose between them. The

[NLI(2), p. 11]

11

<u>Miss Mackenna</u> **I am glad you are a sceptic.**

<u>John Corbet</u> **I thought you were a spritualist.**

<u>Miss Mackenna</u> **I have seen a good many seances and sometimes think it is all coincidence and thought transference. (<u>She says this in a low voice</u>) Then at other times I think as Dr Trench does, and then I feel as Job – you know the quotation – the hair of my head stands up. A spirit passe~~d~~^s before my face.**

<u>Mrs Mallet</u> **Come and sit here, Miss Mackenna.**

<u>Miss Mackenna</u> **No, I am going to sit beside Mr Corbet** (<u>Mr Corbet and Miss Mackenna sit down</u>)

<u>John Corbet</u> **You feel ~~that way~~** like Job **tonight?**

<u>Miss Mackenna</u> **I feel that something is going to happen, that is why I am glad you are a sceptic.**

<u>John Corbet</u> **You feel safer?**

<u>Miss Mackenna</u> **Yes, safer.**

<u>Mrs Henderson</u> **I am glad to meet all my dear friends again and to welcome Mr Corbet amongst us. As he is a stranger I must explain that we do not call up spirits, we make the right conditions and they come. I do not know who is going to come, sometimes there are a great many and the guides choose between them. The**

---

1 you] that you *H(2), NLI(5)*

6 as Job *revised to* like Job *BL(2)*

8 passes] passed *NLI(3), NLI(4), LCP, H(2), NLI(5)* passes *revised to* passed *BL(2)*

8/9 Mrs Mallet Turn the key, Dr Trench, we dont want anybody blundering in here. (Dr Trench locks door) *NLI(3), NLI(4), LCP, NLI(5); so H(2) but* door] the door*; NLI(4) adds marginal stage direction:* sits behind table

9–11 *marginal stage directions added:* Corbet sits chair below window. Mrs Malett sits below fire. *and* (pulls chair from below table near to Corbet) *NLI(4)*

13 you] that you *H(2)*

19 do not *revised to* don't *NLI(4)*

Mrs Henderson guides try to send somebody for everybody but do not always succeed. If you want to speak to some dear friend who has passed over do not be discouraged. If your friend cannot come this time, may be he can next time. My control is a dear little girl called Lulu who died when she was six or seven years old. She describes the spirits present, and tells us what spirit wants to speak. Miss Mackenna, a verse of a hymn please the same we had last time, and will everyone join in the singing.

(they sing the following lines)

(Mrs Henderson is leaning back in her chair asleep)

Miss Mackenna (to Jhn Corbet) She always snores like that when she is going off.

[NLI(2), p. 12]

12

<u>Mrs Henderson</u> **guides try to send somebody for everybody but do not always succeed. If you want to speak to some dear friend who has passed over do not be discouraged. If your friend cannot come this time, may be he can next time. My control is a dear little girl called Lulu who died when she was six or seven years old. She describes the spirits present, and tells us what spirit wants to speak. Miss Mackenna, a verse of a hymn please the same we had last time, and will everyone join in the singing.**

(<u>they sing the following lines</u>)

(<u>Mrs Henderson is leaning back in her chair asleep</u>)

<u>Miss Mackenna</u> **(to <u>John Corbet)</u> She always snores like that when she is going off.**

1–2 do not *revised to* don't *NLI(4)*

6 died *revised in pencil to* passed over *LCP* passed over *H(2)*

7 six or seven] five or six *NLI(3), NLI(4), LCP, H(2), NLI(5)*

8 us *omitted H(2)*

9 Miss Mackenna *revised to* Mr Patterson *NLI(4), LCP* Miss Patterson *H(2)*

12/13 "Sun of my soul, Thou Saviour dear,
It is not night if Thou be near:
O may no earth-born cloud arise
To hide Thee from Thy servant's eyes."

(sung to the tune of Stillorgan, hymn 564, p. 752 Church Hymnal. Dublin, 1919 *NLI(3), NL(4), LCP, H(2); so NLI(5) and NLI 30,185 but NLI(5) rearranges material in note, and deletes* 1919.

13

Mrs Henderson (in a child's voice) Lulu glad to see everybody.

Mrs Mallet And we are glad you have come, Lulu.

Mrs Henderson (in a child's voice) Lulu glad to see strange man.

Miss Mackenna (to John Corbet) She is speaking to you.

John Corbet Thank you, Lulu.

Mrs Henderson (in a child's voice) You mustnt laugh at the way I speak.

John Corbet I am not laughing, Lulu.

Mrs Henderson (in achild's voice) Nobody must laugh. Little girl does her best but cann t speak queer words and make sounds that fill up mouth. Tall man here, lots of hair on face and not much high up, not much here, (Mrs Henderson touches the top of her head) red necktie funny sort of pin.

Mrs Mallet Yes..yes...

Mrs Henderson (in a childå voice) Lulu cannot hear. He is far off. He has come near. Lulu can hear now. He says, he says, "drive that man away!" He ispointing to somebody in the corner, that corner over there. He says it is the bad man who spoilt everything last time. If they

[NLI(2), p. 13]

13

Mrs Henderson **(in a child's voice) Lulu glad to see everybody.**

Mrs Mallet **And we are glad you have come, Lulu.**

Mrs Henderson **(in a child's voice) Lulu glad to see strange man.**

Miss Mackenna **(to Jo^h^n Corbet) She is speaking to you.**

John Corbet **Thank you, Lulu.**

Mrs Henderson **(in a child's voice) You mustnt laugh at the way I speak.**

John Corbet **I am not laughing, Lulu.**

Mrs Henderson **(in a child's voice) Nobody must laugh. Little girl does her best but cannot speak queer words and make sounds that fill up mouth. Tall man here, lots of hair on face and not much high up, not much here, (Mrs Henderson touches the top of her head) red necktie funny sort of pin.**

Mrs Mallet **Yes . . yes . . .**

Mrs Henderson **(in a child's voice) Lulu cannot hear. He is far off. He has come near. Lulu can hear now. He says, he ~~says~~, "drive that man away!" He is pointing to somebody in the corner, that corner over there. He says it is the ~~loud~~ ^bad^ man who spoilt everything last time. If they**

---

1 Lulu . . . everybody] Lulu so glad to see all her friends. *NLI(3), NLI(4), LCP, H(2), NLI(5)*

3 strange man] new friend *NLI(3), NLI(4), LCP, H(2), NLI(5)*

7 speak] talk *NLI(3), NLI(4), LCP, H(2), NLI(5)*

9–14 Mrs Henderson (in a childs voice) Nobody must laugh. Lulu does her best but cant say big long words. Lulu sees a tall man here, lots of hair on face (Mrs Henderson passes her hand over her cheeks and chin ~~without touching her face~~ not much on the top of his head (Mrs Henderson passes her hand over the top of her head ~~without touching it)~~ red necktie, and such a funny sort of pin *NLI(3); so NLI(4), H(2) with no deletions; so LCP and NLI(5) but* without touching her face *and* without touching it *omitted*

15/16 Mrs Henderson (in a child's voice) Pin like a horseshoe.
Mrs Mallet It's my husband.
Mrs Henderson (in a child's voice) He has a message
Mrs Mallet Yes. *NLI(3), NLI(4), LCP, H(2), NLI(5)*

16 far] too far *NLI(3), NLI(4), LCP, H(2), NLI(5)*

18–19 *marginal stage direction:* Comes down stage R. *NLI(4)*

Mrs Henderson	wont drive him away Lulu will scream.
Miss Mackenna	That horrible spirit again.
Abraham Johnson	Last time he monopolised the seance.
Mrs Mallet	He would not let anybody speak but himself.
Mrs Henderson	(in a child's voice) They have driven bad man away. Young lady here.
Mrs Mallet	Is not my husband here?
Mrs Henderson	(in a child's voice) Man with funny pin gone away - young lady here- queer clothes-fancy dress clothes- hair all curls- crouched on floor near that ~~old~~ old man with glasses.
Dr Trench	No, I do not recognise her.
Mrs Henderson	(in child's voice) May be for young lady, there.
Miss Mackenna	No, I do not recognise her.
Mrs Henderson	(in child's voice) That bad man, that bad man in the corner, they have let him back. Lulu is going to scream, Oh,Oh, (in a mans voice) How dare you write to her. How dare you ask if we were married. How dare you question her!

[NLI(2), p. 14]

14

Mrs Henderson **wont drive him away Lulu will scream.**

Miss Mackenna **That horrible spirit again.**

Abraham Johnson **Last time he monopolised the seance.**

Mrs Mallet **He would not let anybody speak but himself.**

Mrs Henderson **(in a child's voice) They have driven bad man away. Young lady here.**

Mrs Mallet **Is not my husband here?**

Mrs Henderson **(in a child's voice) Man with funny pin gone away - young lady here - queer clothes - fancy dress clothes - hair all curls - crouched on floor near that ~~odd~~** old **man with glasses.**

Dr Trench **No, I do not recognise her.**

Mrs Henderson **(in child's voice) May be for young lady, there.**

Miss Mackenna **No, I do not recognise her.**

Mrs Henderson **(in child's voice) That bad man, that bad man in the corner, they have let him back. Lulu is going to scream, Oh, Oh,**
(in a man's voice) How dare you write to her. How dare you ask if we were married. How dare you question her!

---

5 bad] that bad *NLI(3), NLI(4), HCP, H(2), NLI(5)*

6 Young lady here] Lulu sees a young lady *NLI(3), NLI(4), LCP, H(2), NLI(5)*

9–11 young lady here – Lulu thinks she must be at a fancy dress party, such funny clothes, hair all in curls – all bent down on floor near that old man with glasses. *NLI(3), NLI(4), LCP, H(2), NLI(5), but* all in curls] all curls *H(2)*

13–14 *omitted NLI(3), NLI(4), HCP, H(2), NLI(5)*

15 in child's] in a child's *LCP, H(2), NLI(5)*

15–16 that bad man in the corner] that bad old man in the corner *NLI(3), NLI(4), LCP, NLI(5)*

16 back] come back *NLI(3), NLI(4), LCP, H(2), NLI(5)*

15

Dr Trench A soul in its agony - it cannot see us or hear us.

Mrs Henderson (upright and rigid, only her lips moving, and still in a man's voice) You sit crouching there. Did you not hear what I said? How dared you question her? I found you an ignorant little girl, without intellect, without moral ambition. How many times did I not stay from great men's houses, how many times forsake the Lord Treasurer, how many times neglect the business of the State that we might read Plutarch together. I taught you to think in every situation of life not as Hester Vanhomrigh would think in that situation but as Cato or Brutus would and now you behave like some common slut, some tavern slut, her ear against the key-hole.

John Corbet (to Miss Mackenna) It is Swift, Jonathan Swift, speaking to the woman he called Vanessa. She was christened Hester Vanhomrigh.

Mrs Henderson (in Vanessa's voice) I questioned her, Jonathan, because I love. Why have you let me spend hours in your company if you did not want me to love you? (in Swift's voice) When I rebuilt Rome in your mind it was as though I walked its streets. (in Vanessa's voice) Was that all, Jonathan? Was I nothing but a painter's canvas? (in Swift's voice) My God, do you think it was easy?

[NLI(2), p. 15]

15

Dr Trench A soul in its agony – it cannot see ~~her~~ us or ~~question~~ hear us.

Mrs Henderson (upright and rigid, only her lips moving, and still in a man's voice) You sit crouching there. Did you not hear what I said? How dared you question her? I found you an ignorant little girl, without intellect, without moral ambition. ~~How~~ How many times did I not stay from great men's houses, how many times forsake the Lord Treasurer, how many times neglect the business of the State that we might read Plutarch together. I taught you to think in every situation of life not as Hester Vanhomrigh would think in that situation but as Cato or Brutus would and now you behave like some common slut, some tavern slut , her ear against the key-hole.

John Corbet (to Miss Mackenna) It is Swift, Jonathan Swift, speaking to the woman he called Vanessa. She was christened Hester Vanhomrigh.

Mrs Henderson (in Vanessa's voice) I questioned her, Jonathan, because I love. Why have you let me spend hours in your company if you did not want me to love you? (in Swift's voice) When I rebuilt Rome in your mind it was as though I walked its streets. (in Vanessa's voice) Was that all, Jonathan? Was I nothing but a painter's canvas? (in Swift's voice) My God, do you think it was easy?

---

7 stay] stay away *NLI(3), NLI(4), LCP, H(2), NLI(5)*

9 Treasurer *revised to* Treasurer's *NLI(5)*

10 *inserted following* together *in NLI(3):*

(Abraham Johnson half rises. D[r] Trench motions to remain seated.)

D[r] Trench. Silence.

M[rs] Mallet. But D[r] Trench.

D[r] Trench. Hush. we can do nothing.

insertion retained LCP, H(2), NLI(5) but motions] motions him *and* Mrs Mallet] Abraham Johnson *H(2), NLI(5)*
inserted before I taught: Mrs Henderson (speaking as before) *LCP, H(2), NLI(5)*

13–14 some tavern slut *omitted NLI(3), NLI(4), LCP, H(2), NLI(5)*

14 her ear] with her ear *LCP, H(2), NLI(5)*

15 speaking] talking *NLI(3), NLI(4), LCP, H(2), NLI(5)*

Mrs Henderson (in Swift's voice) I was a man of strong passions and I had sworn never to marry. (in Vanessa's voice) If you andh she are not married, why should we not marry like other men and women? I loved you from the first moment when you came to my mother's house and began to teach me. I thought it would be enough to look at you, to speak to you, to hear you speak. I followed you to Ireland five years ago and I can bear it no longer. It is not enough to look, to speak, to hear. Jonathan, Jonathan, I am a woman, the women Brutus and Cato loved were not different. (in Swift's voice) I have something in my blood that no child must inherit. I have constant attacks of dizziness, I pretend they come from a surfeit of fruit when I was a child. I had them in Londo - there was a great doctor there, Dr Arbuthnot, I told him of those attacks of dizziness, I told him of worse things. It was he who explained. Pope knew - there is a line of his. (in Vanessa's voice) O, I know - "Great Wit to madness ~~how~~ [near] allied". If you had children, Jonathan, my blood would make them healthy. I will take your hand, I will lay it upon my heart -upon the Vanhomrigh blood that has been healthy for generations(Mrs Hende slowly raises her left hand) That is the first time you have touched my body, Jonathan. (She stands up and and remains rigid) (in Swift's voice) What do I care

[NLI(2), p. 16]

16

<u>Mrs Henderson</u> **(<u>in Swift's voice</u>) I was a man of strong passions and I had sworn never to marry. (<u>in Vanessa's voice</u>) If you and she are not married, why should we not marry like other men and women? I loved you from the first moment when you came to my mother's house and began to teach me. I thought it would be enough to look at you, to speak to you, to hear you speak. I followed you to Ireland five years ago and I can bear it no longer. It is not enough to look, to speak, to hear. Jonathan, Jonathan, I am a woman, the women Brutus and Cato loved were not different. (<u>in Swift's voice</u>) I have something in my blood that no child must inherit. I have constant attacks of dizziness, I pretend they come from a surfeit of fruit when I was a child. I had them in London – there was a great doctor there, Dr Arbuthnot, I told him of those attacks of dizziness, I told him of worse things. It was he who explained. Pope knew – there is a line of his. (<u>in Vanessa's voice</u>) O, I know – "Great Wit to** near **madness ~~now~~ allied". If you had children, Jonathan, my blood would make them healthy. I will take your hand, I will lay it upon my heart – upon the Vanhomrigh blood that has been healthy for generations (<u>Mrs Henderson slowly raises her left hand</u>) That is the first time you have touched my body, Jonathan. (<u>She stands up and and remains rigid</u>) (<u>in Swift's voice</u>) What do I care**

---

1 Mrs Henderson (in Swift's voice) *omitted LCP*

8 you *omitted then inserted and* to . . . five *omitted H(2)* five years ago *revised to* God knows how many years ago *NLI(4), in pencil LCP*

14 from a] from *H(2)*

18 Pope knew *deleted NLI(4), revised in pencil to* Dryden knew *LCP, omitted H(2), NLI(5)* his *revised to* Dryden's *in ink LCP* Dryden's *H(2), NLI(5)* Pope . . . Dryden's *deleted and restored NLI(4)*

19 Great Wit] Great wits are sure *NLI(5)*

25 She] Mrs Henderson *NLI(3), NLI(4), LCP, H(2), NLI(5)*

Mrs Henderson (Swift's voice) if it be healthy, what do I care if I could make mine healthy? Am I to add another to the healthy rascaldom and knavery of the world? (in Vanessa's voice) Look at me, Jonathan. Your arrogant intellect separates us. Give me both your hands. I will put them upon my breast. (Mrs Henderson raises her right hand to the level of her left, and then raises both to her breast) (Vanessa's voice) O it is white - white as the gambler's dice - white ivory dice. think of the uncertainity. Perhaps a mad child - perhaps a rascal, perhaps a knave, perhaps not Jonathan. The dice of the intellect are loaded, but I am the common ivory dice. (her hands are stretched out as though drawing somebody towards her) It is not my hands that draw you back. My hands are weak, they could not draw you back if you did not love as I love. You said that you have strong passions, that is true, Jonathan - no man in Ireland is so passionate. That s why you need me, that is why you need children, nobody has greater need. You are growing old. An old man without children is very solitary. Even his friends, men as old as he, turn away, they turn towards the young, their children or their children's children. They cannot endure an old man like themselves. (Mrs Henderson moves away from the chair, her movements gradually growing con-

[NLI(2), p. 17]

17

~~**Mrs Henderson**~~ ~~**(Swift's voice)**~~

it

if it be healthy, what do I care if ~~I~~ ^ could make mine
healthy? Am I to add another to the healthy
rascaldom and knavery of the world? (<u>in Vanessa's</u>
<u>voice</u>) Look at me, Jonathan. Your arrogant intell-
ect separates us. Give me both your hands. I
will put them upon my breast. (<u>Mrs Henderson raises</u>
<u>her right hand to the level of her left, and then</u>

in

<u>raises both to her breast</u>) (^<u>Vanessa's voice</u>) O it
is white – white as the gambler's dice – white
⊙ T **ivory dice ~~-~~ ~~t~~hink of the uncertainty. Perhaps a**
mad child – perhaps a rascal, perhaps a knave, perhaps
not, Jonathan. The dice of the intellect are loaded,
but I am the common ivory dice. (<u>her hands are stretched</u>
<u>out as though drawing somebody towards her</u>) It is
not my hands that draw you back. My hands are weak,
they could not draw you back if you did not love as
I love. You said that you have strong passions,
that is true, Jonathan – no man in Ireland is so
passionate. That is why you need me, that is why
you need children, nobody has greater need. You
are growing old. An old man without children is
very solitary. Even his friends, men as old as he,
turn away, they turn towards the young, their children
or their children's children. They cannot endure an
old man like themselves. (<u>Mrs Henderson moves away</u>
<u>from the chair, her movements gradually growing con-</u>

---

1 healthy? What *NLI(3), NLI(4)*
8 (in Vanessa's voice) *omitted LCP, H(2), NLI(5)*
8–9 O . . . white] *revised to* My breast is white *NLI(4)*

18

convulsive) You are not too old for the dice, Jonathan, but a few years if you turn away will make you an old miserable childless man. (in Swift's voice) O God, hear the prayer of Jonathan Swift that afflicted man and grant that he may leave to posterity nothing but his intellect that came to him from Heaven, (in Vanessa's voice) Can you face solitude with that mind, Jonathan? (Mrs Henderson goes to the door and finds that it is closed) (in Swift's voice) Dice, white ivory dice. My God, I am left alone with my enemy . (Mrs Henderson sinks to the floor and then speaks as Lulu) Bad old man. Do not let him come back. Bad old man does not know he is dead. Lulu cannot find fathers, mothers, sons that have passed over . Power almost gone. (Mrs Mallet leads Mrs Henderson who seems very exhausted back to her chair. She is still asleep. She speaks again as Lulu) Another verse of hymn. Everybody sing. Hymn bring good influence.

(They sing)

[NLI(2), p. 18]

18

convulsive) You are not too old for the dice, Jonathan, but a few years if you turn away will make you an old miserable childless man. (in Swift's voice) O God, hear the prayer of Jonathan Swift that afflicted man and grant that he may leave to posterity nothing but his intellect that came to him from Heaven. (in Vanessa's voice) Can you face solitude with that mind, Jonathan? (Mrs Henderson goes to the door and finds that it is closed) (in Swift's voice) Dice, white ivory dice. My God, I am left alone with my enemy . (Mrs Henderson sinks to the floor and then speaks as Lulu) Bad old man. Do not let him come back. Bad old man does not know he is dead. Lulu cannot find fathers, mothers, sons that have passed over. Power almost gone. (Mrs Mallet leads Mrs Henderson who seems very exhausted back to her chair. She is still asleep. She speaks again as Lulu) Another verse of hymn. Everybody sing. Hymn bring good influence.

(They sing)

8 and finds] finds *NLI(3), NLI(4), LCP, H(2), NLI(5)*

9 in Swift's] Swift's *NLI(3), NLI(4)*

9–10 Who locked this door? Who locked me in with my enemy *inserted following* Swift's voice *NLI(3), NLI(4), NLI(5); so H(2) but* this door] the door; *NLI(4) adds* (Mrs Henderson beats upon the door) *retained LCP, H(2), NLI(5)*

18 bring] will bring *NLI(3), NLI(4), LCP, H(2), NLI(5)*

19/ *hymn inserted:*

"If some poor wandering child of Thine
Have spurned today the voice divine
Now, Lord, the gracious work begin
Let him no more lie down in sin." *NLI(3), NLI(4), LCP, H(2), NLI(5)*

19

(during the hymn Mrs Henderson has been murmuring "Stella" but the singing has almost drowned her voice. The singers draw one another's attention to the fact that she is speaking until the singing stops.)

Dr Trench I thought she was speaking.

Mrs Mallet I saw her lips move.

Dr Trench She would be more comfortable with a cushion but we might wake her.

Miss Mackenna Nothing can wake her out of a trance like that until she wakes up herself. (She brings a cushion and she and Dr Trench put Mrs Henderson into a more comfortable position)

Mrs Henderson (in Swift's voice) Stella.

Miss Mackenna (to John Corbet) Did you hear that? She said Stella.

John Corbet Vanessa has gone, Stella has taken her place.

Miss Mackenna Did you notice the change while we were singing? The new influence in the room.

John Corbet I thought I did, but it must have been fancy.

Miss Mackenna It was as though we came suddenly out of a crowded lighted room into stillness and darkness.

[NLI(2), p. 19]

19

(during the hymn Mrs Henderson has been murmuring "Stella" but the singing has ^almost drowned her voice. The singers draw one another's attention to the fact that she is speaking until the singing stops.)

Dr Trench — **I thought she was speaking.**

Mrs Mallet — **I saw her lips move.**

~~Mrs~~ Dr Trench — **She would be more comfortable with a cushion but we might wake her.**

Miss Mackenna — **Nothing can wake her out of a trance like that until she wakes up herself. (She brings a cushion and she and Dr Trench put Mrs Henderson into a more comfortable position)**

Mrs Henderson — **(in Swift's voice) Stella.**

Miss Mackenna — **(to John Corbet) Did you hear that? She said Stella.**

John Corbet — **Vanessa has gone, Stella has taken her place.**

Miss Mackenna — **Did you notice the change while we were singing? The new influence in the room.**

John Corbet — **I thought I did, but it must have been fancy.**

Miss Mackenna — **It was as though we came suddenly out of a crowded lighted room into stillness and darkness.**

---

4 speaking until the *revised to* speaking. The *NLI(3); revision retained NLI(4), LCP, H(2), NLI(5)*

9 Miss Mackenna *revised to* Mrs Mallet *NLI(3), NLI(4); revision retained LCP, H(2), NLI(5)*

11 *marginal stage direction:* They sit again in their old places— *NLI(4)*

20–21 lighted *omitted NLI(3), NLI(4) then* 20–21 *deleted NLI(3), LCP omitted H(2), NLI(5)*

John Corbet Hush!

Mrs Henderson (in Swift's voice) Have I wronged ~~[illegible]~~ you, beloved Stella? Are you unhappy? You have no children, you have no lover, you have no husband. A cross and ageing man for friend - nothing but that. But no, do not answer, -you have answered already in that poem you wrote for my last birthday, my fifty-fourth birthday. With what scorn you speak there of the common lot of woman - a woman with no adornment but a face"
"Before the thirtieth year of life
A maid forlorn or hated wife."
It is the thought of the great Chrysostom who wrote in a famous passage that women loved according to the soul, loved as saints can love, as saints can be loved, keep their beauty longer, have greater happiness than women loved according to the flesh. That thought has comforted me, but it is a terrible thing to be responsible for another's happiness. There are moments when I doubt, when I think Chrysostom may have been wrong. But now I have your poem to drive doubt away. You have addressed me in these noble words -

You taught how I might youth prolong
By knowing what is right or wrong;
How from my heart to bring supplies
Of lustre to my fading eyes,

[NLI(2), p. 20]

20

<u>John Corbet</u> **Hush!**

<u>Mrs Henderson</u> **<u>(in Swift's voice)</u> Have I wronged ~~your~~ you,**
beloved Stella? Are you unhappy? You have
no children, you have no lover, you have no husband.
A cross and ageing man for friend – nothing but
that. But no, do not answer, – you have answered
already in that poem you wrote for my last birthday,
my fifty-fourth birthday. With what scorn you
a
speak there of the common lot of woman – ^ wom~~a~~n ¢/ stet
with no adornment but a face"
"Before the thirtieth year of life
A maid forlorn or hated wife."
It is the thought of the great Chrysostom who wrote
in a famous passage that women loved according to
d
the soul, love^ as saints can love, as saints can be
loved, keep their beauty longer, have greater happiness
than women loved according to the flesh. That thought
has comforted me, but it is a terrible thing to be
responsible for another's happiness. There are
moments when I doubt, when I think Crysostom may
have been wrong. But now I have your poem to drive
doubt away. You have addressed me in these noble
words –

You taught how I might youth prolong
By knowing what is right or wrong;
How from my heart to bring supplies
for/ **Of lustre ~~to~~ my fading eyes,**

---

1 John Corbet *revised to* Mrs Mallet *NLI(3), LCP; H(2), NLI(5) as revised*

3–4 You have no lover *moved to follow* unhappy? *LCP, H(2)*

8 my fifty-fourth birthday *omitted LCP, H(2), NLI(5) reinserted in pencil LCP*

9 there *omitted NLI(3), NLI(4), LCP, H(2), NLI(5)* of woman] of women *LCP, H(2), NLI(5)* a woman *omitted NLI(3), NLI(4), LCP, H(2), NLI(5)*

15–16 as saints can be loved *omitted NLI(3), NLI(4), LCP, H(2), NLI(5)*

25 or *revised to* and *BL(2)*

27 for] to *NLI(3), NLI(4), LCP, H(2), NLI(5)*

[NLI(2), p. 22]

22

Mrs Henderson (Swift's voice)

"How soon a beauteous mind repairs
The loss of chang'd or fading hairs,
How wit and virtue from within
Can spread a smoothness o'er the skin."

John Corbet

The words on the window pane.

Mrs Henderson

(in Swift's voice) Then because you understand that I am afraid of solitude, afraid of outliving my friends - and myself - you comfort me in that last verse - you overpraise my moral nature when you attribute to it a rich mantle, but O how touching those words which describe your love -

"Late dying, may you cast a shred
Of that rich mantle o'er my head;
To bear with dignity my sorrow,
One day alone, then die tomorrow."

Yes, you will close my eyes, Stella, but you will live long after me, dear Stella, for you are still a young woman, but you will close my eyes.

(Mrs Henderson sinks back in chair and speaks as Lulu)

Mrs Henderson

(speaking as Lulu) Bad old man gone. Power all used up Lulu can do no more. Good-bye friends, (Mrs Henderson speaking in her own voice) Go away, Go away! (She wakes) I saw him a moment ago, has he spoilt the seance again?

[NLI(2), p. 22]

22

Mrs Henderson (Swift's voice)

"How soon a beauteous mind repairs
The loss of chang'd or fading hairs,
How wit and virtue from within
Can spread a smoothness o'er the skin."

John Corbet **The words on the window pane.**

Mrs Henderson **(in Swift's voice) Then because you understand that I am afraid of solitude, afraid of outliving my friends – and myself – you comfort me in that last verse – you overpraise my moral nature when you attribute to it a rich mantle, but O how touching those words which describe your love -**

"Late dying, may you cast a shred
Of that rich mantle o'er my head;
– – –
To bear with dignity my sorrow,
One day alone, then die tomorrow."

Yes, you will close my eyes, Stella, but you will live long after me, dear Stella, for you are still a young woman, but you will close my eyes.
(Mrs Henderson sinks back in chair and speaks as Lulu)

Mrs Henderson **(speaking as Lulu) Bad old man gone. Power all used up. Lulu can do no more. Good-bye friends, (Mrs Henderson speaking in her own voice) Go away, Go away! (She wakes) I saw him a moment ago, has he spoilt the seance again?**

---

2 fading *revised to* falling *NLI(3), LCP; so H(2), NLI(5)*
5 on *revised to* upon *BL(2)*
12 you may *revised in ink to* may you *LCP*
18 a *omitted NLI(3) restored NLI(4), NLI(5)* woman, but *rev to* woman. Yes, you *BL(2)*
21 Mrs Henderson (speaking as Lulu) *omitted NLI(3), NLI(4), LCP, H(2), NLI(5)*
22 used up] gone *deleted to* used up *NLI(3), NLI(4)*

There is no page numbered 21 in the typescript.

23

Mrs Mallet — Yes, Mrs Henderson, my husband came, but he was driven away.

Dr Trench — Mrs Henderson is very tired. We must leave her to rest. (To Mrs Henderson) You did your best and nobody can do more than that. (he takes out money)

Mrs Henderson — No...No.... I cannot take any money - not after a seance like that.

Dr Trench — Of course you must take it, Mrs Henderso n. (He puts money on the table and Mrs Henderson gives a furtive glance to see how much it is. She does the same as each sitter lays down his or her money)

Mrs Mallet — A bad seance is just as exhausting as a good seance and you must be paid.

Mrs Henderson — No...No.... please dont. It is very wrong to take money for such a failure.
(Mrs Mallet lays down money)

Cornelius Patterson — A jockey is paid whether he wins or not. (he lays down money)

Miss Mackenna — That spirit rather thrilled me. (she lays down money)

[NLI(2), p. 23]

23

Mrs Mallet — **Yes, Mrs Henderson, my husband came, but he was driven away.**

Dr Trench — **Mrs Henderson is very tired. We must leave her to rest. (To Mrs Henderson) You did your best and nobody can do more than that. (he takes out money)**

Mrs Henderson — **No . . . No. . . . I cannot take any money – not after a seance like that.**

Dr Trench — **Of course you must take it, Mrs Henderson. (He puts money on the table and Mrs Henderson gives a furtive glance to see how much it is. She does the same as each sitter lays down his or her money)**

Mrs Mallet — **A bad seance is just as exhausting as a good seance and you must be paid.**

Mrs Henderson — **No . . . No. . . . please dont. It is very wrong to take money for such a failure. (Mrs Mallet lays down money)**

Cornelius Patterson — **A jockey is paid whether he wins or not. (he lays down money)**

Miss Mackenna — **That spirit rather thrilled me. (~~she~~ lays down money)**

---

1 came] cam *rev in ink to* came *LCP*
9–10 *marginal stage direction:* Goes out to R. to get his coat and hat. *NLI(4)*
10 the *omitted NLI(3), NLI(4), LCP, NLI(5)*
18 *inserted stage direction:* goes out— X L. *NLI(4)*
20 *inserted stage direction:* goes out X R. Two others lay down money and exit. *NLI(4)*
21 she *retained NLI(3), NLI(4), LCP, H(2), NLI(5)*

24

Mrs Henderson	If you insist, I must take it.
Abraham Johnson	I shall pray for you tonight. I shall ask God to bless and protect your seances. (he lays down money)
	(all go out, except John Corbet and Mrs Henderson)
John Corbet	I know you are tired, Mrs Henderson, but I must speak to you. I have been deeply moved by what I have heard. This is my contribution to prove that I am satisfied - completely satisfied (he puts a note on the table)
Mrs Henderson	A pound note - nobody ever gives me more than ten shillings, and yet the seance was a failure.
John Corbet	(sitting down near ~~Madam~~ Mrs Henderson) When I say I am satisfied I do not mean that I am convinced it was the work of spirits. I prefer to think that you created it all whether awake or asleep; that you are an accomplished actress and scholar. In my essay for my Cambridge doctorate I examine all the explanations of Swift's celibacy offered by his biographers, and prove that the explanation you selected was the only plausible one. But there is something I must ask you. Swift was the chief repesentative of the intellect of his

[NLI(2), p. 24]

24

Mrs Henderson **If you insist, I must take it.**

Abraham Johnson **I shall pray for you tonight. I shall ask God to bless and protect your seances. (he lays down money)**
(all go out except John Corbet and Mrs Henderson)

John Corbet **I know you are tired, Mrs Henderson, but I must speak to you. I have been deeply moved by what I have heard. This is my contribution to prove that I am satisfied – completely satisfied (he puts a note on the table)**

Mrs Henderson **A pound note – nobody ever gives me more than ten shillings, and yet the seance was a failure.**

John Corbet **(sitting down near ~~Medium~~** Mrs Henderson**) When I say I am satisfied I do not mean that I am convinced it was the work of spirits. I prefer to think that you created it all whether awake or asleep, that you are an accomplished actress and scholar. In my essay for my Cambridge doctorate I examine all the explanations of Swift's celibacy offered by his biographers, and prove that the explanation you** s**~~d~~elected was the only plausible one. But there is something I must ask you. Swift was the chief representative of the intellect of his**

---

4 *inserted stage direction:* Goes out Other man lays down money and exits — *NLI(4)*
5 out *omitted H(2)*
5–6 *marginal stage direction:* X behind table *NLI(4)*
9 completely satisfied *omitted H(2)*
13 down near *revised to* down behind table near *NLI(4)*
16 whether . . . asleep *deleted LCP, omitted H(2), NLI(5)*

[NLI(2), p. 25]

25

John Corbet	epoch, that arrogant intellect free at last from superstition. He foresaw its collapse. He foresaw democracy, he must have ~~decided~~ dreaded the future. Did he refuse to beget children because of that dread? Was Swift mad? Or was it the intellect itself that was mad?
Mrs Henderson	Who are you talking of, Sir?
John Corbet	Swift, of course.
Mrs Henderson	Swift? I do not know anybody called Swift.
Jn Corbet	Jonathan Swift, whose spirit seemed to be present tonight.
Mrs Henderson	What? That dirty old man?
John Corbet	He was neither old nor dirty when Stella and Vanessa loved him.
Mrs Henderson	I saw him very clearly just as I woke up. ~~I saw him very clearly.~~ His clothes ~~[deleted]~~ were dirty, his face dirty, his face covered with boils. He was horrible. Some disease had made one of his eyes swell up, it stood out from his face like a hens ~~duck's~~ egg.

[NLI(2), p. 25]

25

John Corbet — **epoch, that arrogant intellect free at last from superstition. He foresaw its collapse. He**
dreaded
foresaw democracy, he must have ~~decided~~ ^ the future. Did he refuse to beget children because of that dread? Was Swift mad? Or was it the intellect itself that was mad?

Mrs Henderson — **Who are you talking of, Sir?**

John Corbet — **Swift, of course.**

Mrs Henderson — **Swift? I do not know anybody called Swift.**

John Corbet — **Jonathan Swift, whose spirit seemed to be present tonight.**

Mrs Henderson — **What? That dirty old man?**

John Corbet — **He was neither old nor dirty when Stella and Vanessa loved him.**

Mrs Henderson — **I saw him very clearly just as I woke up. ~~I saw him very clearly.~~ His clothes [?~~dirty~~] were dirty his face dirty, his face covered with boils. He was horrible. Some disease had made one of his eyes swell up, it stood out from his face like a**
hens
~~duck's~~ egg.
^

1 That arrogant intellect *omitted NLI(5)*
9 do not *revised to* don't *NLI(4)*
17 his face dirty *omitted NLI(3), NL(4), LCP, H(2), NLI(5)*
17–18 He was horrible *omitted NLI(3), NLI(4), LCP, H(2), NLI(5)*

26

John Corbet — He looked like that in his old age. Stella had been dead a long time. His brain had gone, his friends had deserted him. The man appointed to take ~~charge~~ care of him beat him to keep him quiet.

Mrs Henderson — Now they are ~~[illegible]~~ old, now they are young. They change all in a moment as their thought changes. It is sometimes a terrible thing to be out of the body. God help us all.

Dr Trench — (at doorway) Come ~~Mr~~ along Corbet, Mrs Henderson is tired out.

John Corbet — Goodbye, Mrs Henderson. (He goes out with Dr Trench)

(Mrs Henderson counts the money, finds her purse which is in a vase on the mantelpiece and puts the money in it.)

Mrs Henderson — How tired I am! Id be the better of a cup of tea. (she finds the teapot and puts it on table and puts kettle on fire, and then as she crouches down by the hearth suddenly lifts up her hands and counting her fingers speaking in Swift's voice) Four great ministers that were my friends are gone (she wakes with a start and speaks in her own voice) Where did I put that tea caddy? Ah! there it is. . and there should be a cup and saucer. (she finds the saucer ~~cup~~) but where 's the ~~sugar~~ cup (she moves aimlessly

[NLI(2), p. 26]

26

John Corbet — **He looked like that in his old age. Stella had been dead a long time. His brain had gone, his friends had deserted him. The man appointed to**
care
take ~~charge~~ ^ of him beat him to keep him quiet.

Mrs Henderson — **Now they are [~~?~~] old, now they are young. They change all in a moment as their thought changes. It is sometimes a terrible thing to be out of the body, God help us all.**

along
Dr Trench — **(at doorway) Come ~~Mr~~ ^ Corbet, Mrs Henderson is tired out.**

John Corbet — **Goodbye, Mrs Henderson. (He goes out with Dr Trench)**

(Mrs Henderson counts the money, finds her purse which is in a vase on the mantelpiece and puts the money in it.)

Mrs Henderson — **How tired I am! Id be the better of a cup of tea. (she finds the teapot and puts it on the table and puts kettle on fire, and then as she crouches down by the hearth suddenly lifts up her hands and counting her fingers speaking in Swift's voice) Four great ministers that were my friends are gone (she wakes with a start and speaks in her own voice) Where did I put that tea caddy? Ah! there it is. . and there should be a cup and saucer. (she finds the**
saucer cup
~~cup~~ ^) but where's the ~~sugar~~ (she moves aimlessly

---

2 a *omitted then inserted H(2)*

8/9 *inserted stage direction:* All pass in hall from R. to L. Trench last — *NLI(4)*

11 *inserted stage direction:* shuts the door. *NLI(4)*

11/12 (all the sitters except Miss Mackenna who has returned to her room pass along the passage on their way to front door,) *added in NLI(3); so LCP, H(2), NLI(5) but* front] the front

16 and puts it on the table *omitted NLI(3), NLI(4), LCP, H(2), NLI(5) then inserted in NLI (4) as* puts it on table

18 counting *revised to* counts *BL(2);*

19 speaking] speaks *NLI(5); so NLI 30,185 but restored to* speaking *with* stet four] five *NLI(3), NLI(4), LCP, H(2), NLI(5)*

20 *inserted before* she wakes *NLI(3), NLI(4), LCP, H(2), NLI(5):* ten great ministers that were my friends are gone. I have not fingers enough to count the great ministers that were my friends and that are gone.

22 *stage direction:* on mantel-piece *inserted before* Ah *then moved to follow* it is *NLI(4)*

23–24 *marginal stage direction:* brings it to table ~~brings it to —~~ *NLI(4)*

[NLI(2), p. 27]

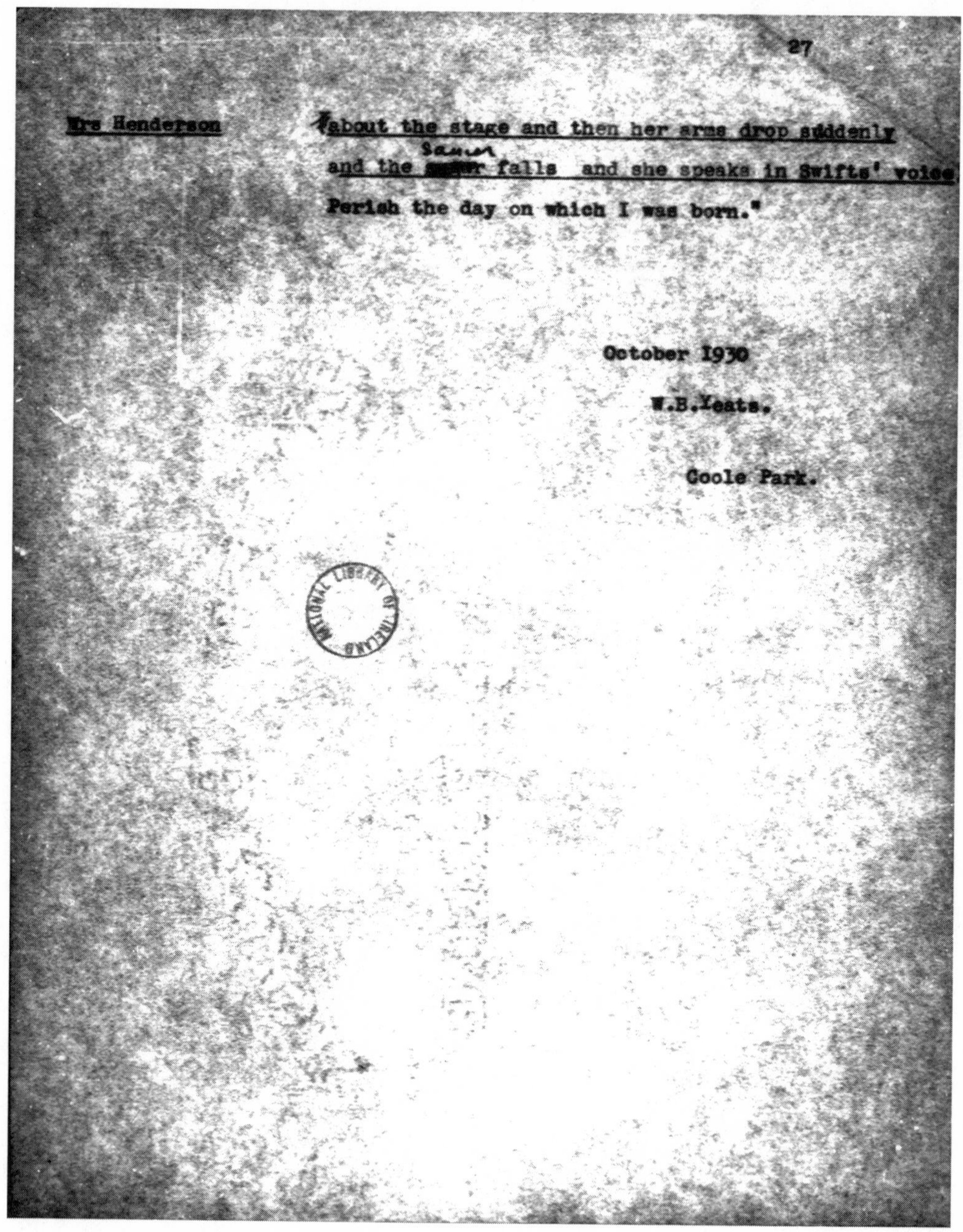
27

Mrs Henderson ~~"~~about the stage and then her arms drop suddenly and the ~~saucer~~ Saucer falls and she speaks in Swifts' voice. Perish the day on which I was born."

October 1930

W.B.Yeats.

Coole Park.

[NLI(2), p. 27]

27

Mrs Henderson **~~(~~about the stage and then her arms drop suddenly**

saucer

and the ~~sugar~~ falls and she speaks in Swifts' voice)

Perish the day on which I was born."

October 1930

W. B.Yeats.

Coole Park.

1–2 her arms drop suddenly *deleted to* and the saucer falls and she *in turn deleted to* letting the saucer fall and break *NLI(3); so LCP, H(2), NLI(5)*

2 and the saucer falls *inserted after* suddenly *NLI(4) along with marginal stage direction:* between table and fire —

4–6 *omitted NLI(5)*

The Cuala Press Edition

1934

THE WORDS UPON THE WINDOW PANE: A PLAY IN ONE ACT, WITH NOTES UPON THE PLAY AND ITS SUBJECT, BY WILLIAM BUTLER YEATS.

THE CUALA PRESS
DUBLIN, IRELAND
MCMXXXIV

In Memory of Lady Gregory
in whose house it was written.

[xi]

THE WORDS UPON THE WINDOW PANE: A PLAY IN ONE ACT, BY WILLIAM BUTLER YEATS

[xii]

PERSONS OF THE PLAY

Doctor Trench
Miss Mackenna
John Corbet
Cornelius Patterson
Abraham Johnson
Mrs. Mallet
Mrs. Henderson

[xiv]

THE WORDS UPON THE WINDOW [p. 34]
PANE.

A lodging house room, an armchair, a little table in front of it, chairs on either side. A fireplace and window. A kettle on the hob and some tea-things on a dresser. A door at back and towards the right. Through the door one can see an entrance hall. The sound of a knocker. Miss Mackenna passes the door, returns bringing with her John Corbet, a man of twenty-two or twenty three, and Doctor Trench, a man of between sixty and seventy.

DOCTOR TRENCH *(in hall)* May I introduce John Corbet, one of the Corbets of Ballymoney, but at present a Cambridge student? This is Miss Mackenna our enthusiastic secretary. (*They come into room, and take off their coats).*

MISS MACKENNA I thought it better to let you in myself. This country is still sufficiently medieval to make spiritualism an undesirable theme for gossip. Give me your coats and hats, I will put them in my own room. It is just across the hall. Better sit down, your watches must be fast. Mrs. Henderson is lying down, as she always does before a séance. We wont begin for ten minutes yet. *(She goes out with hats and coats*).

DOCTOR TRENCH Miss Mackenna does all the real work of the Dublin Spiritualists Association.

[p. 35] She did all the correspondence with Mrs. Henderson and persuaded the landlady to let her this big room and a small room upstairs. We are a poor society and could not guarantee anything in advance. Mrs. Henderson has come from London at her own risk. She was born in Dublin and wants to spread the movement here. She lives very economically and does not expect a great deal. We all give what we can. A poor woman with the soul of an apostle.

JOHN CORBET Have there been many séances?

DOCTOR TRENCH Only three so far.

JOHN CORBET I hope she will not mind my skepticism. I have looked into Myers' 'Human Personality' and a wild book by Conan Doyle, but am unconvinced.

DOCTOR TRENCH We all have to find the truth for ourselves. Lord Dunraven, then Lord Adare, introduced my father to the famous David Home. My father often told me that he saw David Home floating in the air in broad daylight, but I did not believe a word of it. I had to investigate for myself, and I was very hard to convince. Mrs. Piper, an American trance medium, not unlike Mrs. Henderson, convinced me.

JOHN CORBET A state of somnanbulism and voices coming through her lips that purport to be those of dead persons?

DOCTOR TRENCH Exactly: quite the best [p. 36] kind of mediumship if you want to establish the identity of a spirit. But do not expect too much. There has been a hostile influence.

JOHN CORBET You mean an evil spirit?

DOCTOR TRENCH The poet Blake said that he never knew a bad man that had not something very good about him. I say a hostile influence, an influence that disturbed the last séance very seriously. I cannot tell you what happened, for I have not been at any of Mrs. Henderson's séances. Trance mediumship has nothing new to show me. I told the young people when they made me their President that I would probably stay at home, that I could get more out of Emanuel Swedenborg than out of any séance. *(A knock).* That is probably old Cornelius Patterson; he thinks they race horses and whippets in the other world and is, so they tell me, so anxious to find out if he is right that he is always punctual. Miss Mackenna will keep him to herself for some minutes. He gives her tips for Harold's Cross.

(Miss Mackenna crosses to hall door and admits Cornelius Patterson. She brings him to her room across the hall).

JOHN CORBET *(who has been wandering about)* This is a wonderful room for a lodging house.

DOCTOR TRENCH It was a private house until about fifty years ago. It was not so near the town in those days and there are large stables at the [p. 37] back. Quite a number of notable people lived here. Grattan was born upstairs, no, not Grattan, Curran perhaps—I forget—but I do know that this house in the early part of the eighteenth century belonged to friends of Jonathan Swift, or rather of Stella. Swift chaffed her in the *Journal to Stella* because of certain small sums of money she lost at cards probably in this very room. That was before Vanessa appeared upon the scene. It was a country house in those days surrounded by trees and gardens. Somebody cut some lines from a poem of hers upon the window-pane—tradition says Stella herself. *(A knock).* Here they are but you will hardly make them out in this light. *(They stand in the window. Corbet stoops down to see better. Miss Mackenna and Abraham Johnson enter and stand near door).*

ABRAHAM JOHNSON Where is Mrs. Henderson?

MISS MACKENNA She is upstairs, she always rests before a séance.

ABRAHAM JOHNSON I must see her before the séance. I know exactly what to do to get rid of this evil influence.

MISS MACKENNA If you go up to see her there will be no séance at all. She says it is dangerous even to think, much less to speak, of an evil influence. [p. 38]

ABRAHAM JOHNSON Then I shall speak to the President.

MISS MACKENNA Better talk the whole thing over first in my room. Mrs. Henderson says that there must be perfect harmony.

ABRAHAM JOHNSON Something must be done. The last séance was completely spoilt. *(A knock).*

MISS MACKENNA That may be Mrs. Mallet, she is a very experienced spiritualist. Come to my room, old Patterson and some others are there already. *(She brings him to the other room and later crosses to hall-door to admit Mrs. Mallet).*

JOHN CORBET I know these lines well—they are part of a poem Stella wrote for Swift's fifty-fourth birthday. Only three poems of hers—and some lines she added to a poem of Swift's—have come down to us, but they are enough to prove her a better poet than Swift. Even those few words on the window make me think of a seventeenth century poet, Donne or Crashaw. (He quotes):

'You taught how I might youth prolong
By knowing what is right and wrong,
How from the heart to bring supplies
Of lustre to my fading eyes'

---

6 perfect harmony] See the Census entry for NLI(4), p. xii, above.

How strange that a celibate scholar, well on in life, [p. 39] should keep the love of two such women. He met Vanessa in London at the height of his political power. She followed him to Dublin. She loved him for nine years, perhaps died of love; but Stella loved him all her life.

DOCTOR TRENCH I have shown that writing to several persons and you are the first who has recognised the lines.

JOHN CORBET I am writing an essay on Swift and Stella for my doctorate at Cambridge. I hope to prove that in Swift's day men of intellect reached the height of their power—the greatest position they ever attained in Society and the State—that everything great in Ireland and in our character, in what remains of our architecture, comes from that day; that we have kept its seal longer than England.

DOCTOR TRENCH A tragic life, Ormonde, Harley, Bolingbroke, all those great Ministers that were his friends, banished and broken.

JOHN CORBET I do not think you can explain him in that way—his tragedy had deeper foundations. His ideal order was the Roman Senate, his ideal men Brutus and Cato; such an order and such men had seemed possible once more; but the movement passed and he foresaw the ruin to come, Democracy, Rousseau, the French Revolution, that is why he hated the common run of men,—'I hate lawyers, I hate doctors' he said 'though I love Doctor So-and-so and Judge So-and-so',—that is why he wrote Gulliver, that is why he wore out his brain, that is why he felt *saevo indignatio*, that is why he sleeps under the greatest epitaph in history. You remember how it goes? It is almost finer in English than in Latin:—'He has gone where fierce indignation can lacerate his heart no more.' [p. 40]

(Abraham Johnson comes in, followed by Mrs. Mallet and Cornelius Patterson).

ABRAHAM JOHNSON Something must be done, Doctor Trench, to drive away the influence that has destroyed our séances. I have come here week after week at considerable expense. I am from Belfast. I am by profession a minister of the Gospel, I do a great deal of work among the poor and ignorant. I produce considerable effect by singing and preaching, but I know that my effect should be much greater than it is. My hope is that I shall be able to communicate with the great Evangelist Sankey. I want to ask him to stand invisible beside me when I speak or sing, and lay his hands upon my head and give me such a portion of his power that my work may be blessed as the work of Moody and Sankey was blessed.

MRS. MALLET What Mr. Johnson says about the hostile influence is quite true. The last two séances were completely spoilt. I am thinking of starting a teashop in Folkestone. I followed Mrs. Henderson to Dublin to get my husband's advice, but two spirits kept talking and would not let any other spirit say a word. [p. 41]

DOCTOR TRENCH Did the spirits say the same thing and go through the same drama at both séances?

MRS. MALLET Yes—just as if they were character in some kind of horrible play.

DOCTOR TRENCH That is what I was afraid of.

MRS. MALLET My husband was drowned at sea ten years ago but constantly speaks to me through Mrs. Henderson as if he were still alive. He advises me about everything I do, and I am utterly lost if I cannot question him.

CORNELIUS PATTERSON I never did like the Heaven they talk about in churches, but when somebody told me that Mrs. Mallet's husband ate and drank and went about with his favourite dog, I said to myself, 'That is the place for Corney Patterson.' I came here to find out if it was true and I declare to God I have not heard one word about it.

ABRAHAM JOHNSON I ask you, Doctor Trench, as President of the Dublin Spiritualist Association, to permit me to read the ritual of exorcism appointed for such occasions. After the last séance I [p. 42] copied it out of an old book in the library of Belfast University. I have it here. *(He takes paper out of his pocket).*

DOCTOR TRENCH The spirits are people like ourselves, we treat them as our guests and protect them from discourtesy and violence, and every exorcism is a curse or a threatened curse. We do not admit that there are evil spirits. Some spirits are earth-bound—they think they are still living and go over and over some action of their past lives, just as we go over and over some painful thought, except that where they are thought is reality. For instance, when a spirit which has died a violent death comes to a medium for the first time, it re-lives all the pains of death.

MRS. MALLET When my husband came for the first time the medium gasped and struggled as if she was drowning. It was terrible to watch.

DOCTOR TRENCH Sometimes a spirit re-lives not the pain of death but some passionate or tragic moment of life. Swedenborg describes this and gives the reason for it. There is an incident of the kind in the *Odessey*, and many in Eastern literature; the murderer repeats his murder, the robber his robbery, the lover his serenade, the soldier hears the trumpet once again. If I were a Catholic I would say that such spirits were in Purgatory. In vain do we [p. 43] write *requiescat in pace* upon the tomb, for they must suffer, and we in our turn must suffer until God gives peace. Such spirits do not often come to séances unless those séances are held in houses where those spirits lived, or where the event took place. This spirit which speaks those incomprehensible words, and does not answer when spoken to, is of such a nature. The more patient we are, the more quickly will it pass out of its passion and its remorse.

ABRAHAM JOHNSON I am still convinced that the spirit which disturbed the last séance is evil. If I may not exorcise it I will certainly pray for protection.

DOCTOR TRENCH Mrs. Henderson's control, Lulu, is able and experienced and can protect both medium and sitters, but it may help Lulu if you pray that the spirit find rest.

(Abraham Johnson sits down and prays silently moving his lips. Mrs. Henderson comes in with Miss Mackenna and others. Miss Mackenna shuts the door).

DOCTOR TRENCH Mrs. Henderson, may I introduce to you Mr. Corbet, a young man from Cambridge and a sceptic, who hopes that you will be able to convince him.

MRS. HENDERSON We were all sceptics

once. He must not expect too much from a first séance. He must persevere. *(She sits in the armchair, and the others begin to seat themselves. Miss Mackenna goes to John Corbet and they remain standing).* [p. 44]

MISS MACKENNA I am glad that you are a sceptic.

JOHN CORBET I thought you were a spiritualist.

MISS MACKENNA I have seen a good many séances and sometimes think it is all coincidence and thought-transference. *(She says this in a low voice).* Then at other times I think as Doctor Trench does, and then I feel as Job—you know the quotation—the hair of my head stands up. A spirit passed before my face.

MRS. MALLET Turn the key, Doctor Trench, we dont want anybody blundering in here. *(Doctor Trench locks door).* Come and sit here, Miss Mackenna.

MISS MACKENNA No, I am going to sit beside Mr. Corbet. *(Corbet and Miss Mackenna sit down).*

JOHN CORBET You feel like Job to-night?

MISS MACKENNA I feel that something is going to happen, that is why I am glad you are a sceptic.

JOHN CORBET You feel safer?

MISS MACKENNA Yes, safer. [p. 45]

MRS HENDERSON I am glad to meet all my dear friends again and to welcome Mr. Corbet amongst us. As he is a stranger I must explain that we do not call up spirits; we make the right conditions and they come. I do not know who is going to come; sometimes there are a great many and the guides choose between them. The guides try to send somebody for everybody but do not always succeed. If you want to speak to some dear friend who has passed over, do not be discouraged. If your friend cannot come this time, may-be he can next time. My control is a dear little girl called Lulu who died when she was five or six years old. She describes the spirits present and tells us what spirit wants to speak. Miss Mackenna, a verse of a hymn, please, the same we had last time, and will everyone join in the singing. *(They sing the following lines from Hymn, 564, Dublin Church Hymnal, Tune Stillorgan).*

'Sun of my soul, Thou Saviour dear,
It is not night if Thou art near:
O may no earth-born cloud arise
To hide Thee from Thy servant's eyes.'

(Mrs. Henderson is leaning back in her chair asleep).

MISS MACKENNA *(to John Corbet).* She always snores like that when she is going off. [p. 46]

MRS HENDERSON *(in a child's voice).* Lulu so glad to see all her friends.

MRS MALLET And we are glad you have come, Lulu.

MRS HENDERSON *(in a child's voice).* Lulu glad to see new friend.

MISS MACKENNA *(to John Corbet).* She is speaking to you.

JOHN CORBET Thank you, Lulu.

MRS HENDERSON *(in a child's voice).* You mustn't laugh at the way I talk.

JOHN CORBET I am not laughing, Lulu.

MRS HENDERSON *(in a child's voice).* Nobody must laugh. Lulu does her best but can't say big long words. Lulu sees a tall man here, lots of hair on face *(Mrs. Henderson passes her hands over her cheeks and chin)*, not much on the top of his head *(Mrs. Henderson passes her hand over the top of her head)*, red necktie, and such a funny sort of pin.

MRS MALLET Yes. . . . Yes. . . .

MRS HENDERSON *(in a child's voice).* Pin like a horseshoe.

MRS MALLET It's my husband.

MRS HENDERSON *(in a child's voice).* He has a message.

MRS MALLET Yes. [p. 47]

MRS HENDERSON *(in a child's voice).* Lulu cannot hear. He is too far off. He has come near. Lulu can hear now. He says. . . . he says, 'Drive that man away!' He is pointing to somebody in the corner, that corner over there. He says it is the bad man who spoilt everything last time. If they wont drive him away, Lulu will scream.

MISS MACKENNA That horrible spirit again.

ABRAHAM JOHNSON Last time he monopolised the séance.

MRS MALLET He would not let anybody speak but himself.

MRS HENDERSON *(in a child's voice).* They have driven that bad man away. Lulu sees a young lady.

MRS MALLET Is not my husband here?

MRS HENDERSON *(in a child's voice).* Man with funny pin gone away. Young lady here—Lulu thinks she must be at a fancy dress party, such funny clothes, hair all in curls—all bent down on floor near that old man with glasses.

DOCTOR TRENCH No, I do not recognise her.

MRS HENDERSON *(in a child's voice).* That bad man, that bad old man in the corner, they have

[p. 48]

let him come back. Lulu is going to scream. O. . . . O. . . . *(in a man's voice)*. How dare you write to her? How dare you ask if we were married ? How dare you question her?

DOCTOR TRENCH A soul in its agony—it cannot see us or hear us.

MRS HENDERSON *(upright and rigid, only her lips moving, and still in a man's voice)*. You sit crouching there. Did you not hear what I said? How dared you question her? I found you an ignorant little girl without intellect, without moral ambition. How many times did I not stay away from great men's houses', how many times forsake the Lord Treasurer's, how many times neglect the business of the State that we might read Plutarch together.

(Abraham Johnson half rises. Doctor Trench motions him to remain seated).

DOCTOR TRENCH Silence.

ABRAHAM JOHNSON But, Doctor Trench.

DOCTOR TRENCH Hush—we can do nothing.

MRS HENDERSON *(speaking as before)*. I taught you to think in every situation of life not as Hester Vanhomrigh would think in that situation but as Cato or Brutus would, and now you behave like some common slut with her ear against the keyhole.

JOHN CORBET *(to Miss Mackenna).* It is Swift, Jonathan Swift, talking to the woman he called Vanessa. She was christened Hester Vanhomrigh. [p. 49]

MRS HENDERSON *(in Vanessa's voice).* I questioned her, Jonathan, because I love. Why have you let me spend hours in your company if you did not want me to love you? *(In Swift's voice).* When I re-built Rome in your mind it was as though I walked its streets. *(In Vanessa's voice).* Was that all Jonathan? Was I nothing but a painter's canvas? (In Swift's voice). My God, do you think it was easy? I was a man of strong passions and I had sworn never to marry. *(In Vanessa's voice).* If you and she are not married, why should we not marry like other men and women? I loved you from the first moment when you came to my mother's house and began to teach me. I thought itwould be enough to look at you, to speak to you, to hear you speak. I followed you to Ireland five years ago and I can bear it no longer. It is not enough to look, to speak, to hear. Jonathan, Jonathan, I am a woman, the women Brutus and Cato loved were not different. *(In Swift's voice).* I have something in my blood that no child must inherit. I have constant attacks of dizziness; I pretend they come from a surfeit of fruit when I was a child. I had them in London—there was a great doctor there, Doctor Arbuthnot, I told him of those attacks [p. 50] of dizziness, I told him of worse things. It was he who explained.—there is a line of Dryden's. . . . *(In Vanessa's voice).* O, I know—'Great wits are sure to madness near allied'. If you had children, Jonathan, my blood would make them healthy. I will take your hand, I will lay it upon my heart—upon the Vanhomrigh blood that has been hcalthy for generations. *(Mrs Henderson slowly raises her left hand).* That is the first time you have touched my body, Jonathan. *(Mrs. Henderson stands up and remains rigid. In Swift's voice).* What do I care if it be healthy? What do I care if it could make mine healthy? Am I to add another to the healthy rascaldom and knavery of the world ? *(In Vanessa's voice).* Look at me, Jonathan. Your arrogant intellect separates us. Give me both your hands. I will put them upon my breast. *(Mrs Henderson raises her right hand to the level of her left and then raises both to her breast).* O it is white—white as the gambler's dice —white ivory dice. Think of the uncertainty. Perhaps a mad child—perhaps a rascal—perhaps a knave—perhaps not, Jonathan. The dice of the intellect are loaded, but I am the common ivory dice. *(Her hands are stretched out as though drawing somebody towards her).* It is not my hands that draw you back. My hands are weak, they could not draw

21 white ivory dice] See the Census entry for NLI(4), p. xii, above.

you back if you did not love as I love. You said that [p. 51] you have strong passions; that is true, Jonathan—no man in Ireland is so passionate. That is why you need me, that is why you need children, nobody has greater need. You are growing old. An old man without children is very solitary. Even his friends, men as old as he, turn away, they turn towards the young, their children or their children's children. They cannot endure an old man like themselves. *(Mrs Henderson moves away from the chair, her movements gradually growing convulsive).* You are not too old for the dice, Jonathan, but a few years if you turn away will make you an old miserable childless man. *(In Swift's voice).* O God hear the prayer of Jonathan Swift, that afflicted man, and grant that he may leave to posterity nothing but his intellect that came to him from Heaven. *(In Vanessa's voice).* Can you face solitude with that mind, Jonathan? *(Mrs Henderson goes to the door, finds that it is closed).* Dice, white ivory dice. *(In Swift's voice).* My God, I am left alone with my enemy. Who locked the door, who locked me in with my enemy? *(Mrs. Henderson beats upon the door, sinks to the floor and then speaks as Lulu).* Bad old man. Do not let him come back. Bad old man does not know he is dead. Lulu cannot find fathers, mothers, sons that have passed over. Power almost gone. *(Mrs Mallet leads*

Mrs Henderson who seems very exhausted back to her chair. She is still asleep. She speaks again as Lulu). [p. 52] Another verse of hymn. Everybody sing. Hymn will bring good influence. *(They sing).*

> ‘If some poor wandering child of Thinc
> Have spurned today the voice divine,
> Now, Lord, the gracious work begin;
> Let him no more lie down in sin.’

(During the hymn Mrs Henderson has been murmuring ‘Stella’ but the singing has almost drowned her voice. The singers draw one another’s attention to the fact that she is speaking. The singing stops).

DOCTOR TRENCH I thought she was speaking.

MRS MALLET I saw her lips move.

DOCTOR TRENCH She would be more comfortable with a cushion but we might wake her.

MRS MALLET Nothing can wake her out of a trance like that until she wakes up herself. *(She brings a cushion and she and Doctor Trench put Mrs Henderson into a more comfortable position).*

MRS HENDERSON *(in Swift’s voice).* Stella.

MISS MACKENNA *(to John Corbet).* Did you hear that? She said Stella.

JOHN CORBET Vanessa has gone, Stella has taken her place. [p. 53]

MISS MACKENNA Did you notice the change while we were singing? The new influence in the room?

JOHN CORBET I thought I did, but it must have been fancy.

MRS MALLET Hush!

MRS HENDERSON *(in Swift's voice)*. Have I wronged you, beloved Stella? Are you unhappy? You have no children, you have no lover, you have no husband. A cross and ageing man for friend—nothing but that. But no, do not answer—you have answered already in that poem you wrote for my last birthday. With what scorn you speak of the common lot of women 'with no adornment but a face—

> Before the thirtieth year of life
> A maid forlorn or hated wife.'

It is the thought of the great Chrysostom who wrote in a famous passage that women loved according to the soul, loved as saints can love, keep their beauty longer, have greater happiness than women loved according to the flesh. That thought has comforted me, put it is a terrible thing to be responsible for another's happiness. There are moments when I doubt, when I think Chrysostom may have been wrong. [p. 54] But now I have your poem to drive doubt away. You have addressed me in these noble words—

'You taught how I might youth prolong
By knowing what is right or wrong;
How from my heart to bring supplies
Of lustre to my fading eyes;
How soon a beauteous mind repairs
The loss of chang'd or falling hairs,
How wit and virtue from within
Can spread a smoothness o'er the skin.'

JOHN CORBET The words on the window-pane.

MRS HENDERSON *(in Swift's voice)*. Then, because you understand that I am afraid of solitude, afraid of outliving my friends—and myself—you comfort me in that last verse—you overpraise my moral nature when you attribute to it a rich mantle, but O how touching those words which describe your love—

'Late dying may you cast a shred
Of that rich mantle o'er my head;
To bear with dignity my sorrow,
One day alone, then die tomorrow.'

Yes, you will close my eyes, Stella, but you will live long after me, dear Stella, for you are still a young woman, but you will close my eyes. *(Mrs Henderson sinks back in chair and speaks as Lulu).* Bad old man gone. Power all used up. Lulu can do no more Goodbye, friends. *(Mrs Henderson speaking in her own voice).* Go away, go away! *(She wakes).* I saw him a moment ago, has he spoilt the séance again? [p. 55]

MRS MALLET Yes, Mrs. Henderson, my husband came, but he was driven away.

DOCTOR TRENCH Mrs. Henderson is very tired. We must leave her to rest. *(To Mrs Henderson).* You did your best and nobody can do more than that. *(He takes out money).*

MRS HENDERSON No. . . . No. . . . I cannot take any money, not after a séance like that.

DOCTOR TRENCH Of course you must take it, Mrs Henderson. *(He puts money on table and Mrs. Henderson gives a furtive glance to see how much it is. She does the same as each sitter lays down his or her money).*

MRS MALLET A bad séance is just as exhausting as a good séance, and you must be paid.

MRS HENDERSON No. . . . No. . . . Please don't. It is very wrong to take money for such a failure. *(Mrs. Mallet lays down money).*

CORNELIUS PATTERSON A jockey is

paid whether he wins or not. *(He lays down money)* [p. 56]

MISS MACKENNA That spirit rather thrilled me. *(She lays down money).*

MRS HENDERSON If you insist, I must take it.

ABRAHAM JOHNSON I shall pray for you tonight. I shall ask God to bless and protect your séances. *(He lays down money. All go out except John Corbet and Mrs. Henderson).*

JOHN CORBET I know you are tired, Mrs. Henderson, but I must speak to you. I have been deeply moved by what I have heard. This is my contribution to prove that I am satisfied, completely satisfied. *(He puts a note on the table).*

MRS HENDERSON A pound note—nobody ever gives me more than ten shillings, and yet the séance was a failure.

JOHN CORBET *(sitting down near Mrs. Henderson).* When I say I am satisfied I do not mean that I am convinced it was the work of spirits. I prefer to think that you created it all, that you are an accomplished actress and scholar. In my essay for my Cambridge doctorate I examine all the explanations of Swift's celibacy offered by his biographers and prove that the explanation you selected was the only plausible one. But there is something I must ask you. Swift was the chief representative of the intellect of his epoch free at last from superstition. He foresaw its collapse. He foresaw democracy, he must have dreaded the future. Did he refuse to beget children because of that dread? Was Swift mad? Or was it the intellect itself that was mad? [p. 57]

MRS HENDERSON Who are you talking of, sir?

JOHN CORBET Swift, of course.

MRS HENDERSON Swift? I do not know anybody called Swift.

JOHN CORBET Jonathan Swift, whose spirit seemed to be present tonight.

MRS HENDERSON What? That dirty old man?

JOHN CORBET He was neither old nor dirty when Stella and Vanessa loved him.

MRS HENDERSON I saw him very clearly just as I woke up. His clothes were dirty, his face covered with boils. Some disease had made one of his eyes swell up, it stood out from his face like a hen's egg.

JOHN CORBET He looked like that in his old age. Stella had been dead a long time. His brain had gone his friends had deserted him. The man appointed to take care of him beat him to keep him quiet.

MRS HENDERSON Now they are old, now they are young. They change all in a moment as their thought changes. It is sometimes a terrible thing to be out of the body, God help us all. [p. 58]

DOCTOR TRENCH *(at doorway).* Come along, Corbet. Mrs. Henderson is tired out.

JOHN CORBET Good-bye, Mrs. Henderson.

(He goes out with Doctor Trench. All the sitters except Miss Mackenna, who has returned to her room, pass along the passage on their way to the front door. Mrs. Henderson counts the money, finds her purse which is in a vase on the mantelpiece and puts the money in it).

MRS HENDERSON How tired I am! I'd be the better of a cup of tea. *(She finds the teapot and puts kettle on fire, and then as she crouches down by the hearth suddenly lifts up her hands and counting her fingers, speaks in Swift's voice).* Five great Ministers that were my friends are gone, ten great Ministers that were my friends are gone. I have not fingers enough to count the great ministers that were my friends and that are gone. *(She wakes with a start and speaks in her own voice).* Where did I put that tea-caddy? Ah! there it is. And there should be a a cup and saucer. *(She finds the saucer).* But where's the cup? *(She moves aimlessly about the stage and then,* letting the saucer fall and break, speaks in Swift's *voice).* Perish the day on which I was born.

Here ends 'Words Upon the Window Pane;' A Play in one Act: by William Butler Yeats. Three hundred and fifty copies of this book have been printed and published by Elizabeth Corbet Yeats, (on paper made in Ireland) at The Cuala Press 133 Lower Baggot Street, Dublin, Ireland. Finished in the last week of January nineteen hundred and thirty four. [p. 59]

Appendix

Introduction to the Cuala Press Edition, 1934

In the text given below of Yeats's Introduction to the Cuala Press edition of *The Words Upon the Window Pane*, brackets enclose corrections of words misspelled by the printer or punctuation marks that the printer omitted. Drafts and pre-publication forms of the Introduction are listed in the Census of Manuscripts. In this first publication Yeats included three footnotes, which appear below on page 228.

INTRODUCTION

I

Somebody said the other night that in Dublin were many clubs—he himself knew four—that met in cellars and garrets and had for their object our general improvement. He was scornful, said that they had all begun by drawing up a programme and passing a resolution against the censorship and would never do anything else. When I began my public life Dublin was full of such clubs that passed resolutions and drew up programmes and, though the majority stopped there, some did much to find an audience for a school of writers. The fall of Parnell had freed imagination from practical politics, from agrarian grievance and political enmity and turned it to imaginative nationalism, to Gaelic, to the ancient stories, and at last to lyrical poetry and to drama. Political failure and political success have had the same result except that to-day imagination is turning full of uncertainty to something it thinks European, and whether that something will be 'arty' and provincial, or a form of life, is as yet undiscoverable. Hitherto we but walked the road, but now we have shut the door and turned up the lamp. What shall occupy our imagination? We must, I think, decide among these three ideas of national life; that of Swift; that of a great Italian of his day; that of modern England. If the Garrets and the Cellars listen I may throw light upon the matter, and I hope if all the time I seem thinking of something else I shall be forgiven. I must speak of things that come out of the common consciousness where every thought is like a bell with many echoes[.]

II

My little play *The Words upon the Window Pane* came to me amidst considerations such as these, as a reward, as a moment of excitement. John O'Leary read, during an illness, the poems of Thomas Davis and though he never thought them good poetry they shaped his future life, gave him the moral simplicity that made him so attractive to young men in his old age, but we can no longer permit life to be shaped by a personified idea, we must serve with all our faculties some actual thing. The old service was moral, at times lyrical; we discussed perpetually the character of public men; we never asked were they able and well-informed but what would they sacrifice? How many times did I hear on the lips of J. F. Taylor these words: 'Holy, delicate white hands'? His patriotism was a religion, never a philosophy. More extreme in such things than Taylor and O'Leary, who often seemed to live in the eighteenth century, to acknowledge its canons alone in literature and in the arts, I turned from Goldsmith and from Burke because they had come to seem a part of the English system, from Swift because, being a romantic, I acknowledged no verse between Cowley and Smart's *Song to David*, no prose between Sir Thomas Brown and the dialogues of Landor. But now I read Swift for months together, Burke and Berkeley less often but always with excitement, and Goldsmith lures and waits. I collect materials for my thought and work, for some identification of my beliefs with the nation itself, I seek an image of the modern mind's discovery of itself, of its own permanent form, in that one

Irish century that escaped from darkness and confusion. I would that our fifteenth, sixteenth or even our seventeenth century had been the clear mirror, but fate decided against us.

III

Swift haunts me; he is always just round the next corner. Sometimes it is a thought of my great-great-grandmother, a friend of that Archbishop King who sent him to England about the 'First Fruits,' sometimes it is Saint Patrick's, where I have gone to wander and meditate, that brings him to mind, sometimes I remember something hard or harsh in O'Leary or in Taylor, or in the public speech of our statesmen, that reminds me by its style of his verse or prose. Did he not speak, perhaps, with just such an intonation? This instinct for what is near and yet hidden is in reality a return to the sources of our power, and therefore a claim made upon the future. Thought seems more true, emotion more deep spoken by someone who touches my pride, who seems to claim me of his kindred, who seems to make me a part of some national mythology, nor is mythology mere ostentation, mere vanity if it draws me onward to the unknown; another turn of the gyre and myth is wisdom, pride discipline. I remember the shudder in my spine when Mrs. Patrick Campbell said, speaking words Hofmannstahl put into the mouth of Electra 'I too am of that ancient race'

Swift has sailed into his rest:
Savage indignation there
Cannot lacerate his breast.
Imitate him if you dare,
World-besotted traveller; he
Served human liberty.

IV

'In Swift's day men of intellect reached the height of their power, the greatest position they had reached in society and the state. . . . His ideal order was the Roman Senate, his ideal men Brutus and Cato; such an order and such men seemed possible once more.' The Cambridge undergraduate into whose mouth I have put these words may have read similar words in Oliver 'the last brilliant addition to English historians,' for young men such as he read the newest authorities; probably Oliver and he thought of the influence at Court and in public life of Swift and of Leibnitz, of the spread of science and of scholarship over Europe, its examination of documents, its destruction of fables, a science and a scholarship modern for the first time, of certain great minds that were medieval in their scope but modern in their freedom. I must, however, add certain thoughts of my own that affected me as I wrote. I thought about a passage in the *Grammont Memoirs* where some great man is commended for his noble manner, as we commend a woman for her beauty or her charm; a famous passage in the *Appeal from the New to the Old Whigs* commending the old Whig aristocracy for their intellect and power and because their doors stood open to like-minded men; the palace of Blenheim, its pride of domination that expected a thousand years, something Asiatic in its carved intricacy of stone. 'Everything great in Ireland, in our character, in what remains of our architecture, comes from that day . . . . we have kept its seal longer than England'. The overstatement of an enthusiastic Cambridge student, and yet with its measure of truth. The battle of the Boyne overwhelmed a civilization full of religion and myth, and brought in its place intelligible laws planned out upon a great blackboard; a capacity for horizontal lines, for rigid shapes; buildings, attitudes of mind that could be multiplied like an expanding bookcase; the modern world, and something that appeared and perished in its dawn, an instinct for Roman rhetoric, Roman elegance. It established a Protestant aristocracy some of whom neither called themselves English[1] nor looked with contempt nor dread upon conquered Ireland. Indeed the battle was scarcely over when Molyneux, speaking in their name, affirmed the sovereignty of the Irish Parliament.[2] No one had the right to make our laws but the King, Lords and Commons of Ireland; the battle had been fought to change not an English but an Irish Crown; and our Parliament was almost as ancient as that of England. It was this doctrine[3] that Swift uttered in the fourth *Drapier Letter* with such astringent eloquence that it passed from the talk of study and parlour to that of road and market, and created the political nationality of Ireland. Swift found his nationality through the *Drapier Letters*, his conviction came from action and passion, but Berkeley, a much younger man, could find it through contemplation. He and his fellow students but knew the war through the talk of the older men. As a boy of eighteen or nineteen he called the Irish people 'natives' as though he were in some foreign land, but two or three years later, perhaps while still an undergraduate, defined the English materialism of his day in three profound sentences, and wrote after each that 'we Irishmen' think otherwise—'I publish . . . . to know whether other men have the same ideas as we Irishmen'—and before he was twenty five had fought the Salamis of the Irish intellect. The Irish landed aristocracy who knew more of the battle of the Boyne delineated on vast tapestries for their House of Lords by Dublin Huguenots, than of philosophy, found themselves masters of a country demoralised by generations of war and famine and shared in its demoralisation. In 1730 Swift said from the pulpit that their houses were in ruins and no new building anywhere, that the houses of their rack-ridden tenants were no better than English pigsties, that the bulk of the people trod barefoot and in rags. He exaggerated for already the Speaker, Connolly, had built that great house at Celbridge where slate, stone and furniture were Irish, even the silver from Irish mines; the Parliament House had perhaps been planned; and there was a general stir of life. The old age of Berkeley passed amid art and music, and men had begun to boast that in these no country had made such progress; and some dozen years after Berkeley's death Arthur Young found everywhere in stately Georgian houses scientific agriculturalists, benefactors of their countryside, though for the half-educated drunken, fire-eating, impoverished lesser men he had nothing but detestation. Goldsmith might have found likeable qualities,

1 Nor were they English: the newest arrivals soon intermarried with an older stock, and that older stock had intermarried again and again with Gaelic Ireland. All my childhood the Coopers of Markree, County Sligo, represented such rank and fashion as the County knew, and I had it from my friend the late Bryan Cooper that his supposed Cromwellian ancestor being childless adopted an O'Brien; while local tradition thinks that an O'Brien, promised the return of her confiscated estate if she married a Cromwellian soldier, married a Cooper and murdered him three days after. Not, however, before he had founded a family. The family of Yeats, never more than small gentry, arrived, if I can trust the only man among us who may have the seen the family tree before it was burnt by Canadian Indians, 'about the time of Henry VII.' Ireland, divided in religion and politics, though the last division began to disappear ten years ago, is as much one race as any modern country.

2 'Until 1691 Roman Catholics were admitted by law into both Houses of Legislature in Ireland' [MacNeill's Constitutional and Parliamentary History of Ireland: page 10].

3 A few weeks ago the hierarchy of the Irish Church addressed, without any mandate from Protestant Ireland, not the Irish people as they had every right to even in the defence of folly, but the Imperial Conference and begged that the Irish Courts might remain subservient to the Privy Council. Terrified into intrigue where none threatened they turned from Swift and Molyneux. I remind them that when the barons of the Irish Court of Exchequer obeyed the English Privy Council in 1719 our ancestors clapped them into gaol. (1931)

a capacity for mimicry perhaps, among these lesser men, and Sir Jonah Barrington made them his theme, but, detestable or not, they were out of fashion. Miss Edgeworth described her *Castle Rackrent* upon the title page of its first edition as the habits of the Irish squirearchy before 1782. A few years more and the country people would have forgotten that the Irish aristocracy was founded like all aristocracies upon conquest, or rather, would have remembered, and boasted in the words of a medieval Gaelic poet 'We are a sword people and we go with the sword.' Unhappily the lesson first taught by Molyneux and Swift had been but half learnt when the test came—country gentlemen are poor politicians—and Ireland's 'dark, insipid period', began. During the entire eighteenth century the greatest land-owning family of the neighbourhood I best knew in childhood sent not a single man into the English army and navy, but during the nineteenth century one or more in every generation; a new absenteeism, forseen by Miss Edgeworth, began; those that lived upon their estates bought no more fine editions of the classics; separated from public life and ambition they sank, as I have heard Lecky complain, 'into grass farmers.' Yet their genius did not die out; they sent everywhere administrators and military leaders, and now that their ruin has come—what resolute nation permits a strong alien class within its borders?—I would, remembering obscure ancestors that preached in their churches or fought beside their younger sons over half the world, and despite a famous passage of O'Grady's, gladly sing their song.

V

'He foresaw the ruin to come, democracy, Rousseau, the French Revolution, that is why he hated the common run of men,—"I hate lawyers, I hate doctors" he said "though I love Doctor So-and-so and Judge So-and-So,"—that is why he wrote *Gulliver*[,] that is why he wore out his brain, that is why he felt *saeva indignatio*, that is why he sleeps under the greatest epitaph in history.' His *Discourse of the Contests and Dissensions of Athens and Rome* published in 1703 to warn the Tory Opposition of the day against the impeachment of Ministers, is Swift's one philosophical work. All States depend for their health upon a right balance between the One, the Few and the Many. The One is the executive, which may in fact be more than one—the Roman republic had two Consuls—but must for the sake of rapid decision be as few as possible; the Few are those who through the possession of [hereditary] wealth, or great personal gifts, have come to identify their lives with the life of the State, whereas the lives and ambitions of the Many are private. The Many do their day's work well and so far from copying even the wisest of their neighbours affect 'a singularity' in action and in thought; but set them to the work of the state and every man's Jack is 'listed to a party'[,] becomes the fanatical follower of men of whose characters he knows next to nothing, and from that day on puts nothing into his mouth that some other man has not already chewed and digested. And furthermore, from the moment of enlistment thinks himself above other men and struggles for power until all is in confusion. I divine an Irish hatred of abstraction expressed likewise by that fable of Gulliver among the inventors and men of science, by Berkeley in his *Commonplace Book*, by Goldsmith in the satire of *The Good-Natured Man*, in the picturesque, minute observation of *The Deserted Village*, and by Burke in his attack upon mathematical democracy. Swift enforced his moral by proving that Rome and Greece were destroyed by the war of the Many upon the Few; in Rome, where the Few had kept their class organisation, it was a war of classes, in Greece, where they had not, war upon character and genius. Miltiades, Aristides, Themistocles, Pericles, Alcibiades, Phocion, 'impeached for high crimes and misdemeanours . . . . were honoured and lamented by their country as the preservers of it and have had the veneration of all ages since paid justly to their memories. In Rome parties so developed that men born and [bred] among the Few were compelled to join one party or the other and to flatter and bribe. All civilisations must end in some such way, for the many obsessed by emotion create a multitude of religious sects but give themselves at last to some one master of bribes and flatteries and sink into the ignoble tranquility of servitude. He defines a tyrant as the predominance of the One, the Few, or the Many, but thinks that of the Many the immediate threat. All states at their outset possess a ruling power seated in the whole body as that of the soul in the human body, a perfect balance of the three estates, the king[,] some sort of chief magistrate, and then comes 'a tyranny: first either of the Few or the Many; but at last infallibly of a single person.' He thinks the English balance most perfect in the time of Queen Elizabeth but that in the next age a tyranny of the Many produced that of Cromwell, and that, though recovery followed, 'all forms of government must be mortal like their authors,' and he quotes from Polybius 'those abuses and corruptions, which in time destroy a government, are sown along with the very seed of it' and destroy it 'as rust eats iron or worms wood.' Whether the final tyranny is created by the Many—in his eyes all Cæsars were tyrants—or imposed by foreign power the result is the same. At the fall of liberty came 'a dark insipid period through all Greece'—had he Ireland in his mind also?—and the people became in the words of Polybius 'great reverencers of crowned heads.'

Twenty-two years later Giambattista Vico published that Scienza Nuova which Mr. James Joyce is expounding or symbolising in the strange fragments of his *Work in Progress*. He was the opposite of Swift in everything, an humble, peaceful man, son of a Neapolitan bookseller and without political opinions; he wrote panegyrics upon men of rank, seemed to admire all that they did, took their gratuities and yet kept his dignity. He thought civilisation passed through the phases Swift has described, but that it was harsh and terrible until the Many prevailed, and its joints cracked and loosened, happiest when some one man surrounded by able subordinates dismissed the Many to their private business, that its happiness lasted some generations until, sense of the common welfare lost, it grew malicious and treacherous, fell into 'the barbarism of reflection' and after that into an honest, plain barbarism accepted with relief by all and started upon its round again. Rome had conquered surrounding nations because those nations were nearer than it to humanity and happiness; was not Carthage already almost a democratic state when destruction came? Swift seemed to shape his narrative upon some clairvoyant vision of his own life, for he saw civilisation pass from comparative happiness and youthful vigour to an old age of violence and self-contempt, whereas Vico saw it begin in penury like himself and end as he himself would end in a long inactive peace. But there was a greater difference, Swift a practical politician in everything he wrote ascribed its rise and fall to virtues and vices all could understand, whereas the philosophical Vico ascribed them to 'the rhythm of the elemental forms of the mind,' a new idea that would dominate philosophy. Outside Anglo-Saxon nations where progress, impelled by moral enthusiasm and the Patent Office, seems a perpetual straight line, this 'circular movement' as Swift's master, Polybius, called it has long been the friend and enemy of public order. Both Sorel and Marx, their eyes more Swift's than Vico's, have preached a return to a primeval state, a beating of all down into a single class that a new civilisation may arise with its Few, its Many, and its One. Students of contemporary Italy, where Vico's thought is current through its influence upon Croce and Gentile, think it created, or in part created, the present government of one man surrounded by just such able assistants as Vico foresaw. Some philosopher has added this further thought: the classes rise out of the matrix, create all mental and bodily riches, sink back, as Vico saw civilisation rise and sink, and government is there to keep the ring and see to it that combat never ends. These thoughts in the next few generations, as elaborated by Oswald Spengler, who has followed Vico without essential change, by Flinders Petrie, by the German traveller, Frobenius, by Henry Adams, and perhaps by my friend Gerald Heard, may affect the masses. They have already deepened our sense of tragedy and somewhat checked the naiver among those creeds and parties who push their way to power by flattering our moral hopes. Pascal thought there was evidence for and against the existence of God, but that if a man kept his mind in suspense about it he could not live a rich and active life, and I suggest to the Cellars and Garrets that though history is too short to change the idea of progress or that of the eternal circuit into scientific fact, that the eternal circuit may best suit our preoccupation with the soul's salvation, our individualism, our solitude. Besides we love antiquity, and that other idea, progress, the sole religious myth of modern man, is only two hundred years old.

VI

Swift's pamphlet had little effect in its day; it did not prevent the impeachment and banishment a few years later of his own friends; and although he was in all probability the first—if there was another 'my small reading cannot trace it,'—to describe in terms of modern politics the discord of parties that compelled revolutionary France, as it has compelled half a dozen nations since the war, to accept the 'tyranny' of a 'single person,' it was soon forgotten; but for the understanding of Swift it is essential. It shows that the defence of liberty boasted upon his tombstone did not come from political disappointment (when he wrote it he had suffered none) and what he meant by liberty. Gulliver, in those travels written twenty years later, calls up from the dead 'a sexumvirate to which all the ages of the world cannot add a seventh'; Epaminondas and Socrates, who suffered at the hands of the Many; Brutus, Junius Brutus, Cato the Younger, Thomas More, who fought the tyranny of the One; Brutus with Cæsar still his inseparable friend, for a man may be a tyrant without personal guilt.

Liberty depended upon a balance within the state, like that of the 'humours' in a human body, or like that 'unity of being' Dante compared to a perfectly proportioned human body, and for its sake Swift was prepared to sacrifice what seems to the modern man liberty itself: The odds were a hundred to one, he wrote, that 'violent zeal for the truth' came out of 'petulancy, ambition, or pride.' He himself might prefer a republic to a monarchy, but did he open his mouth upon the subject would be deservedly hanged. Had he religious doubts he was not to blame, for God had given him reason, so long as he kept them to himself. It was the attitude of many a modern Catholic who thinks, though upon different grounds, that our civilisation may sink into a decadence like that of Rome. But sometimes belief itself must be hidden. He was devout; had the Communion Service by heart; read the Fathers and prayed much, yet would not press the mysteries of his faith upon any unwilling man. Had not the early Christians kept silent about the divinity of Christ; should not the missionaries to China 'soften' it? He preached as law commanded; a man could save his soul doubtless in any religion which taught submission to the Will of God, but only one state could protect his body; and how could it protect his body if rent apart by those cranks and sectaries mocked in his *Tale of a Tub*? Had not French Huguenots and English Dissenters alike sinned against the state? Except at those moments of great public disturbance, when a man must choose his creed or his king, let him think his own thoughts in silence.

What was this liberty bought with so much silence, and served through all his life with so much eloquence? 'I think' he wrote in the *Discourse* 'that the saying *vox populi, vox dei* ought to be understood of the universal bent and current of a people, not of the bare majority of a few representatives, which is often produced by little arts and great industry and application wherein those who engage in the pursuit of malice and revenge are much more sedulous than those who would prevent them.' That *vox populi* or 'bent and current,' or what we even more vaguely call national spirit, was the sole theme of his *Drapier Letters*; its right to express itself as it would through such men as had won or inherited general consent. I doubt if a mind so contemptuous of average men thought, as Vico did, that it found expression also through all individual lives or asked more for those lives than protection from the most obvious evils. I remember J. F. Taylor, a great student of Swift, saying 'individual liberty is of no importance, what matters is national liberty.'

VII

The will of the State, whether it build a cage for a dead bird or remain in the bird itself, must always, whether interpreted by Burke or Marx, find expression through some governing class or company identified with that 'bent and current,' with those 'elemental forms,' whether by interest or training. The men of Swift's day would have added that class or company must be placed by wealth above fear and toil, though Swift thought that every properly conducted State must limit the amount of the wealth the individual could possess. But the old saying that there is no wisdom without leisure has somewhat lost its truth. When the physical world became rigid; when curiosity inherited from the Renaissance, and the soul's anxiety inherited from the Middle Ages, passed, man ceased to think; his work thought in him. Spinoza, Leibnitz, Swift, Berkeley, Goethe, the last typical figure of the epoch, recognised no compulsion but the 'bent and current' of their lives; the Speaker, Connolly, could still call out a posse of gentlemen to design the façade of his house, and though Berkeley thought their number too great, that work is still admired; Swift called himself a poor scholar in comparison to Lord Treasurer Harley. Unity of being was still possible though somewhat over-rationalised and abstract, more diagram than body; whereas the best modern philosophers are professors, their pupils compile notebooks that they may be professors some day; politicians stick to their last or leave it to plague us with platitudes; we poets and artists may be called, so small our share in life, 'separated spirits', words applied by the old philosophers to the dead. When Swift sank into imbecility or madness his epoch had finished in the British Isles, those 'elemental forms,' had passed beyond him; more than the 'Great Ministers' had gone. I can see in a sort of nightmare vision the 'primary qualities' torn from the side of Locke, Johnson's ponderous body bent above the letter to Lord Chesterfield, some obscure person somewhere inventing the spinning-jenny, upon his face that look of benevolence kept by painters and engravers from the middle of the eighteenth century to the time of the Prince Consort for such as he, or to simplify the tale—

Locke sank into a swoon;
The Garden died;
God took the spinning-jenny
Out of his side.

VIII

'That arrogant intellect free from superstition at last': A young man's overstatement full of the unexamined suppositions of common speech. I saw Asia in the carved stones of Blenheim, not in the pride of great abstract masses, but in that humility of flower-like intricacy—the particular blades of the grass;—nor can chance have thrown into contiguous generations Spinoza and

Swift, an absorption of the whole intellect in God, a fakir-like contempt for all human desire; 'take from her', Swift prayed for Stella in sickness, 'all violent desire whether of life or death'; the elaboration and spread of Masonic symbolism, its God made in the image of Sir Christopher Wren; Berkeley's declaration, modified later, that physical pleasure is the *Summum Bonum*, Heaven's sole reality: his counter truth to that of Spinoza.

In judging any moment of past time we should leave out what has since happened; we should not call the Swift of the *Drapier Letters* nearer truth because of their influence upon history than the Swift who attacked in *Gulliver* the inventors and logicians; we should see certain men and women as if at the edge of a cliff, time broken away from their feet. Spinoza and the Masons, Berkeley and Swift, speculative and practical intellect, stood there free at last from all prepossessions and touched the extremes of thought; the Gmnosophists of Strabo close at hand, could they but ignore what was harsh and logical in themselves, or the China of the Dutch cabinet-makers, of the *Citizen of the World*, the long-settled rule of powerful men, no great dogmatic structure, few great crowded streets, scattered unprogressive communities, much handiwork, wisdom wound into the roots of the grass.

IX

'I have something in my blood that no child must inherit.' There have been several theories to account for Swift's celibacy; Sir Walter Scott suggested a 'physical defect,' but that seems incredible. A man so outspoken would have told Vanessa the truth and stopped a tragic persecution, a man so charitable have given Stella the protection of his name. The refusal to see Stella when there was no third person present suggests a man that dreaded temptation; nor is it compatible with those stories still current among our country people of Swift sending his servant out to fetch a woman, and dismissing that servant when he woke to find a black woman at his side. Lecky suggested dread of madness—the theory of my play, of madness already present in constant eccentricity; though with a vagueness born from distaste of the theme, he saw nothing incompatible between Scott's theory and his own. Had Swift dreaded transmitting madness he might well have been driven to consorting with the nameless barren women of the streets. Somebody else suggests syphilis contracted doubtless between 1799 when he was engaged to Varina and some date soon after Stella's arrival in Ireland. Mr. Shane Leslie thinks that Swift's relation to Vanessa was not platonic and that whenever his letters speak of a cup of coffee they mean the sexual act; whether the letters seem to bear him out I do not know, for that excited bluestocking bores me; but whether they seem to or not he must, if he is to get a hearing, account for Swift's relation to Stella. It seems certain that Swift loved her though he called it by some other name, and she him, and that it was platonic love.

'Thou, Stella, wert no longer young,
When first for thee my harp was strung,
Without one word of Cupid's darts,
Of killing eyes or bleeding hearts;
With friendship and esteem possest,
I ne'er admitted Love a guest.
In all the habitudes of life,
The friend, the mistress, and the wife,
Variety we still pursue,
In pleasure seek for something new;

Or else comparing with the rest,
Take comfort that our own is best;
The best we value by the worst,
As tradesmen show their trash at first;
But his pursuits are at an end,
Whom Stella chooses for a friend.'

If the relation between Swift and Vanessa was not platonic there must have been some bar that affected Stella as well as Swift. Doctor Delany is said to have believed that Swift married Stella in 1716 and found in some exchange of confidences that they were brother and sister, but Sir William Temple was not in Ireland during the year that preceded Swift's birth and so far as we know Swift's mother was not in England.

There is no satisfactory solution. Swift, though he lived in great publicity, wrote and received many letters, hid two things which constituted perhaps all that he had of private life: his loves and his religious beliefs.

X

'Was Swift mad? or was it the intellect itself that was mad?' The other day a scholar in whose imagination Swift has a pre-eminence scarcely possible outside Ireland said 'I sometimes feel that there is a black cloud about to overwhelm me, and then comes a great jet of life; Swift had that black cloud and no jet. He was terrified'. I said 'Terrified perhaps of everything but death' and reminded him of a story of Doctor Johnson's. There was a reward of five hundred pounds for the identification of the author of the *Drapier Letters*. Swift's butler who had carried the manuscript to the printer stayed away from work. When he returned Swift said 'I know that my life is in your hands, but I will not bear, out of fear, either your insolence or negligence.' He dismissed the butler and when the danger had passed he restored him to his post, rewarded him and said to the servants 'No more Barclay, henceforth Mr. Barclay.' 'Yes,' said my friend, 'He was not afraid of death but of life, of what might happen next, that is what made him so defiant in public and in private and demand for the State the obedience a Connaught priest demands for the Church.' I have put a cognate thought into the mind of John Corbet. He imagines, though but for a moment, that the intellect of Swift's age, persuaded that the mechanicians mocked by Gulliver would prevail, that its moment of freedom could not last, so dreaded the historic process that it became in the half mad mind of Swift a dread of parentage: 'Am I to add another to the healthy rascaldom and knavery of the world?' Did not Rousseau within two years of the death of Swift publish his *Discourse Upon Arts and Sciences* and discover the instinctive harmony not in heroic effort, not in Cato and Brutus, not among impossible animals—I think of that noble horse Blake drew for Hayley—but among savages and thereby beget the sans-culottes of Marat: after the arrogance of power the humility of a servant.

XI

When I went into the theatre café after the performance a woman asked a question and I replied with some spiritualistic anecdote. 'Did that happen with the medium we have seen to-night?' she said: and yet May Craig who played the part had never seen a séance. I had however assisted her by self-denial. No character upon the stage spoke my thoughts. All were people I had met or might have met in just such a séance. Taken as whole, the man who expected to find whippet-racing beyond the grave not less than the old man who was half a Swedenborgian, they express the attitude of mind of millions who have substituted the séance room for the Church. At most séances there is somebody who finds symbol where his neighbour finds fact, but the average man or woman thinks that the dead have houses, that they eat and sleep, hear lectures, or occasionally talk with Christ as though He were a living man; and certainly the voices are at times so natural, the forms so solid, that the plain man can scarce think otherwise.

If I had not denied myself, if I had allowed some character to speak my thoughts what would he have said? It seems to me that after reading many books and meeting many phenomena, some in my own house, some of it when alone in my room, I can see clearly at last. I consider it certain that every voice that speaks, every form that appears, whether to the medium's eyes and ears alone or to some one or two others or to all present, whether it remains a sight or sound or affects the sense of touch, whether it is confined to the room or can make itself apparent at some distant place, whether it can or cannot alter the position of material objects, is first of all a secondary personality or dramatisation of the medium's. Perhaps May Craig, when alone in her room after the play, went, without knowing what she was doing, through some detail of her performance. I once saw an Abbey actor going up the stairs to his dressing-room, after playing the part of a lame man, and saw that he was still limping. I see no necessary difference except of degree between such unconscious movements and the powerful grotesque faces imprinted by the controls of Eusapia Paladino upon paraffin wax. The Polish psychologist Ochorowicz, vexed by the mischievous character of his medium's habitual control, created by suggestion a docile and patient substitute that left a photograph of its hand and arm upon an unopened coil of film in a sealed bottle. But at most séances the suggestions come from subconscious or unspoken thought. I found the preacher who wanted Sankey's help at a séance where the mind of an old doting general turned all into delirium. We sat in the dark and voices came about us in the air; crowned head after crowned head spoke until Cromwell intervened and was abused by one of the sitters for cutting off the head of 'Charles the Second', while the preacher kept repeating 'He is monopolising the séance, I want Mr. Moody, it is most important I should get Mr. Moody.' Then came a voice 'King George is here.' I asked which of the George's, and the sitter who hated Cromwell said 'King George, our George, we should all stand up,' but the general thought it would be enough if we sang 'God save the King.' We sang, and then there was silence, and in the silence from somewhere close to the ceiling the clear song of a bird.

Because mediumship is dramatisation: even honest [mediums] cheat at times either deliberately or because some part of the body has freed itself from the control of the waking will, and almost always truth and lies are mixed together. Swedenborg, lacking our experimental proof of the complicity of medium and sitter, denounced all spirits that had not reached their final rest for jugglers and cheats. But what shall we say of their knowledge of events, their assumption of forms and names beyond the medium's knowledge or ours? What of the arm photographed in the bottle?

The Indian ascetic passing into his death-like trance knows that if his mind is not pure, if there is anything there but the symbol of his God, some passion, ambition, desire or fantasy will confer upon him its shape or purpose for he is entering upon a state where thought and existence are the same. One remembers those witches described by Glanvil who course the field in the likeness of hares while their bodies lie at home, and certain mediumistic phenomena. The ascetic would say did we question him that the unpurified dead are subject to transformations that would be similar were it not that in their case no physical body remains in cave or bed or chair, all is transformed. They examine their past, if undisturbed by our importunity, tracing events to their source, and as they take the form their thought suggests, seem to live backward through time; or if incapable of such examination, creatures not of thought but of feeling, renew, as shades, detached events of their past lives, taking the greater excitement first.

When Achilles comes to the edge of the blood pool (an ancient substitute for the medium) he was such a shade. Tradition affirms that deprived of the living present by death they can create nothing, or, in the Indian phrase, can originate no new Karma. Their aim, like that of the ascetic in meditation, is to enter at last into their own timeless being, into the whole of being, that which is there always. They are not however the personalities which haunt the séance room, these when they speak from, or imply supernormal knowledge, when they are more than transformations of the medium, are as it were new beings begotten by spirit upon medium to live short but veritable lives, whereas the secondary personalities resemble those eggs brought forth without the assistance of the male bird. They within their narrow limits create, they speak truth when they repeat some message suggested by the past lives of the spirit, remembered like some prenatal memory, or, when, though such instances must be few, begotten by some spirit obedient to its source, or, as we might say, blessed; but when they neither repeat such message nor were so begotten they may justify passages in Swedenborg that denounce them as the newspapers denounce cheating mediums, seeing that they find their fragmentary knowledge or vague conscience but little check upon invention.

Let images of basalt, black, immovable,
Chiselled in Egypt, or ovoids of bright steel
Hammered and polished by Brancusi's hand,
Represent spirits; if spirits seem to stand
Before the bodily eyes, speak into the bodily ears
They are not present but their messengers.
Of double nature these; one nature is,
Compounded of accidental phantasies;
We question; it but answers what we would
Or as phantasy directs—because they have drunk the blood.

I have not heard of spirits in an European séance room re-enacting their past lives; our séances take their characteristics from the desire of those present to speak to or perhaps obtain the counsel of their dead; yet under the conditions described in my play such re-enacting might occur, indeed most hauntings are of that nature. Here however is a French traveller's account of a séance in Madagascar, quoted by César de Vesme:—

'One, Taimandebakaka, of the Bara race, and renowned in the valley of the Menamaty as a great sorceror, evoked one day in my presence in his village the soul of Captain Flayelle and of Lieutenant Montagnole, both killed at Vohingheso in a fight with the Baras four years before. Those present—myself and some privileged natives—saw nothing when Taimandebakaka claimed to see the two persons in question; but we could hear the voices of officers issuing orders to their soldiers, and these voices were European voices which could not be imitated by natives. Similarly, at a distance we could hear the echoes of firing and the cries of the wounded and the lowing of frightened cattle—oxen of the Fahavalos.'

XII

It is fitting that Plotinus should have been the first philosopher to meet his daimon face to face, though the boy attendant out of jealousy or in convulsive terror strangled the sacrificial dove, for he was the first to establish as sole source the timeless individuality, or daimon, instead of the Platonic Idea, to prefer Socrates to his thought. This timeless individuality contains archetypes of all possible existence whether of man or of brute, and as it traverses its 'period' or series of lives, now one, now another, prevails. We may fail to express an archetype, or alter it by reason, but all done from nature is its unfolding into time. In that sense the dramatisation that kept the actor lame though the curtain had fallen, and some apparition that describes its suicide, are both spirits. Another existence may take the place of Socrates, yet Socrates can never cease to exist. Once a friend of mine was digging in a long neglected garden and suddenly out of the air came a voice thanking her, an old owner of the garden she was told later, long since reborn, but still in the garden. Plotinus thought that we should not 'baulk at this limitlessness of the intellectual; it is an infinitude having nothing to do with number or part' (Ennead V.7.I.) yet it seems that it can at will re-enter number and part and thereby make itself apparent to our minds. If we accept this idea many strange or beautiful things become credible. The Indian pilgrim has not deceived us; he did hear the bed, where the sage of his devotion slept thousands of years ago, creak as though someone turned over in it, and he did see the blankets all tossed about at dawn as if someone had just risen; the Irish country-woman did see the ruined castle lit up, the bridge across the river dropping; those two Oxford ladies did find themselves in the garden of the Petit Trianon with Marie Antoinette and her courtiers and see that garden as she saw it; the gamekeeper did hear those footsteps the other night that sounded like the footsteps of a stag where stag has not passed these hundred years. All about us there seems to start up a precise, inexplicable, [teeming] life, and the earth becomes once more, not in rhetorical metaphor, but in reality, sacred.